Planters and the Making of a "New South"

Planters and the Making of a "New South"

Class, Politics, and Development in North Carolina, 1865–1900

by Dwight B. Billings, Jr.

The University of North Carolina Press
Chapel Hill

© 1979 The University of North Carolina Press
All rights reserved
Manufactured in the United States of America
ISBN 0-8078-1315-X
Library of Congress Catalog Card Number 78-25952

Library of Congress Cataloging in Publication Data

Billings, Dwight B   1948–
   Planters and the making of a "new South."

   Bibliography: p.
   Includes index.
   1. North Carolina—Industries—History.   2. North
Carolina—Economic conditions.   3. North Carolina—
Social conditions.   I. Title.
HC107.N8B5   330.9'756'04   78-25952
ISBN 0-8078-1315-X

To the working people
of Roanoke Rapids, North Carolina,
and Sterns, Kentucky,
where southern labor stirs.

Contents

Acknowledgments . . . xiii

1. *Introduction . . . 3*

2. *Underdevelopment in Plantation Societies . . . 9*

   Plantations and the World Capitalist System . . . 9

   Economic Dependence and Underdevelopment—
   The External Relationship . . . 13

   Class Relations and Persistent Poverty—
   The Internal Dimension . . . 17

3. *The Political Economy of the American South:
   Persistence and Change . . . 25*

   The South: An Economically Peripheral Region . . . 25

   The Transition from Old South to New . . . 35

4. *Social Origins of the New South:
   The Case of North Carolina . . . 42*

   Antebellum North Carolina . . . 43

   Social Origins of Industry in North Carolina . . . 50

   A Test of the Middle-Class Thesis . . . 62

5. *Modernization in the South:
   North Carolina's Revolution from Above . . . 70*

6. *Labor Relations and Ideology in the New South:
   Consequences of North Carolina's Revolution
   from Above . . . 96*

   A Different Ethos along Tobacco Road . . . 113

   Understanding the New South's Creed . . . 121

   Conclusion . . . 130

7. *Populism, Progressivism, and Paternalism:
   The Politics of Development . . . 132*

   Who Made North Carolina "Modern"? . . . 136

8. *Uneven Development and the Agrarian Revolt* . . . 145
   Who Were the North Carolina Populists? . . . 155
   *The Politics of Participation
   in the North Carolina Senate, 1895 and 1897* . . . 167
9. *The Conservative Triumph* . . . 188
   White Supremacy and the Senate of 1899 . . . 190
   Progressivism and Paternalism: The Aycock Regime . . . 197
   Education, Modernization, and the Middle Class . . . 203
   Conclusion . . . 212
10. *"Softly, Do You Not Hear . . . ?"* . . . 215
   Notes . . . 233
   Bibliography . . . 261
   Index . . . 275

Tables

3.1 *Regional Manufacture of Agricultural Implements . . . 28*

3.2 *Percentage of Average Wage Earners, 1879,*
and of Employees, 1947, in Selected Manufacturing Industries
Employed in the South . . . 31

4.1 *Economic Indicators for North Carolina and the South,*
1880 . . . 51

5.1 *North Carolina Farm Ownership in 1900 . . . 72*

5.2 *Control of Tenants in North Carolina in 1900 . . . 74*

5.3 *Concentration within North Carolina's*
Landholding Elite in 1900 . . . 76

8.1 *North Carolina Populist Gubernatorial Vote, 1896,*
by Selected County Characteristics . . . 160

8.2 *Occupational Composition*
of the North Carolina Senate, 1897 . . . 171

8.3 *Religious Composition*
of the North Carolina Senate, 1897 . . . 171

8.4 *Educational Composition*
of the North Carolina Senate, 1897 . . . 171

8.5 *Comparison of 1897 Senate Voting Clusters*
by Average County Background of Populist Senators . . . 181

8.6 *Class Structure in Rural North Carolina . . . 186*

9.1 *Occupational Composition of the Democrats*
in the 1899 Senate . . . 193

10.1 *Comparison of Estimated Long-Run Price Elasticities*
for Cotton Growing (1883–1914) and Total Value
Added by Manufacturing Per Capita (1890 and 1900),
for Ten Southern States . . . 224

Figures

3.1 *Regional Income Shares, 1840–1950* . . . *29*

4.1 *Aggregate Real and Personal Wealth Per Capita (Free), 1860* . . . *48*

7.1 *Turnover in North Carolina Senate* . . . *141*

7.2 *Total State Disbursements (in millions)* . . . *143*

8.1 *Two-Dimensional Representation of the Fusion Senate, 1895* . . . *173*

8.2 *Two-Dimensional Representation of the Fusion Senate, 1897* . . . *179*

Acknowledgments

I wish to express my appreciation to the many people who supported me in the preparation of this book. Gerhard Lenski, at The University of North Carolina at Chapel Hill, gave personal encouragement and made numerous suggestions that have contributed much to the final product. Lester Salamon gave valuable comments, and his analysis of Mississippi as a developing society provided a chief exemplar for my research. Had I not discovered Salamon's work, my own would have had far less coherence. Robert Gallman, John Reed, and Everett Wilson, all at The University of North Carolina at Chapel Hill, were most helpful.

I want to thank my family for their years of love and encouragement and also many friends and colleagues whose human support and intellectual contributions during this writing have been invaluable. These include Brian Anderson, Doug Arnett, Lars Bjorn, Larry Busch, Dan Chirot, Ron Eller, Robert Goldman, Jack Hoadley, Floyd Hunter, Al Imershein, Charles Ragin, Gregg Sampson, Rachael Tayar, and Dave Walls. Three of these deserve special mention. Dan Chirot introduced me to historical sociology and political economy. Bob Goldman and Rachael Tayar were constant sources of ideas and support. I also wish to thank the staffs of the North Carolina Collection and the Southern Historical Collection of the Louis Round Wilson Library, The University of North Carolina at Chapel Hill, as well as the Danforth Fellowship program. Finally, Marlene Pettit did a cheerful and skilled job typing the manuscript.

Planters and the Making of a "New South"

1. Introduction

The history of the American South provides many challenges to the sociologist studying social classes and social change. Although the region's commercial agriculture developed as part of the modern world market system, slavery is reputed to have produced a society in the South whose aristocratic tendencies and economic interests were at odds with the rest of American society. Slaveholding conflicted with the dynamic, expansionist, middle-class capitalism of the North. The political expression of this conflict was the Civil War, a bloody fight to determine which pattern of social relations would be dominant on the American continent.

Historians have been fascinated by the effects of the war on southern society. C. Vann Woodward in *Origins of the New South* is an example of one who claims that no other class in our history fell so rapidly or so completely as the South's planter aristocracy after the Civil War. A number of French aristocrats who never lived to see the nineteenth century or Russian aristocrats who did not see much of the twentieth century might argue the point were they here to do so. Nevertheless, apart from its accuracy, which I shall discuss later, this prevalent view dramatizes the extent of social change in the South: a rich agricultural South based on the labor of African slaves; a wartorn South first conquered by northern troops and then by northern railroads; and, finally, a "New South," rich in industry and poor in wages.

This drama creates fascinating problems for sociologists interested in the process of stratification; they could correlate the rise and fall of social classes with the confusing patterns of southern politics. The South's uneven development poses important problems for students of political and economic development. Why have some formerly backward areas of the South, such as the Carolina Piedmont, industrialized and others, such as the Delta region, seem never to change? I shall try to make sense of the patterns of social stratification and social change in the South by analyzing the economic and political development in the state of North Carolina after the Civil War.

In 1860, North Carolina was the poorest southern state. Compared with the grandeur of its neighbors, Virginia and South Carolina, North Carolina appeared humble. Its eastern counties supported a patrician class of slaveholders who dominated the state politically, but its vast western territories housed a huge population of yeomen and subsistence farmers whose life styles, in comparison, must have seemed frontierlike. Despite its comparative backwardness, however, by 1900, North Carolina was becoming the industrial leader of the New South. If we could return to the North Carolina of 1880, at the midpoint of this transition, it would not be clear at all how such a remarkable transformation could be possible.

In 1880 the effects of Civil War were still highly visible in North Carolina. The last of the federal troops had been withdrawn from the South only three years earlier. Roughly forty thousand North Carolinians (the greatest number in any Southern state) died in a war many had opposed. Approximately 350,000 slaves had been emancipated, but proprietary control was restored with the development of the sharecropping system. Much of the land was still in ruins. Because slaves and land had been the South's capital, there was little money for rebuilding.[1] North Carolina's financial assets in 1880 were the lowest in the South.[2] The ruinous costs of war were further compounded by chronic agricultural depression. There were more white than black sharecroppers because yeomen fell increasingly into debt and were forced into the tenancy system. By 1880 one-third of the state's farms were operated by tenants.

North Carolina's transportation system had been inadequate during the antebellum years. Postbellum capital deficiency crippled its rebuilding and extension. If we could again travel North Carolina's sparse, rugged roads from the Tidewater across the rolling, red clay Piedmont and up into the wild, majestic mountains west of the Blue Ridge, we would realize how separate and hostile were its geographical subregions. Even compared with the rest of the South, North Carolina was extremely rural. A rugged coast, outlined with deadly sandbars, permitted no great seaport cities like Charleston to the south. Poor internal transportation prevented urban growth. Only four towns in North Carolina in 1880 numbered more than four thousand people and only one of these—Charlotte, with a population just over seven thousand—was not in the coastal region.[3]

Despite such obstacles, or perhaps because of them, North Carolina distinguished itself by launching an industrial revolution. In 1880 the value of farm products had exceeded the value of manufactured products by more than 250 percent. Twenty years later, however, the pattern was reversed, when manufactured products outstripped agricultural production by several million dollars.[4] For its cotton mills and tobacco towns, its development of a fine system of public highways, and its regional leadership in school building and public health, North Carolina began to acquire a new popular image. Its reputation for progress seems almost to have set it apart from the rest of the South. V. O. Key, for instance, wrote: "Many see in North Carolina a closer approximation to national norms, or national expectations of performance, than they find elsewhere in the South. In any competition for national judgment they deem the state far more 'presentable' than its southern neighbors. It enjoys a reputation for progressive outlook and action in many phases of life, especially industrial development, education, and race relations."[5] Key—a southern liberal who saw the South's "way out" in urbanization, industrialization, and outmigration of blacks—shared in and took hope from this view of North Carolina. He reported that from 1900 to 1939 the state ranked first among southern states in its 1,397 percent increase in value added by manufacturing and second in its 194 percent increase in the value of its farm products. He called the profound political and economic changes that occurred at the turn of the century a "political and educational renaissance" that "set in motion the progressive, productive forces that today distinguish the state."[6]

Yet North Carolina's economic development has been uneven. The state ranks thirteenth nationally in absolute value added by manufacturing. In 1976, North Carolina unseated Florida as the South's business leader. A recent report notes that "thirty-five North Carolina firms made the [region's] Top 200 . . . posting $13.77 billion in sales."[7] Two of the five largest southern corporations are in North Carolina, and no southern state has larger banks. The same report reveals that more of the chief executives of the region's top businesses were natives of North Carolina than of any other state and that more had been educated at its state university than at any other educational institution. North Carolina also remains the seventh most rural state in the United States. Although it has the second highest proportion of nonagricultural employees in goods-producing industries in the United States, it ranks fiftieth in proportional union membership. North Carolina ranks fiftieth in average hourly earnings for production workers and forty-third in total per capita income. The state has the fifth most poorly educated population, despite its celebrated education "renaissance," and the seventh highest rate of infant mortality in the nation.

Just as the pattern of North Carolina's economic development has not been unambiguous, neither has its politics. Joseph Steelman, for example, concluded that his "search for an explanation of why North Carolina acquired the reputation, early in the 20th century, of being a 'preeminent' state of the 'New South,' progressive in outlook, enlightened in political, social, and economic matters has probably raised more issues than it has resolved."[8] No writer has made adequate sense of the paradoxical nature of North Carolina's politics. In a recent critical bibliography on New South politics, J. Morgan Kousser remarked: "North Carolina's historians have assiduously uncovered the facts of that state's political history, but have been less successful in arranging them into patterns which advance our understanding of Southern history or institutions."[9]

My goal in this book is as much to develop hypotheses about the South as to test them with the facts of North Carolina's development. My strategy has been to use class as an analytic tool for studying social change. Gerhard Lenski's *Power and Privilege* and Barrington Moore's *Social Origins of Dictatorship and Democracy* have shown that theories of social stratification provide powerful analytical tools for understanding social change. Lenski redefined stratification analysis as the study of the dynamics of distribution, the age-old question of who gets what and why. He integrated economics, political sociology, and the sociology of social movements to explain long-term trends and comparative patterns of inequality. Moore demonstrated the lasting effects of historical factors in modernization. In a number of case studies, he related the technological and social aspects of agricultural production to subsequent patterns of economic and political development. These two studies have provided the empirical foundations for several recent theoretical discussions, and they return social stratification to the central place it held in classical sociology.[10]

When Karl Marx wrote that all history is the history of class struggle, he was stating a methodological principle. Marx examined the potential conflicts of economic life. He argued that profound social changes occur when productive classes (defined by their relationship to the means of production) become aware of their common interests and organize into political parties to advance or defend these interests. The renewed interest in classical sociology among students of social change results in a heightened appreciation for the methodology of political-economic analysis.[11]

This approach focuses on how an economic surplus is socially obtained. Since an economic surplus is "socially and politically defined from the very start," a political economy "is characterized by a particular class structure—that is, the way in which a surplus is extracted from the economy, how and by whom it is distributed, and for what purposes."[12] Tied up with changes in how a surplus is generated or used are profound changes in many aspects of social life. These include not only class structures and the nature of work relations, but authority relationships in general, politics, and aspects of daily life such as family patterns and community membership as well as cultural standards and expressions. These factors are affected by political-economic changes and permit them to occur although in historical situations their interplay is usually most difficult to analyze.[13] Given the fact that in the past few centuries such changes have occurred in a worldwide context, this approach invites—indeed, requires—comparative and historical investigation. A comparative perspective, in particular, has been absent from much of the literature on the South because so much attention has focused on the region's unique experience within American society.

It is important to remember that class relations are sociological abstractions that can be inferred only from the actions of real people. The principal methodological strategy throughout this book will be an attempt to understand the actions of key economic and political actors and to infer from these interpretations of class structures, class interests, and class consciousness. I accept quite literally C. Wright Mills's claim that sociological imagination consists of grasping the relationship between history and social structure as these interact in biography.[14] Throughout this work I propose to keep an eye not only on abstract social configurations but on the real lives, at least sketched in broad strokes, of North Carolina leaders. Close attention is paid to planters, industrialists, and politicians. It is hoped that the lives of North Carolina planters such as Paul Carrington Cameron, mill builders such as Daniel Tompkins, tobacco magnates such as James B. Duke, agrarian leaders such as Leonidas Polk and Marion Butler and the lives of middle-class reformers such as Walter Hines Page and Josephus Daniels will show the changing patterns and continuities of social life in the early postbellum South.[15]

2. Underdevelopment in Plantation Societies

Persistent poverty and a multitude of other social and economic indications of backwardness characterize all societies and regions dominated by plantation agriculture. This is true whether the case is the Caribbean, South and Central America, Southeast Asia, Africa, or the southern region of the United States. In this chapter I shall discuss a macrosociological approach to this problem, the political economy of plantation society. This approach locates plantation production in its context of the world capitalist market system and explains its persistent underdevelopment in terms of both its external trade dependency and its internal class structure.

Plantations and the World Capitalist System

Modern economic stagnation cannot be understood apart from the fact of worldwide economic interdependence, as a number of scholars, especially Gunnar Myrdal, Andre Gunder Frank, and Immanuel Wallerstein, have stressed.[1] Frank, for instance, criticizes modernization theories for their emphasis on the spread of psychological modernity. In their assumption that economic backwardness is a consequence of cultural isolation, these theories, he says, fail "to take account of the economic and other relations between the metropolis and its economic colonies throughout the history of the worldwide expansion and development of the mercantilist and capitalist system." Frank argues that economic growth and underdevelopment are often products of the same historical process. He laments most of all the failure of social theory "to explain the structure and development of the capitalist system as a whole and to account for its simultaneous generation of underdevelopment in some of its parts and of economic development in others."[2] The structure and dynamics of the capitalist world system have been the object of extensive macrosociological research by Immanuel Wallerstein. His research is one of the foundations for my investigation of the American South.

Interpretations vary regarding the complex technological, demographic, economic, and sociopolitical changes that resulted in the emergence of the worldwide capitalist market in the sixteenth century.[3] It is clear, however, that the most important fact about this social system has been its complex division of labor. "This division," according to Wallerstein, "is not merely functional—that is, occupational—but geographical. That is to say, the range of economic tasks is not evenly distributed throughout the world system. In part this is the consequence of ecological considerations, to be sure. But for the most part, it is a function of the social organization of work, one which magnifies and legitimates the ability of some groups within the system to exploit the labor of others, that is, to receive a larger share of the surplus." The methodological implications of this division are clear for comparative studies in social stratification. As Wallerstein says, "The emergence, consolidation, and political roles of classes and status groups must be appreciated as elements of this world system."[4] Political economists such as Karl Marx have always understood this relationship, yet sociological studies of stratification often fail to recognize it.

The operation of the world market system also reveals aspects of the development process that are not otherwise apparent. One fundamental principle is that the "on-going process of a world-economy tends to expand the economic and social gaps among its varying areas in the very process of its development."[5] According to Wallerstein, this occurs because economic activities requiring high levels of skill and capitalization tend to concentrate in "core" metropolitan areas of the system. Since capitalism typically rewards accumulated capital at a higher rate than it does labor, "the geographical maldistribution of skills involves a steady trend toward self-maintenance." Indeed, poor nations today struggle to prevent the widening gap between themselves and the rich nations from widening even further.[6]

Not all regions of the world economy share equally in the benefits of economic growth. Most deprived are those regions on the "periphery" of capitalist development. Wallerstein defines the periphery of a world economy as "that geographical sector of it wherein production is primarily of lower-ranking goods (that is, goods whose labor is less well rewarded) but which is an integral part of the overall system of the division of labor, because the commodities involved are essential for daily use."[7] Plantation agriculture is a mode of production frequently found in peripheral regions of the world economy. The plantation cultivation of cotton in the American South and its international marketing are typical peripheral developments.

For a variety of historical reasons, including periods of labor shortage, the peasantry of western Europe was able to resist some of the exploitation inherent in the economic growth that marked the transition from feudalism to capitalism. This resistance set limits on the pace of bourgeois development and encouraged western Europe to turn outward for other lands and other labor supplies to exploit.[8] Although capitalism matured in its core commercial regions, the expansion of trade in its periphery "encouraged social retrogression and the reinstitution of older"—archaic—"modes of production in Eastern Europe and the New World."[9]

The extension of western trade relations into eastern Europe produced what Marx and Engels called a "second serfdom." Formerly free peasants in eastern Europe were enserfed by landlords who previously had been unconcerned about agricultural profits. In the sixteenth century feudal dues were raised and peasants were tied to the demesne when the nobility entered the world grain market.[10] The result was a landed aristocracy with interests in commercial agriculture, labor repression, limited local markets, and a feeble bourgeoisie.[11] Primary production for export in the American South had the same result. In the following chapters I shall argue that the identification of similar development patterns and class relations in eastern Europe and the American South is an important insight into the nature of the South, and I shall suggest that this similarity reveals as much about the character of the New South as it explains the peculiar institutions of the Old South. The South's peculiar institutions cannot be understood without an understanding of the region's relationship to world capitalism.

Researchers are prompted by the similarities among plantation societies to consider their labor relations as a distinct mode of production. The classical Marxist typology identified communal, city, asiatic, feudal, capitalist, and socialist modes of production. Daniel Chirot has defined "servile labor," the characteristic mode of production in plantation societies, as that in which "agricultural laborers are bound to the land which they work, and in which a significant portion of their product winds up in markets where it is sold in order to pay (directly or indirectly through dues) for manufactured goods which are largely consumed by the landowning elite."[12] This arrangement is a solution to the problem of labor scarcity.

Plantation agriculture is described as a distinct mode of production in order to distinguish it from feudalism. George Beckford,[13] Frank, Eugene Genovese, and Wallerstein all agree that the persistent poverty characteristic of peripheral or plantation lands must be seen in part as a product of the dynamics of world capitalism. Feudalism assumes manorial self-sufficiency, not worldwide interdependence. The development strategy for a feudal region would be incorporation into interregional trade. Despite popular opinion, plantation societies are not backward because they lack contact with the modernizing influence of industrial society. Quite the opposite. Trade with industrial societies often perpetuates the chronic underdevelopment of plantation regions.[14]

In addition to the problems of trade dependency, the treatment of plantation production as a distinct mode of production also highlights its characteristic class structure.[15] Many observers believe that this class structure has important implications for economic development. Writing about the South, Genovese, for example, has argued that "the very fact of slave labor introduced precapitalist distortions into the economy and into [southern] society as a whole"[16] He interprets the southern planter as a capitalist with a bourgeois inheritance producing for a world market and yet, he says, the master-slave relationship resulted in "interests and tendencies antithetical to metropolitan bourgeoisie." The blood spilled in the American Civil War confirms this clearly enough.

Economic Dependence and Underdevelopment—
The External Relationship

Scholars have identified several preconditions for the rise of plantation production. Beckford summarizes one of the most useful approaches, the Wolf and Mintz framework, as follows:

> Preconditions for the establishment of the plantation as a settlement institution include (1) *capital* sufficient to allow the plantation organization to secure needed factors of production; (2) *land* in sufficient quantity and of adequate quality for present and future production; (3) *labor* in sufficient quantity to minimize production costs and so maximize profit; (4) *technology* of a sufficiently high level for "modern" production; and (5) *sanctions* of a political-legal sort to maintain a disciplined labor force and to regulate distribution of the surplus. In addition, the system needs (6) a sizeable industrial *market* for its staple and (7) a system of class *stratification* that differentiates those with capital from those with only labor services to sell.[17]

Plantations are parts of a wider economic system at the center of which are distant commercial and industrial cities. Plantations provide these cities with primary products and often with new markets for manufactured goods.[18] The plantation is thus an instrument for modernization. It opens up new regions, expands production and income, contributes technology to undeveloped lands, stimulates peasant output and income, and, to a limited degree, introduces an economic multiplier effect.[19] But, as

Beckford dramatically puts it, if the plantation is a solution to the problem of *un*development, it is itself the cause of *under*development—that is, plantation production goes only so far in promoting regional economic growth.

The expansion of primary exports can lead to agricultural diversification and industrialization. Citing the case of California and the Pacific Northwest, Douglass North has shown that "a successful agricultural export trade can and has induced urbanization, improvements in the factor markets, and a more efficient allocation of investment funds."[20] Why, then, do plantation societies remain tied to single export staples? And why, after four hundred years of participation in the world economy, do they remain poor?

Part of the answer is that plantation societies are economically dependent on trade with urban and industrial centers. Theotonio dos Santos has provided a widely accepted definition of dependence as "a situation in which the economy of certain countries is conditioned by the development and expansion of another economy to which the former is subjected. The relation of interdependence between two or more economies, and between these and world trade, assumes the form of dependence when some countries (the dominant ones) can expand and can be self-sustaining, while other countries (the dependent ones) can do this only as a reflection of that expansion, which can have either a positive or a negative effect on their immediate development."[21] Such dependence on faraway metropolises is one factor that operates to keep plantation societies economically underdeveloped. This problem is worsened by the fact that there is an observed tendency for market exchanges to increase rather than to diminish inequalities between unequal exchange partners. Gunnar Myrdal has written, "If things were left to market forces unhampered by any policy interferences, industrial production, commerce, banking, insurance, shipping, and indeed almost all those economic activities which in a developing economy tend to give a bigger than average return—and, in addition, science, art, literature, education, and higher culture generally—would cluster in certain localities and regions leaving the rest of the country more or less in a backwater."[22]

Wallerstein stresses the importance of state power in maintaining and challenging unequal exchanges. "Once we get a difference in the strength of state-machineries, we get the operation of 'unequal exchange' which is enforced by strong states on weak ones, by core states on peripheral areas." According to Wallerstein, only when a single nation dominates the whole world system does it favor unrestricted market forces. He sees mercantilism, for example, the creation of national economic barriers, as "a defense mechanism of capitalists located in states which are one level below the high point of strength in the system."[23] Planters are considerably more defenseless because they typically operate in societies with states that are comparatively weak in an international context.

Backwater regions can and do overcome initial disadvantages.[24] Agricultural expansion and diversification may increase the division of labor and lead to the growth of subsidiary industries that contribute to the efficiency of production and marketing. In addition, other industries may arise to serve local consumers, and some of these may eventually broaden the export base. As a consequence, urban areas begin to develop; they tend to stimulate investment in education, which further expands the region's economic potential.[25] These stages of growth tend *not* to occur in plantation societies, however, which have tremendous comparative advantages for particular commodities, such as cotton, and remain tied to a single export staple. Herein lies the problem. Single-product agricultural producers are disadvantaged in the world market. They exchange raw primary products grown on the plantation for goods manufactured in the metropolis. Agricultural producers can secure terms of trade favorable for development only when productivity in manufactured goods is greater than productivity in primary products both in the plantation society and in the industrial society. This is rarely the case. Typically, the benefits of increased productivity in exports are transferred to the manufacturing society or region, not to the producer.[26]

Plantation societies want the products industrial societies

offer. Because of trade disadvantages, however, they find themselves increasingly indebted to these societies, thus limiting the capital available for their development of home industries. Ironically, whatever amounts of capital are available for investment —apart from the usual investments in land and, in the case of the antebellum South, in slaves—often tend to be invested outside the plantation society. Roads, power facilities, railroads, and the like must exist in underdeveloped areas before local businessmen can be induced to invest in the plantation society. The building of such facilities is often viewed as too risky for individual capitalists in underdeveloped societies, especially when compared with more secure investment opportunities in the developed societies, as Paul Baran notes.[27]

Primary producers can break out of this vicious circle of underdevelopment. It has been observed historically that development occurs most rapidly when plantation societies have the least contact with the world market. This is considered to have been true for Latin American producers during both world wars and the Great Depression.[28] A classic case of protection from world trade is that of Tokugawa Japan, a period of great stability, when the political elite created a unified nation-state while isolation permitted the slow growth of agricultural surpluses, internal markets, and industry—preconditions for the rapid development that followed the Meiji Restoration.[29] Plantation societies can close off from the world market, substitute domestic products for imports, and aim at economic diversification. State power could be used to eliminate luxury imports, and it could stimulate local demand through income equalization and land reform. Further, it could absorb short-run losses in high-risk development ventures.[30] Given the political status quo of plantation societies, however, such policies are not likely. State policies aimed at reallocating the productive resources and changing the demand structure of plantation societies are tantamount to political revolution. Paul Baran writes:

> The alliance of property-owning classes controlling the destinies of most underdeveloped countries cannot be expected to design and to execute a set of measures running counter to each and all of their immediate vested interests.

> Set up to guard and to abet the existing property rights and privileges, [the state] cannot become the architect of a policy calculated to destroy the privileges standing in the way of economic progress and to place the property and incomes derived from it at the service of society as a whole.
>
> The keepers of the past cannot be the builders of the future.[31]

Concern with interests within plantation society that oppose development raises the general question of how class structures within plantation societies, in addition to external trade disabilities, influence development.

Class Relations and Persistent Poverty— The Internal Dimension

Dynamic forces that are external to plantation societies help keep these societies underdeveloped. Internal forces also inhibit change. The plantation is not only a system of production, but a community as well. Its class structure is a consequence of plantation production and a cause of further development limitations. A number of studies describe the social relations characteristic of plantation regions.[32] Servile labor developed as a solution to the problem of labor scarcity. Slavery in America, for example, developed in response to the effects of the frontier on the southern labor supply. Edgar Thompson describes the process as follows: "In the American colonies with an abundance of free or cheap natural resources there was no reason for a man voluntarily to enter or remain long in the employ of another. On the frontier he had every opportunity to become an independent squatter or farmer. Forced labor in America was, therefore, mainly a defensive measure against the effects of the frontier on the labor market."[33] Plantation organization substitutes supervision for skilled labor.[34] Thus the plantation is a highly authoritarian institution with power centralized in the hands of its owner. The owner's authority is supported by law and by a rigid class structure. Because all decisions regarding the lives of its workers are made by the planter without interference from outside, such as the church or state, the plantation has been called—borrowing the language of Erving Goffman—a "total institution."[35]

Because they are characterized by high levels of compulsion and exploitation, plantation societies are "pregnant with conflict."[36] Usually, the planters' power is enforced by castelike barriers on mobility between themselves and their workers that are often defended by racial distinctions. Thompson has described the plantation as a "race-making situation."

> The naked force of the planter was never sufficient to keep men working at low place. There had to develop some kind of myth, like race, which not only those who ruled but those who are ruled accepted. It was not sufficient to assert the superiority of the white man and the inferiority of the black man; it was much more important to persuade the black man to accept the allegation of his own inferiority. This is what the idea of race achieved. . . . As cultural differences between whites and Negroes receded, visible physical differences loomed larger to become the chief marks around which to organize doctrines and beliefs of deeper biological differences.
>
> In Virginia the plantation took two peoples originally differentiated as Christian and heathen and before the first century was over it had made two races.[37]

In following chapters, I shall discuss how stratification by race was also an important element in the planters' hegemony over the nonslaveholding white farmers in the South and how manipulation of working-class fears of economic competition with blacks was an important control device in the industrial villages of the New South as well. Status distinctions, however, should not obscure the basic class character of plantation societies. No one has contributed more to an understanding of the latter than Eugene Genovese.[38]

Genovese has led in the comparative study of plantation societies, but most of his insights into the effects of class relations on economic development are drawn from the American South. Slavery, he argues, gave the South a social system and a civilization that was fundamentally at odds with the rest of the bourgeois world. "The planters," he says, "were not mere capitalists; they were precapitalist, quasi-aristocratic landowners who had to adjust their economy and ways of thinking to a capitalist world market. Their society, in its spirit and fundamental direction represented the antithesis of capitalism, however many compromises it had to make."[39] This was so because the master-slave relationship was much more than simply an economic arrangement. It was a class relationship that implied distinct politics, ideology, and social behavior for the plantation region. According to Genovese, since the whole civilization rested on this relationship, its preservation was more important than the pursuit of profit. Plantation cultivation was pursued even when it was economically irrational. Changes that threatened it were resisted. In particular, industrialization—the typical solution to the vicious circle of trade dependency—was resisted.

Planters needed some industrial products—cheap clothing, shoes, and farm equipment—but, according to Genovese, they "could not sustain economically or tolerate politically a general industrialization." They faced a number of economic handicaps that limited the capital they had for investment. Genovese believes that the South was a "colonial" area. Much of its capital was drained off by imports as well as by northern financiers and shippers who moved its exports. The available money tended to be invested in more land and more slaves or it was spent on lavish consumption. Capital for industrial development therefore was limited, but expenditures on slaves and conspicuous consumption enhanced the social status of the planter and helped to preserve his class hegemony. This expenditure pattern was reinforced by southern banking institutions, which were not sources of industrial capital but, rather, "clearing houses of mercantile finance."[40] They extended credit to planters on the basis of production expectations and guaranteed the export of staple crops, thus ensuring the planters' dependence on the world market.

According to Genovese's hotly debated interpretation, another serious inhibition of economic development resulting from southern class structure was the fact that slavery limited the home market for manufactured goods. Genovese writes:

> In the slave South the home market consisted primarily of the plantations, which bought foodstuffs from the West and manufactured goods from the East. The planters needed increased Southern manufacturing, but only for certain purposes. . . . This narrow market could not compare with the tremendous Western demand for industrial commodities of all kinds, especially for agricultural implements and machinery on the more capital-intensive Western farms. The Northeast had the capital and skilled labor for fairly large-scale production and had established its control over existing markets in the North and West. Southern manufacturers could not hope to compete with Northerners outside the South, and the same conditions that brought about Northern control of the Northern market made possible Northern penetration of the Southern market despite its costs of transportation.[41]

A few antebellum southerners, such as Hinton Helper of North Carolina and Cassius Clay of Kentucky, also believed that slavery limited this home market, and they opposed slavery for that reason. The following is from an antislavery appeal made by Cassius Clay:

> Lawyers, merchants, mechanics, laborers, who are your consumers; Robert Wickliffe's two hundred slaves? How many clients do you find, how many goods do you sell, how many hats, coats, saddles, and trunks do you make for these two hundred slaves? Does Mr. Wickliffe lay out as much for himself and his two hundred slaves as two hundred freemen do? . . . All our towns dwindle and our farmers lose, in consequence, all home markets. Every farmer bought out by the slave system sends off the consumers of the manufacturers of the town: when the consumers are gone, the mechanic must go also. . . . A home market cannot exist in a slave state.[42]

If landowning classes in plantation societies fail to carry out modernizing reforms, no other groups have power to do so. Certainly the commercial middle classes in plantation societies are too dependent on the planters, who are their best customers, to risk opposing their interests. Genovese describes the position of the middle class in the antebellum South as follows:

> In the South extensive and complicated commercial relations with the world market permitted the growth of a small commercial bourgeoisie. The resultant fortunes flowed into slaveholding, which offered prestige and economic and social security in a planter-dominated society. Independent merchants found their business dependent on the patronage of the slaveholders. The merchants either became planters themselves or assumed a servile attitude toward the planters. The commercial bourgeoisie, such as it was, remained tied to the slaveholding interest, had little desire or opportunity to invest capital in industrial expansion, and adopted the prevailing aristocratic attitudes.[43]

Other observers have noted the tendency for the middle classes of underdeveloped societies to oppose change and ally themselves with the landowning class.[44] Genovese's arguments, if correct, lead to the conclusion that industrialization could have occurred in the South only with the collapse of the planter class or change in their class interests.

Genovese's interpretation of southern class interests is based on the assumption that plantation agriculture yielded a low level of profits and, further, that the planter did not care greatly since he was motivated by values other than economic rationality alone. He clung to a way of life. He persisted in making heavy investments in land and slaves in spite of poor economic returns. This view has recently been challenged by econometricians Robert Fogel and Stanley Engerman in their book *Time on the Cross*. They claim that new investigations show that, in fact, slaveowning was highly profitable and southern agriculture highly productive. Investment in slaves, they claim, earned an average return of 10 percent on the market price, "equal to or in excess of the averages which obtained in a variety of nonagricultural enterprises." Further, they argue that southern plantations were 40 percent more efficient than northern farms in 1860: "The larger slave plantations had achieved, on average, a degree of efficiency that was unmatched by any other major subsector of American agriculture, North or South, during the antebellum era."[45] They reject altogether the argument that the South was an underdeveloped or "colonial" region and as false the thesis that slavery retarded southern growth, pointing out that between 1840 and 1860 the South's per capita income grew 30 percent more rapidly than did income in the North.[46] Finally, Fogel and Engerman claim not only that the effects of conspicuous consumption on capital formation have been "overstated," but that "recent work on the southern wealth distribution reveals that previous scholars have generally exaggerated the degree of inequality" in the antebellum South. They argue,

> This finding strikes at the heart of the claim that the skewed income distribution made the southern market too small to support large-scale manufacturing firms of the type which existed in the Northeast. Even if the income distribution had been more unequal than it was, the fact that planters purchased large quantities of clothing and shoes for slaves from northern firms suggests the existence of a large market for manufacturing goods on plantations. It can, indeed, be argued that the products ordered by planters were more standardized and more amenable to mass production techniques than would have been the situation if slaves were themselves the source of demand.[47]

Fogel and Engerman's research is important because, in their words, "it also throws into doubt the contention that southern slaveholders were a 'pre-capitalist,' 'uncommercial' class which subordinated profit to considerations of power, life style, and 'patriarchal commitments.'" They attribute greater economic rationality to the planters than does Genovese, claiming that the explanation for the South's lag behind the North in industrialization is simply that "during the antebellum era the South's comparative advantage was in agriculture rather than in manufacturing."[48] If the anticapitalist spirit of Southern planters has been overstressed, then perhaps, too, their resistance to industry has been magnified. This is of fundamental importance for an understanding of the class origins of the New South.

The motivations of antebellum slaveholders have not received adequate historical treatment. Paul David and Peter Temin
warn that Fogel and Engerman's "illegitimate methodological
device of arguing from information about rates of return to
conclusions about the behavior and motivation of representative
individuals" simply "fails to illuminate the motives of the *typical* slaveholder."[49] Genovese's claim that industry was actively
opposed in the South is crucial to his argument, but he lacks
historical evidence. In fact, he makes an important acknowledgment that "the extent to which planters and rural slaveholders
owned the South's industrial enterprises cannot as yet be mea-
sured accurately, but it was clearly considerable."[50] In research
on the antebellum textile industry in North Carolina, Richard
Griffin and Diffee Standard report that the plantation-based
Battle family in eastern North Carolina raised a half-million
dollars to enlarge their cotton mill near Rocky Mount during
an antebellum recession, but a sudden rise in cotton prices
led them to reinvest in land and slaves instead.[51] If decisions
not to develop industry can be explained economically, then
Genovese's interpretation is weakened because he assumes that
planters' economic actions cannot be understood in terms of
capitalist economic rationality because their overriding end was
preservation of the slave labor system.

Genovese's insightful interpretation of southern slaveholding avoids the economic determinism of vulgar Marxism by
stressing the dialectical relationship between economy and society, but his characterization of the planter as "precapitalist"
is misleading. Wallerstein defines capitalism as an economic
system in which production is for sale and profit in a market.
"Slavery and so-called 'second-serfdom,'" he says, "are not to
be regarded as anomalies in a capitalist system." They represent
alternative modes of "agricultural capitalism" that are directed
toward the same end as wage-labor capitalism—production for
profit.[52] The apparent conflict between Fogel and Engerman
and Genovese may prove reconcilable if short-run effects of
cotton cultivation are separated from long-run effects. Gavin
Wright, an economist, agrees that Fogel and Engerman have es-

tablished "that the 1850s were a period of enormous profits for slaveholding cotton planters," but he contends that the growth of demand for cotton would not have continued beyond 1860. Great *short-run* profits from cotton production perhaps make the economic decisions of slaveholders more understandable, especially their preference for buying slaves, but this does not invalidate Genovese's interpretation of the *long-run* detrimental effects of slaveholding. Support for this view comes from Wright's argument that Fogel and Engerman confuse the effects of the expansion of demand for cotton with the characteristics of slavery as a mode of production. He contends that "the slave South was typical of many economies in history based essentially on extractive resource-intensive exports, which expand rapidly during a period of rising external demand, but which do not lay the institutional foundations for sustained growth once this era has passed."[53]

3. The Political Economy of the American South: Persistence and Change

The South: An Economically Peripheral Region

Southern historians sometimes claim[1] that the South's position in the American economy has been that of a "colony." Southern states contributed the lion's share of American exports before the Civil War.[2] Ignoring other exports such as rice and tobacco, southern cotton alone made up more than half of the total American exports during the antebellum period. The cash value of cotton exports increased from $17.5 million in 1815 to $191.8 million in 1860.[3] The South soon became aware of its dependency on England and New England, aware that its increased agricultural productivity benefited commercial and manufacturing interests outside the South as much as it did the plantation region itself. As Thomas C. Cochran and William Miller assert in *The Age of Enterprise*, "By 1830, so successful were northern merchants engaged in the cotton trade that forty cents of every dollar paid for the planter's staple went North. . . . As a triangular trade thus developed among the cotton South, commercial New York, and industrial England, southern planters fell deeper and deeper into debt. The more cotton they produced, the more they contributed to the treasuries of northern shippers and northern bankers."[4] The following excerpt from a special legislative report made to the North Carolina General Assembly in 1828 described that state's economic dependency and called for the development of manufacturing industries in the South.

Report on the Establishment of Cotton and Woolen Manufactures to the House of Commons, Jan. 1, 1828
     A crisis is at hand, when our citizens must turn a portion
of their labor and enterprize into other channels of industry;
otherwise, poverty and ruin will fall on every class of our
community. It is a lamentable fact, that the people of North-
Carolina are indebted to one another, and to the Banks, to an
amount appaling to the mind. . . . The debts due to the local
institutions alone, amount to $5,221,877. . . .
     Owing to the want of navigable streams in our state,
leading to good marts, hitherto but few of our Agricultural
products would admit the expense of carrying to market.
Cotton and Tobacco from the interior, are almost the only
articles that will bear transportation, while rice and naval
stores, on the sea board, are the principal exports. When the
prices of these articles were up, the farming interests of
North-Carolina presented something like the appearance of
prosperity, but a great depression has taken place in their
value, and at this time they are scarcely worth producing.
The loss of the West Indian Trade has lessened the demand
for lumber. Tobacco is now taxed in the British markets, more
than 600 percent, while the demand for cotton, our other
great staple, does not keep pace with its increased production. . . . If the planter in North-Carolina can barely afford to
raise cotton at 8 cents per lb. he must soon be driven from its
culture altogether, by the farmers of the West, whose new
rich lands enable them to produce it with less labour and expense. . . . The balance of trade against us, for several years
past, has greatly increased.
     The balance of trade against us, produces another state
of things on the monied concerns of North-Carolina, which
threatens not only the ruin of our local institutions, but as an
inevitable consequence, bankruptcy and distress throughout
the community.
     In setting about to ameliorate our condition, the first step
is to adopt some system that will enable us to buy less and
sell more—that will enable us to supply within ourselves,
our own wants and necessities. . . . But how is this important
revolution to be accomplished? We unhesitatingly answer—
by introducing the Manufacturing System into our own State,

and fabricating, at least to the extent of our own wants. We go further. Instead of sending off at great expense of transportation, our raw material, convert it into fabrics at home, and in that state, bring it into market. In this way, our want of navigation will not be so severely felt. . . .

North-Carolina, during good crop years, is estimated to have shipped for the North and Europe, through her own ports and those of her sister states, at least 80,000 bales of cotton. Eighty thousand bales at $30 per bale, amounts to $2,400,000. But 80,000 bales, thus worth $2,400,000 in the raw state, when converted into fabrics, are increased in value four fold, which will make the sum of $9,600,000 or $7,200,000 more than we obtained for it. . . .

Let the Manufacturing System but take root among us, and it will soon flourish like a vigorous plant in its native soil; it will become our greatest means of wealth and prosperity; it will change the course of trade, and, in a great measure, make us independent of Europe and the North.

Nature has made us far more independent of them than they are of us. They can manufacture our raw material, but they cannot produce it. We can raise it and manufacture it too. Such are our superior advantages, that we may anticipate the time, when the manufactured articles of the South will be shipped to the North, and sold in their markets cheaper than their own fabrics, and when the course of trade and difference of exchange will turn in our favor.[5]

The authors of this legislative report understood all the economic forces affecting plantation regions discussed in the previous chapter—trade dependency and indebtedness, the loss to other regions of the value added to raw materials through manufacturing, the need for partial withdrawal from world trade, and the substitution of home manufactures for imports. But North Carolina's industrial revolution, which the authors foresaw in 1828, was more than a half-century away. North Carolina and the South continued to lag behind the rest of the nation in manufacturing. Table 3.1 compares regions of the United States in terms of their local manufacture of agricultural implements. The South's production increased only 30 percent

Table 3.1. *Regional Manufacture of Agricultural Implements*

Region	Number of Establishments in 1860	Annual Value of Product	
		1860	1850
New England	213	$1,934,924	$1,662,426
Middle Atlantic	678	$5,791,224	$2,471,806
West	840	$8,707,194	$1,923,927
South	241	$1,018,913	$ 784,452

Source: *Eighth Census of the United States, 1860,* Vol. 2 (Agriculture), p. xi.

from 1850 to 1860, whereas the West's production increased over 350 percent. This is consistent with Douglass North's claim that western farmers' demand for manufactured goods generated local industrial expansion that was protected by that region's geographical isolation.[6] The South, lacking such natural protection, saw proportionately more of its capital flow outside the region for farm equipment imports.

Figure 3.1 compares personal income per capita by region as the percentage of the national average for the period from 1840 to 1950. It shows that the income gap between the Northeast and the South increased from 1840 to 1860. In the 1850s, southerners, like their predecessors in the 1820s, foresaw increasing regional divergence, and many urged that the South follow the lead of the North and industrialize. They feared not only that the South would slump behind the North in wealth and economic power, but that the region would lose political parity with the North as well.[7] The reality of this fear was demonstrated politically and militarily in the Civil War.

Fogel and Engerman show that although per capita income was lower in the antebellum South than in the North, it actually grew 30 percent more rapidly. "The myth of Southern backwardness and stagnation," they claim, "thus arose not because of any lack in the southern economic achievement but because the northern achievement was so remarkable, and because the

Figure 3.1. *Regional Income Shares, 1840–1950*

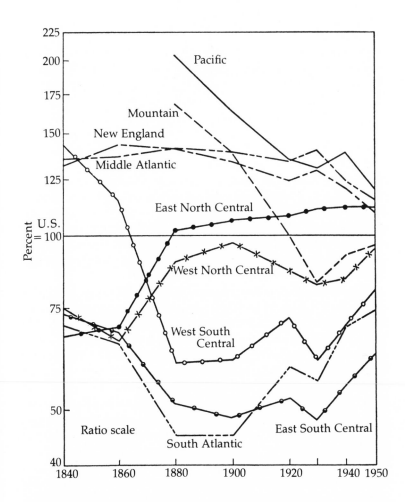

Source: Richard Easterlin, "Regional Income Trends, 1840–1950," in *American Economic History*, ed. Seymour E. Harris (New York: McGraw-Hill Book Co., 1961). Used by permission of the publisher.

continuous comparisons between the North and South were invariably unfavorable to the South. Compared with any country of Europe except England, however, the South's economic performance was quite strong."[8] Gavin Wright agrees that antebellum income was not low but concludes: "Rather than claiming 'backwardness' for 1860 or indeed for the antebellum period generally, critics should instead focus on the *dependent* character of southern growth, and on the region's failure to use its earnings to develop the institutions and acquire the skills needed for sustained growth in the modern era."[9]

The relative economic position of the South Atlantic states fell even more from 1860 to 1880, at least in part because of the devastation that resulted from the war. The region began slowly to catch up only after 1900. By then it had launched its much heralded New South revolution aimed at closing the widening income gap.

In 1880, 75.4 percent of the South's labor force was in agriculture. Agriculture accounted for only 23.3 percent of the work force in the Northeast and 54.5 percent in the North Central region. Only 4.6 percent of the South's population was employed in manufacturing in 1880 compared with 25.7 percent in the Northeast.[10] Today it seems that the South is on the verge of closing the regional economic gap. Per capita income in the South in 1959 was 69 percent of the national average.[11] By 1970 it was 81 percent. But optimism for the region has a long history. The South seems always to have been on the verge of catching up. As George Tindall states dramatically, "Another consistent theme [among southern writers] has been the Vanishing South, forever moving toward the mainstream of American life but somehow never getting there. The Vanishing South, it turns out, has staged one of the most prolonged disappearing acts since the decline and fall of the Roman Empire."[12]

Southern industry is developing at a faster rate than industry in the nation as a whole. Between 1947 and 1962, manufacturing employment in the South increased 42 percent, while it increased by only 13 percent for the nation. The Carolinas now rank first and second among the fifty states with the highest percentage of the labor force employed in industry. Yet North and South Carolina rank, respectively, forty-third and forty-seventh in per capita personal incomes. North Carolina ranks fiftieth for its low average earnings of industrial workers, who are paid only 73 percent of the national average.[13] Table 3.2 shows that the growth of southern industry is closely linked to primary products. The region has experienced little growth of industries that are independent of local resources. As late as

Table 3.2. Percentage of Average Wage Earners, 1879, and of Employees, 1947, in Selected Manufacturing Industries Employed in the South

Industry	1879	1947	Change
First-stage Resource Users			
Food and kindred products	12.5	22.5	10.0
Tobacco manufacturing	28.9	57.8	28.9
Forest products	14.7	44.4	29.7
Products of petroleum and coal	12.5	34.6	22.1
Stone, clay, and glass products	6.6	20.7	13.5
Mean	15.0	35.9	20.9
Second-stage Resource Users			
Paper and allied products	3.3	22.1	18.8
Chemical and allied products	4.7	28.4	23.7
Rubber products	0.0	8.3	8.3
Textiles	3.9	34.0	30.1
Mean	3.0	23.2	20.2
Industries for Which Resources Have Most Indirect Significance			
Printing, publishing, allied products	7.0	14.4	7.4
Leather and its manufacturing	3.6	10.4	6.8
Machinery except transport	5.4	5.1	−0.3
Transport equipment	6.7	9.5	2.8
Mean	5.7	10.0	4.3

Source: Winsborough, "The Changing Regional Character of the South," p. 42. Used by permission of the publisher, Duke University Press (1965).

1954, three of the six poorest paying industries in the South (textiles, apparels, and lumber) accounted for 45 percent of all manufacturing employment.[14] These were the industries experiencing the most growth during the same period.

The fact that the South has lagged behind the North economically does not necessarily mean, however, that the South is a "colony." Fogel and Engerman, writing about the antebellum period, argue that "the South's large purchases of manufactured goods from the North make it no more of a colonial dependency than did the North's heavy purchases of rails from England. The true colonial dependencies, countries such as India and Mexico, had less than one tenth the per capita income of the South in 1860."[15] It is true that, according to their data, the South was richer than any European country in 1860 except England, but that is not the point. It is the South's *relative* economic performance in the American economy—a performance that worsened dramatically after 1860—that is at issue, as well as its relative dependence.

Colonialism has been a common theme among apologists for the slow growth of southern industry. It has been claimed that the North pursued a conscious, aggressively imperialist policy toward the South that retarded southern growth. Much attention, for example, has been focused on the railroad system financed by J. P. Morgan, whose high rates supposedly strangled southern manufacturers. C. Vann Woodward echoes this theme: "Smaller roads were raided, bankrupted, driven to the wall, or suffered to survive at the pleasure of the giant northern systems. The giants divided the Southern Colony at their leisure, according to mutual interest."[16] Those advocating a conspiracy theory of colonialism pointed to discrimination against the South in giving credit, tariff policies, interregional differences in freight rates, monopoly, and absentee ownership. Jonathan Daniels of North Carolina, for example, declared in 1938 that "the cruelest aspects of conquest were not involved in Reconstruction in the South but in the use of national power to entrench sectional advantage elsewhere over the South." Clarence Danhof has reviewed vast evidence on these claims and finds little support for them. He concludes that "the colonial-imperialist thesis of conspiracy must be considered an unfortunate episode—a resurgence of crude sectionalism—that diverted the attention of some of the South's ablest men from constructive approaches to the region's problems."[17]

The historical question of conscious northern "imperialism" is beyond the scope of this analysis, but Danhof identifies colonialism too narrowly with conspiracy. Not all writers who use the colonial imagery to describe the South have conspiracy in mind. Howard Odum, for example, called attention to the South's "international relations" by describing the South as a "colonial economy." He referred to several factors, including "a continuous outflow of money to other regions," outflow of population, low standard of consumption, and deficiency of industry.[18] Rupert Vance cited a complex of problems, including a "losing balance of trade," "over-exploitation of natural resources," a "debtor economy," limited capital accumulation, agricultural overproduction, and "comparative inability to limit output"—all of which he termed "colonial."[19]

The choice of the term "colony" to describe the South's economic dependency is unfortunate. The term suggests foreign political domination of a dependent territory and population. In order to avoid this connotation, the concept of "internal colonialism," advanced by Pablo Gonzales Casonova[20] to describe the relationship between metropolitan and Amerindian regions within Latin America, has been applied to regions within the United States, though there are problems with its usage as well. William Appleman Williams described all of nineteenth-century rural America as existing "in an *internal* colonial relationship *vis-a-vis* the domestic American metropolis (and the larger Western European metropolis of which New York is a part)."[21] Some states have been described as inner colonies including, recently, Maine and Vermont.[22] In an outstanding example of regional analysis, Michael Hechter described Britain's Celtic periphery as an "inner colony." He found that "though the rate of interregional transactions grew rapidly during the period 1801–1921 in the British Isles, and was accompanied by increases in social mobilization in the Celtic regions, nevertheless substantial convergence in regional rates of economic development did not occur."[23] The Celtic periphery remained economically underdeveloped and politically distinct despite national integration. His analysis controlled for regional differences in levels of industry and agricultural productivity. Wage levels were uniform because labor agreements were nationwide. He concluded that regional differences in income shares were the result of "ethnocentrism"—"the socially unanticipated result of the aggregate of . . . individual decisions" and "not part of a planned or even consciously stated policy aiming at the exploitation of the Celtic periphery."[24]

Hechter's stress on the ethnic identity of British regions is a bit strained, but he is aware of the problems in designating regions as internal colonies: "There does not seem to be a general consensus on a small number of essential defining features of internal colonialism. . . . What if all but one or two conditions seem to be met? The danger, of course, is to so relax the meaning of internal colonialism that almost any instance of stratification may fall somewhere within its boundaries."[25] Pierre van den Berghe has urged that inner colonialism be restricted to regions that meet the following conditions: (1) rule of one ethnic group by another within the contiguous boundaries of a single state, (2) territorial separation, (3) the presence of an internal government created to rule the subject peoples, and (4) economic dependency and inferiority.[26] Using this strict definition, which I think is appropriate, the American South is not an internal colony.

The South is best defined as an economically peripheral region within the American economy. Southerners are not ethnically distinct and, except for the brief period of military occupation following the Civil War, the South was never a conquered and incorporated territory such as Ireland or Wales. North and South were equal partners in the American republic, although ultimately it took civil war to determine whose needs would dominate.[27] As a peripheral region devoted to cotton growing, the postbellum South was a dependent economy. The literature on dependency discussed above thus suggests handicaps in economic development which the South shared with other peripheral regions, but caution is urged. The South's position within the American political economy was stronger than that of an overseas possession. The South did industrialize, and the sources of this change were internal.

The Transition from Old South to New

Despite caveats concerning the quality of southern industrialization, the South has changed profoundly. Tobacco rows and cotton fields now share the land with tobacco factories and cotton mills. Cities have arisen and, with them, new classes and new political forces. How has all of this come about? Economic constraints frequently keep plantation societies underdeveloped. Policies that benefit plantation societies in the long run are often resisted by landowning classes. How did the South overcome these obstacles to change? One answer is that the South has advanced through industrialization and diversification only where its dependency on primary production has been broken. In class terms, this is to suggest that change has been possible only where the traditional resistance to change by the planter class has been overcome. Some indirect support for this interpretation comes from research reported by economist William Nicholls.

Having demonstrated the favorable effects of industrial-urban development on the rural economy of the Upper East Tennessee Valley, Nicholls asks the fundamental question of why some areas in the South had substantial industrial-urban growth while others experienced none. Specifically, he was puzzled by why this section of Tennessee, a relatively undeveloped region during the antebellum period, should outstrip the rest of the South even prior to TVA. He concluded that the answer was noneconomic, arguing that "the outstanding economic progress of this area was in significant part the result of its failure to share with other southern areas most of the tenets of southern tradition." More generally, he argued that "the

South's lag in industrial development is in substantial part the result of its stubborn adherence to a set of values inconsistent with a high rate of industrialization."[28]

To explain the persistence of behavior by "tradition," however, is not to explain but merely to describe, for one must still explain the persistence of tradition. As Barrington Moore has said,

> The assumption of inertia, that cultural and social continuity do not require explanation, obliterates the fact that both have to be recreated anew in each generation, often with great pain and suffering. To maintain and transmit a value system, human beings are punched, bullied, sent to jail, thrown into concentration camps, cajoled, bribed, made into heroes, encouraged to read newspapers, stood up against a wall and shot, and sometimes even taught sociology. To speak of cultural inertia is to overlook the concrete interests and privileges that are served by indoctrination, education, and the entire complicated process of transmitting culture from one generation to the next.[29]

The explanation for why some areas of the South—especially, as Nicholls observed, areas that were previously not plantation economies—have modernized more easily than others must be given in terms of social structure. That is, in Moore's language, we must seek the *social origins of southern backwardness and southern change*.

Lester Salamon explains Mississippi's persistent backwardness in terms of the continued hegemony of Mississippi's landed upper class that has dominated that society for generations in cooperation with a dependent commercial middle class.[30] He claims that "the 'alliance of cotton and commerce' constrained economic growth and political freedom in Mississippi by fixing on the society a social and economic system dominated by the labor nexus of the cotton plantation." The massive labor needs of the plantation system have necessitated a policy of strict labor control, discouraged the education of freedmen, and discouraged the development of alternative sources of employment up to the present. "The result has been a regime that is essentially hostile to democracy, that had little incentive to provide public education or to introduce labor-saving improvements, that had little real interest in rapid industrialization, but was willing to support limited industrial growth geared to the needs of the cotton plantation and respectful of plantation-inspired labor policies. In short, the result has been economic backwardness, the 'closed society,'[31] and limited economic development.''

From Salamon's perspective it is essential to understand that the planter regime, at least until recently, has gone unchallenged. Barrington Moore has demonstrated historically that challenges to landed elites have come from urban middle classes, the lower classes (peasants), or revenue-hungry central governments. According to Salamon, all of these forces were absent in Mississippi except, briefly, the lower-class challenge that arose during Reconstruction. The political reforms of Reconstruction were soon swept away by what Salamon calls "a counter-revolutionary reign of terror." According to Moore, a strong urban middle class is "an indispensable element in the growth of parliamentary democracy."[32] No challenge to the planters' hegemony came from Mississippi's middle classes, who were rural, scattered throughout the state, and lacked an urban basis for unification as a class. They were divided by sectional rivalries; many were socially insecure because of their foreign and ethnic statuses. Most important, they were economically dependent on the planters. Lacking a mass market, they could not afford to alienate their best customers. According to Salamon, they emulated the planter aristocracy and tended to invest their commercial and industrial profits in land (and, during the antebellum period, in slaves). This was facilitated by southern banking and credit institutions. When they were "faced with threats from organized small farmers in the later nineteenth century, and enticed by the prospects of acquiring land themselves, the commercial middle class formed a rough working coalition with larger farmers, exchanging support for the anti-democratic labor control policies of the farmers in return for guaranteed commercial profits, and, later, state subsidies for small scale industry."

Some industry developed in Mississippi after the Civil War, but only to a limited degree. Its products (such as fertilizer) were geared to the needs of the planters. In pointing to the fact that Mississippi planters opposed thoroughgoing modernization but sponsored some local manufacture of useful products, Salamon draws parallels between Mississippi's repressive "alliance of cotton and commerce" and a pattern of modernization Barrington Moore has called "revolutions from above."[33] In contrast with the English pattern of industrialization—frequently taken as paradigmatic of modernization itself—where change originates in the urban-commercial sector of society, "revolutions from above" are relatively rare instances in which agrarian ruling classes encourage industrial development. This tends to be an unusually harsh process that often leads to industrial fascism, as in Germany and Japan. The traditional authority of the landed upper class is used simultaneously to force greater agricultural production and rapid industrial development.

Salamon refers to Mississippi's limited economic development as a revolution from above in order to emphasize the planters' dominance in economic affairs and to explain the absence of political democracy in Mississippi. He does not suggest that Mississippi's economic development was "revolutionary" in its extent or its rapidity. Quite the contrary. His interpretation of the failure of Mississippi's middle class to promote change is similar in implication to Baran's claim that in peripheral societies the middle classes are often "keepers of the past."[34] This suggests that an important condition for change in the South may have been the strength and independence of its middle classes and makes sense of Nicholls's findings that change has come most readily to southern areas not previously devoted to plantation agriculture. The following hypothesis is suggested: *Southern economic development has best flourished in those regions (and during those historical periods) where a strong commercial middle class has countered the negative power of the landed interests and promoted industrial development.*

This hypothesis is compatible with the mainstream interpretation of southern history. C. Vann Woodward has most forcefully endorsed this middle-class thesis to explain the dramatic rise of the New South from the ashes of the Old. As one reviewer summarized it, Woodward's *Origins of the New South* "is the story of the decay and decline of the aristocracy, the suffering and betrayal of the poor whites, and the rise and transformation of a middle class."[35] According to Woodward, the Civil War weakened and in some places destroyed altogether the planter aristocracy. "No ruling class of our history ever found itself so completely stripped of its economic foundations as did that of the South in this period. Involved in the downfall of the old planter class were the leading financial, commercial, and industrial families of the region." This made room for the rise of a new class of men, men with a vision of a New South, an industrial South. These new men carried out an industrial revolution comparable to England's, only in less time. "The 'victory of the middle classes' and 'the passing of power from the hands of landowners to manufacturers and merchants,' which required two generations in England, were substantially achieved in a much shorter period in the South."[36]

Empirical support for Woodward's interpretation comes mainly from Broadus Mitchell's *Rise of Cotton Mills in the South*, which claimed that lawyers, bankers, farmers, merchants, teachers, preachers, doctors, and public officials built the mills of the New South. This theory has influenced most subsequent views of the southern textile industry though thorough research is absent. Thus Glenn Gilman, in *Human Relations in the Industrial Southeast*, drawing also on Holland Thompson's *The New South*, believed that to the "middle class—professional people, merchants, independent farmers, small manufacturers, and skilled craftsmen—fell the greater share of the task of rebuilding the South. This is not to say that the planters did not help; but there were neither enough of them, nor did they possess the experience that was needed for the major part of the work. Many of them clung grimly to the land. They still had it, though it be ridden with mortgages, and it was the only life they knew."[37] The middle-class thesis is also reflected in Howard Odum's *The Way of the South*. In *Millhands and Preachers*, Liston Pope claimed that "up to 1910 the mills in Gaston County were owned to large degree, by small investors—farmers, merchants, clerks, wage earners, ministers."[38] Recent students of southern labor history repeat this interpretation, relying on older scholarship. For example, Harry Boyte, in "The Textile Industry: Keel of Southern Industrialization," notes that mill building "represented a significant shift of power from the rulers of the Old Slave South," and Melton McLaurin, in *Paternalism and Protest*, claimed that "since Southern mill owners seldom came from the old planter class, their acceptance of industrialism did not represent a sharp break with the past. Rather they most often represented low country commercial families, Piedmont merchants, and the larger yeomen farmers."[39]

Woodward's interpretation of the class origins of the New South is thus widely accepted. As Sheldon Hackney has said after reviewing all the research that Woodward's thesis has generated, "The remarkable thing is that there has been so little fundamental challenge to the outlines of the story established by Woodward twenty years ago."[40] The middle-class thesis is also consistent with sociological writings of both the Marxist and liberal traditions. Genovese reminds us that "industrialization is unthinkable without an agrarian revolution which shatters the old regime on the countryside."[41] In fact, in the sociological literature, development has implicitly come to mean the rise of the middle class. The following quotation from Leonard Reissman's "Social Development and the American South" suggests how strongly this association is made.

> The importance of the middle class for the process of change comes from the forced restructuring of society that this class sets into motion. The middle class in a developing area provides the leading personnel for social modernization. It is the social segment most committed to such development for its future power and prestige depend upon it.
>
> In our own history, in the history of other western nations, and again today in the events of the newly emerging nations, the middle class has assumed the pivotal role of promoting social development. . . .

The middle class pulls the rest of Society along with it toward higher living standards, broader educational opportunity, and wider participation in society.

In addition to these considerable functions, the rise of the middle class in a developing area challenges and, if successful, finally replaces the dominance of the aristocracy. *It could not be otherwise.* The values that the middle class seeks to legitimate are those that attack the traditional bases of aristocratic domination.[42]

Despite all the change in its occupational structure, when one controls statistically for the level of industrialization, the southern states have too small a middle class relative to the rest of the nation.[43] Reissman is aware of this deficiency when he admits that "evidence for the growth of a middle class to challenge the former aristocratic elite is hard to come by." Nevertheless, he is so committed to the middle-class thesis that he says, "There is really no other valid way to explain the revolutionary changes now taking place, since there must be human agents who are behind that change."[44]

North Carolina, as I shall show, provides a good test of the middle-class thesis. In 1860, North Carolina was the least prosperous southern state, yet by 1900 it was the model of southern development. From a backward state with only a small planter aristocracy it developed into a leader of the postbellum industrial South. To borrow Trotsky's phrase, North Carolina's limited plantation development during the antebellum period may have been a "privilege of historical backwardness" that helps to explain the state's rapid recovery after the Civil War and its shift of economic and political supremacy from the plantation region of the coastal plain to its industrializing Piedmont hinterland. Does this reflect the dramatic rise of a strong, independent middle class? Or were the paternalism of the mill village and the paternalism of rural tenancy and sharecropping—one industrial, the other agricultural, each highly profitable to its owners—complementary aspects of a social process closer akin to the revolutions from above that modernized Germany and Japan than to the history of American democratic capitalism outside the South?

4. Social Origins of the New South: The Case of North Carolina

North Carolina provides an interesting test of the middle-class hypothesis that southern economic development has flourished best in those regions (and during those historical periods) where a strong commercial middle class has countered the negative power of the landed interests and promoted industrial development. From the vantage point of the antebellum South, when North Carolina was a poor, isolated, undistinguished rural state with fewer slaves and big plantations than any other southern state except Tennessee,[1] one would not have predicted that North Carolina would soon become a brawny manufacturing power, yet, somehow, North Carolina evolved from the sleepy "Rip Van Winkle state" of the Old South to become the acknowledged industrial leader of the New South. From 1880 to 1900 its textile manufacturing increased 1,100 percent and an average of six new cotton mills were built each year. Along with these mills, new tobacco factories, furniture plants, railroads, highways, and schools began to dot the rural landscape, heralding the birth of a new era.

Was North Carolina's dramatic post–Civil War industrial success the result of its being a state of small farmers and merchants, lacking an aristocracy with the power to oppose change? This view seems to fit the state's popular image. In comparison with its aristocratic neighbors, Virginia and South Carolina, North Carolina commonly has been called "a vale of humility between two peaks of pride." Writing in the *Nation* in 1923, Judge Robert Winston called North Carolina a "militant mediocracy." He anticipated C. Vann Woodward by claiming that "North Carolina's development is the triumph of a vigorous middle class. The state never had the aristocratic tradition of either Virginia or South Carolina. To be sure it had its planter class . . . but this favored company never established itself so firmly in a holy of holies as its blood brethren to the north and south."[2] Still another North Carolinian of the same period, Robert Wilson, reflecting on the family fortunes based on New South industry, claimed that the state's millionaires were "self made." There were, he contended, "few if any millionaires by virtue of descent."[3] Is this popular image of the state mythical or does North Carolina provide support for the middle-class thesis?

To answer this question I shall describe briefly antebellum North Carolina and examine the extent of planter influence there prior to the war by comparing the state with Virginia and South Carolina. Then I shall explore the social origins of industry in post–Civil War North Carolina by examining the leaders and early history of the textile industry, for it was in the relationship between cotton manufacturing and the agrarian order during the first decades after the war that the modern configuration of class, culture, and politics that we call the "New South" was constructed. Textile manufacturing was a new departure and an old hope. A new market for southern cotton, an occupational outlet for displaced yeomen farmers, a new beginning for depressed southern towns, a businessman's dream—cotton manufacturing, and how it was developed, is a key to understanding the social pattern of those years in the South marked by the slow recovery from war and Reconstruction, the rise of vast personal fortunes alongside the spread of general human suffering, black political disfranchisement and economic oppression, agricultural depression and rural poverty, agrarian unrest, middle-class protest, and the rise of new towns, new hopes, and new myths.

Antebellum North Carolina

There was little in North Carolina's antebellum history to portend the rise of an industrial power. Although her culturological ascriptions do little to explain historical conditions,

Guion Johnson's inventory of the "Social Characteristics of Ante-Bellum North Carolina"—individualism, conservatism, sectionalism, provincialism, superstition—suggests the state's comparative backwardness: "Society in North Carolina in the period prior to the Civil War was permeated by superstitious notions; but this was only one characteristic of a people whose chance of getting ahead in life was limited and whose opportunity of learning new ways of doing things was circumscribed by conditions which made travel difficult and expensive. Isolation had produced a provincial and sectional society which reacted conservatively to the introduction of innovations; enough of the frontier characteristics still clung to the people to make them individualistic."[4] According to Hugh Lefler and Albert Newsome, "During the first third of the nineteenth century North Carolina was so undeveloped, backward, and indifferent to its condition that it was often called 'the second Nazareth,' the 'Ireland of America,' and the 'Rip Van Winkle' state." They attribute this condition to two factors, "handicaps imposed by nature and an ill-suited system of government."[5]

Geography, no doubt, has influenced the social development of North Carolina. Though later the state's rivers would power the region's numerous manufacturing plants, prior to the building of railroads they inhibited North Carolina's urban and commercial growth. Of the state's six principal rivers, only one, the Cape Fear, flows directly into the ocean, affording North Carolina only one good harbor at Wilmington. Of its other rivers, two flow into South Carolina and three into shallow sounds.[6] This meant that much of North Carolina's trade benefited urban centers outside the state such as Charleston, South Carolina, and Petersburg and Norfolk, Virginia. Even as late as 1880 only Mississippi and Arkansas remained more rural than North Carolina. Geographical isolation inhibited cultural as well as economic development. In 1840 one-third of the adult white population was illiterate.[7]

Geography, reinforced by politics, contributed to profound regional inequalities that continue to figure in North Carolina's development. The Piedmont and mountain sections were rich in natural resources and population, but the lack of transportation prevented their development, so they were poor in comparison with the plantation-rich East that used its political supremacy in the early part of the nineteenth century to maintain its advantage. According to Lefler and Newsome,

> The landlocked, undeveloped, but more populous West, where the prevailing regime of small-farm agriculture based on free white labor had produced a greater degree of social, economic, and political democracy, found its every effort for self-development by state action blocked by the dominance of the eastern landlords. These landlords, living a patriarchal life on their plantations in the East, supported chiefly by Negro slave labor, with reasonably satisfactory trade outlets for their produce and enough money for comfortable subsistence and the education of their children, enjoying political control and choice seats at the table of special privilege, looked with an aristocratic air upon the common people. They were pleased with the maintenance of the blessed status quo and were distinctly hostile to such innovations as the extension of political power to the masses or costly improvement projects, for the wealthier East would bear the major cost of these, and the poorer West would reap the major benefit.[8]

Such conditions limited opportunity in North Carolina, forcing a large portion of the population to emigrate. According to the 1850 census, approximately one-third of the free native population born in North Carolina was living outside the state.

Improvements were made during the last decades of the antebellum period as the West gained more political clout. Piedmont leaders Archibald Murphy, John Motley Morehead, and William A. Graham called for vast internal development projects and the latter two, as governors, used state resources to build railroads and schools and to provide minimally for social needs and economic development—a program too soon interrupted by a war few North Carolinians wanted.[9] By 1860 North Carolina was still economically backward in comparison with its aristocratic neighbors, Virginia and South Carolina.

Census data support North Carolina's image as a poor state made up of small farms. According to the United States census of 1860, North Carolina had proportionately fewer slaves and fewer slaveholders than either Virginia or South Carolina. Slaves comprised 33 percent of the state's total population, while they made up 40 percent of Virginia's population and 57 percent of South Carolina's population. In only fourteen of North Carolina's eighty-nine counties were slaves 50 percent or more of the population. In twenty-nine counties at least 40 percent of the population were slaves. North Carolina had proportionately fewer slaveholders than Virginia and South Carolina and proportionately fewer large slaveholders than South Carolina. North Carolina slaveholders were 5 percent of the total free population, whereas slaveholders represented 7 and 9 percent of the free populations of Virginia and South Carolina, respectively. North Carolina slaveholders averaged 9.6 slaves each; slaveholders in Virginia averaged 9.5 and those in South Carolina averaged 15.1 slaves each. In North Carolina 62 percent of the farms were less than one hundred acres each, whereas only 46 percent of South Carolina's farms were less than one hundred acres.[10]

North Carolina lagged slightly behind South Carolina in railroad construction (889 miles versus 988 miles, respectively, in a much smaller area) and fell significantly behind Virginia, which had 1,771 miles of railroads. North Carolina had the lowest percentage of population born out of state among all the American states, another indicator of its isolation and its limited economic growth. It was next to the lowest state in 1860 in its percentage of foreign-born residents. It paid the lowest wages in the nation, averaging only $1.84 per week. Virginia averaged $1.98 and South Carolina averaged $2.08 per week. Not only was antebellum North Carolina low in wages; it was also poor in capital. Virginia had sixty-five banks in 1860 and South Carolina had fifty, but North Carolina had only twenty banks, and these were concentrated in the East. Between 1850 and 1860, Virginia opened eighteen new banks and South Carolina opened thirty-two. In the same period North Carolina added only six new banks. The state's total real and personal property increased only 58 percent in the decade prior to the war, while Virginia's economic worth increased 84 percent and South Carolina's increased 90 percent. The United States economy as a whole grew 68 percent.

Antebellum North Carolina was divided into several distinct economic subregions. In contrast with states of the Deep South, where large plantation regions were rimmed by small hill regions populated by yeomen farmers, the heartland of North Carolina's plantation economy centered in a relatively small coastal plain. It was bordered on the east by infertile Tidewater counties and on the west by the expansive upland farm regions of the Appalachian Mountain and Piedmont territories. Tobacco and cotton cultivation and the plantation mode of production were extensive in many counties of the Piedmont, but in others grain and livestock predominated. Poor internal transportation prevented the economic and political integration of the state as a whole.[11]

North Carolina was a comparatively poor state in 1860, but there were nonetheless pockets of great wealth. Figure 4.1 shows per capita aggregate wealth by counties, ranging from very rich Warren County with a per capita valuation of $3,091.94 to very poor Yancey County with the low of $216.79 per capita. Warren County was a rich tobacco plantation area with a population that was 66 percent slave; Yancey was a mountainous subsistence farm economy on the Tennessee border and was only 4 percent slave. Though North Carolina's plantation region was smaller than that of other southern states, it was populated by men of great wealth and influence. Sectional differences between the rich, export-oriented East and the poor, subsistence-oriented West were issues in state politics dating back to the early Republic involving conflicts over taxation and internal improvements. The rise of manufacturing in the Piedmont is conventionally interpreted as the West's eventual triumph over eastern planters—a sectional as well as a class triumph.[12]

The only detailed picture of the antebellum stratification system is Guion Johnson's *Ante-Bellum North Carolina*, which

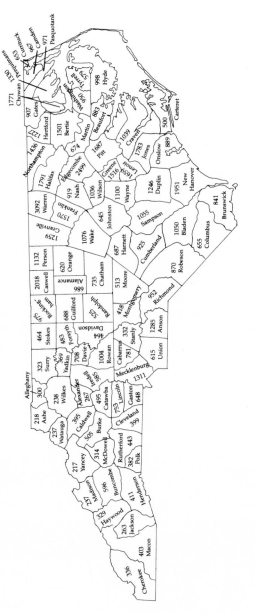

Figure 4.1. Aggregate Real and Personal Wealth Per Capita (Free), 1860

Source: *Eighth Census of the United States 1860*, Vol. 1, pp. 389–59: Vol. 2, p. 309.

reports, "If occupations, land, and slaves be taken as indices of wealth, it is evident that the average per capita wealth in the state was not large. There were few overgrown estates, and the majority of the inhabitants lived upon the produce of their labors."[13] According to Johnson, 27.7 percent of the farm families in North Carolina were slaveholders in 1860, but of these 71 percent owned less than ten slaves.[14] She estimates that only 12 percent of the slaveholders—less than 2 percent of the total free families—were in the planter class. She claims that North Carolina's stratification system was topped by a small "gentry class" comprising 6 percent of the population, who were planters, professionals, large merchants, and manufacturers.[15]

Johnson does not evaluate the extent of the planters' hegemony in North Carolina other than to note the property requirements for antebellum officeholding. She reported that the Constitution of 1776 gave the landed upper class a monopoly of state and county offices. A candidate for state senate had to possess at least three hundred acres; a candidate for governor was required to possess a "freehold in land and tenants above the value of 1000 pounds." The gradual relaxation of these requirements throughout the antebellum period suggests that the planters' hegemony was not absolute, although it was not until 1857 that senatorial suffrage was vested in "every free white man" who "shall have paid public taxes." Lefler and Newsome, discussing the absence of local democratic government, claim that the county court was "the organ of the dominant propertied class and it shaped county policy primarily for the interest of the upper class rather than that of the entire population."[16] Noting that "leading families often dominated local government as if by feudal or divine right," they illustrate planter hegemony by showing, for example, that in forty of the fifty-eight sessions of the General Assembly from 1779 to 1835 a member of the rich Hawkins family from Warren County served. Similarly, members of the Arrington-Brodie family served thirty-five terms in the state senate and seventeen in the house; the Riddick family of Gates and Perquimans did even better, serving fifty terms in the senate and twenty-six in the house.

Two recent studies on the county level suggest further that the planters' influence in North Carolina was disproportionate to their number even in the Piedmont. Gail O'Brien studied power and influence in Mecklenburg County from 1844 to 1854.[17] She used newspaper accounts to identify prominent members of the Charlotte–Mecklenburg County community who appeared to be influential in local affairs, and she used individual manuscript schedules of the United States census to evaluate their wealth. She discovered that planters who owned more than the average number of slaves dominated both routine and crisis politics in the community. In a more ambitious project, O'Brien studied change from 1840 to 1880 in the power structure of Guilford County, a small farm and plantation county in the North Carolina Piedmont, whose county seat is Greensboro.[18] She found that landed slaveholders were dominant during the four decades despite the abolition of slavery and the social disorganization that resulted from the Civil War. These studies are especially interesting because Charlotte and Greensboro, today North Carolina's two largest cities, developed, in part, as textile manufacturing centers. If planter influence, at least in Guilford County, continued into the period of postwar industrialization, the relationship between southern industry and the agrarian order should be reexamined.

Social Origins of Industry in North Carolina

Aggregate data weaken the expectation that North Carolina was distinguishable from other southern states by a strong and independent middle class. Table 4.1 shows the state's relative standing on a number of social and economic dimensions twenty years after the Civil War. The year 1880 is frequently taken as the starting point for the state's industrial revolution. The table shows that North Carolina ranked ninth among eleven southern states in per capita agricultural productivity but third in agricultural diversification. To the extent that diversification reflects independence from plantation production, this suggests some

Table 4.1. Economic Indicators for North Carolina and the South, 1880

Agricultural Productivity Per Capita, Dollars		Agricultural Diversification as Percent of Improved Acres in Cotton, Tobacco	
State Rank	Value	State Rank	Percent
Mississippi	56.29	Virginia	2.2
Arkansas	54.47	Tennessee	9.0
Louisiana	45.62	North Carolina	14.7
Alabama	45.05	Texas	17.2
Georgia	43.46	Florida	25.9
South Carolina	42.16	Arkansas	29.1
Texas	40.96	Louisiana	31.6
Tennessee	40.25	Georgia	31.9
North Carolina	36.96	South Carolina	33.0
Virginia	30.23	Alabama	36.6
Florida	27.61	Mississippi	40.4

Total Value of Manufacturing Per Capita, Dollars		Diversification of Manufacturing as Percent of Total by Two Top Products, Dollars	
State Rank	Value	State Rank	Percent
Virginia	34.23	Louisiana	23
Louisiana	25.75	Tennessee	39
Tennessee	24.04	South Carolina	40
Georgia	23.63	Georgia	45
Florida	20.58	North Carolina	45
South Carolina	16.81	Mississippi	49
North Carolina	14.36	Virginia	49
Texas	13.02	Alabama	51
Alabama	10.74	Texas	54
Arkansas	8.42	Arkansas	60
Mississippi	6.64	Florida	79

Table 4.1, continued

Percent Urban (Towns, Cities 4,000 and above)		Cash and Productive Assets, Per Capita, Dollars	
State Rank	Percent	State Rank	Value
Louisiana	24.6	Virginia	4.11
Virginia	11.8	Texas	3.22
Florida	9.0	Mississippi	2.83
Georgia	7.7	Alabama	2.61
Texas	7.2	Florida	2.58
Tennessee	6.8	Tennessee	2.29
South Carolina	6.6	Arkansas	2.27
Alabama	4.6	Louisiana	1.80
North Carolina	2.9	Georgia	1.13
Mississippi	2.5	South Carolina	.23
Arkansas	1.6	North Carolina	.08

Source: *Tenth Census of the United States, 1880*, Vol. 3, pp. 212, 250; *Compendium*, pp. 380–405, 684–85, 944–1029.

support for the middle-class thesis. North Carolina's social structure was less dominated by plantation agriculture than were those of Mississippi, Alabama, and South Carolina, the three least diversified agricultural states in the South. This diversification index, however, may reflect North Carolina's large subsistence sector, not necessarily balanced agriculture. North Carolina ranked seventh in total value of manufacturing and tied with Georgia for fourth place in diversification. (Its two chief products, cotton and tobacco, accounted for 45 percent of its manufacturing total.)

Two factors look especially unpromising for economic development. No other southern state was as deficient in cash and productive assets as North Carolina. Virginia ranked first in the South with $4.11 per capita, followed by Texas, Mississippi, and Alabama. North Carolina had, in contrast, only $.08 per capita. This tremendous shortage of capital is perplexing, however, because the three lowest states on this dimension, North Carolina, South Carolina, and Georgia, became industrial leaders, but comparatively wealthy Mississippi and Alabama did not. One might expect that the lack of cash among the state's many poor farmers—along with the comparatively lower agricultural productivity of the Upper South—would have hindered the home market and, consequently, the strength of the commercial middle class. Urbanism strengthens the position of the middle class, and on this dimension also North Carolina ranked low. Only Mississippi and Arkansas were more rural than North Carolina. In 1880 only 2.9 percent of North Carolina's population lived in towns larger than four thousand.

To test the middle-class thesis I shall first concentrate on the textile industry, the largest and historically most important of North Carolina's industries. As was the case for England, New England, Japan, and many other nations, textile manufacturing was the backbone of the South's industrial revolution. As Harriet Herring said in her history of early industrial development in the South,

> It is the [textile] industry that has the longest and most conspicuous history in the South. It was the first to reach the stage of local custom work—the shop stage; the first to supply a local market by the use of machinery—the mill stage; the first to enter the national and international markets—the factory stage and the real entry into the industrial system. Finally, it is the industry upon which have been concentrated, both pro and con, the most frequent and spectacular expressions of southern industrial philosophy.[19]

Surprisingly, there are few reliable historical accounts of the growth of the southern textile industry, nor is there a general history of the North Carolina Piedmont, one of the chief regions of industrial growth. It is unclear who carried out textile industrialization, how they did so, with what sources of capital, and even why. On the last point, one economic history textbook states that even the causes for the massive shift of production from the Northeast to the South "are still in doubt." This book's authors argue that while the abundance of cheap labor explains the opportunity for relative investment in the South over other regions, it does not explain why textile manufacturing should have been the particular avenue.[20]

Commenting on the imagery used to describe southern industrialization, Liston Pope wrote:

> The story of the rise of the cotton mills in the South has been often told. Sometimes it has been told in the mood of a romance, portraying the Herculean efforts of a region, defeated and impoverished in war, to lift itself again from poverty and to regain a respectable place in the national economy through taking upon itself an industrial character formerly despised. Again, the industrial revolution ushered in by the rise of the mills has been depicted as the great betrayal of a culture which, though temporarily broken by war, might have been revived, preserving greater beauty and humanity than its betrayer has been able to bring. Still again, the rise of young industrial giants, unshackled and insolent in power, has been denounced as a farce, a burlesque of a development which, under other conditions or leadership, might have been genuinely beneficial. One mood or other—romance, tragedy, or farce—has generally prevailed in the telling of the tale.[21]

The interpretation I propose stresses the slow evolution of southern manufacturing throughout the antebellum period and its acceleration late in the nineteenth century. This conflicts with another interpretation that I will call the "romantic tradition," which portrays the New South and its leadership as a radical discontinuity from the Old South. Holland Thompson and Broadus Mitchell were the most prominent historians in the romantic tradition.[22] C. Vann Woodward relied heavily on their accounts, echoing many of their themes. They were both interpreters and defenders of southern industry. "The development which brought manufacturers to the South was inevitable," wrote Broadus Mitchell. "It is," he believed, "impossible to halt the industrial march which had begun." Thompson and Mitchell were hostile to the slave South and interpreted the industrial South as a new departure. "Manufacturers," claimed Mitchell, "have brought the South release from the stagnation which was characteristic of slavery."[23] The image of a New South implied

new men and new social principles. Thompson argued, as
Genovese would later, that "the whole structure of industrial
society with all its connotations was obnoxious to a large part of
the [antebellum] articulate South." Industry could develop only
if the old slaveholding regime were to collapse. "The decay of
the plantation after the war has already been discussed," wrote
Thompson. "New men came to the front as the fortunes of the
planter declined." Many of these new men rose from humble
origins to become mill owners and managers. "The manager of
the mill was sometimes an aristocrat but more often a member
of the middle class."[24] Thompson and Mitchell minimized the
antebellum foundations of the textile industry and dated the
industry from 1880. In contrast with the slow evolution of the
industry in the North, in the South, according to Mitchell,
"cotton mills were set down suddenly in cotton fields."[25]

   Two other images—that of an ownership pattern we would
today call "peoples' capitalism" and that of a rare public service
zeal—complete the romantic picture of the southern textile industry. It is frequently asserted that the mills were paid for by
many small investors and that in some cases whole towns sold
subscriptions to raise capital in the scramble to build mills. "In
spirit, scope, and success the cotton mill movement that arose
in the South after 1870 became a project in which all segments of
the community eventually participated."[26] According to this tradition, there was hardly a town in North Carolina, poor though
the state was, that could not accumulate $50,000 to $100,000 to
start a mill. North Carolina industrialist Daniel Tompkins published a handbook to advise towns on how to raise money. The
city of Wilmington, for instance, raised $150,000 from its public.
Charlotte tried and failed, but the local Grange joined other
groups in the Mecklenburg area and raised $60,000 from a thou-
sand farmers who each pledged contributions of $5 per month.
After the Panic of 1873, which depressed cotton prices, the
Granges of Mecklenburg, Cabarrus, Rowan, Iredell, Catawba,
Lincoln, and Gaston counties pooled their capital and raised
$90,000 to build a mill.[27] Until historians thoroughly study this

early mill-building period, we will not know how widespread this pattern was.

Related to the romantic interpretation that the entire community was involved in building the mill was an assumption that the mill benefited the entire community. The mill movement was seen as both popular and moral. Even Woodward says that profit alone "cannot account for the public zeal that . . . converted an economic development into a civic crusade inspired with a vision of social salvation."[28] The following quotation from Mitchell illustrates this view.

> [Southern industrialists] began their work following a period, during Reconstruction, of political humiliation, and their tools were only such as were offered by determination in the midst of poverty. These things gave to the whole movement a social sanction, I might almost say social sanctification, which was largely lacking elsewhere. An added element to this end was the fact that industry, particularly the cotton factories, furnished bread and meat to the hordes of poor whites who waited to be reclaimed after the destitution which slavery entailed upon them. Thus southern manufactures were imbued—often in the minds of the enterprisers themselves, and widely in the thought of the general public—with a philanthropic character.[29]

Thus, along with its stress on the discontinuity of the new industrial South from the old slaveholding South, the romantic interpretation saw the textile movement as both popular and philanthropic. This image of the textile industry is challenged by another interpretation that stresses the continuity of the textile industry of the Old South and its rapid post–Civil War growth.

According to Herring, southern textile production dates back to the seventeenth century and to a vigorous domestic manufacturing system that thrived in opposition to the mercantilist policy of the British Empire.[30] As early as 1649 there were self-sufficient plantations in the Virginia colony. During the next half-century domestic manufacture spread to the back country, including upland regions like the North Carolina Piedmont. Prior to the American Revolution, planters supplied yarn and cloth to local markets. Some planters used slaves in the industry and sold their products. Others employed poor neighbors to make textiles for their plantation and others.

In chapter 2, I showed that protection is necessary for the growth of local industry and noted that manufacturing increased in Latin America when that region was cut off from Europe by war. This was also true in the American colonies. Herring states that the "widespread skill in manufacturing was put to good use in pre-Revolutionary and War days."[31] When Alexander Hamilton surveyed American industry after the war in 1791, he found that North Carolina was almost self-sufficient in textiles. Some backcountry areas such as the Appalachian Piedmont were geographically protected from English goods, and these developed domestic products. During roughly the same period the Carolina Piedmont benefited from the arrival of Scotch-Irish and German immigrants, who were experienced in textile production. In 1810, North Carolina's domestic production was valued at $2,989,140. Partly because of its good harbors and economic integration with England, New England was much more dependent on English imports at that time. Its domestic production amounted to a value of one-half million dollars less than North Carolina's alone.

The War of 1812 produced further incentives for textile independence in America. Planters in the South, such as Thomas Jefferson, were hostile to the manufacturing system but, according to Herring, they were *least* hostile to cotton manufacturing. Shortly after the War of 1812, the South entered the factory stage of textile production. The region experienced two boom periods, one in the 1820s and another from 1845 to 1852.[32]

Power spinning had existed in the South from at least as early as 1788 in South Carolina.[33] After the War of 1812 it spread throughout the region. North Carolina's earliest mill, the famous Schenck mill in Lincolnton, dates from 1814. At the same time, Moravians in Salem began a mill, one of the longest running in the South, a foundation for the present Winston-Salem industrial complex. A group around Hillsborough, alarmed by the war, proposed a joint stock company, but this was never completed. A boom in mill building did occur, however, in the late 1820s and early 1830s. Twenty mills were built in eighteen North Carolina counties ranging from Northampton County in the East to Caldwell County in the West and from Caswell County on the Virginia border to Richmond County in the South.[34] Other southern states made similar progress. In 1840, North Carolina had twenty-five mills, Virginia had eighteen, South Carolina fifteen, Georgia nineteen, and Tennessee boasted thirty-eight. By 1860 cotton production outstripped that of all other factory products in the South.

It is not clear who built these early mills in North Carolina. Some writers claim that "the first cotton mills in the state were begun as another adjunct to the general store that probably already operated a grist mill and tanning yard"—that is, merchants built the first mills.[35] But planters also provided milling and tanning services on their plantations for themselves and their neighbors and, as we have seen, as early as the seventeenth century, in Virginia, they sold cotton goods manufactured by their slaves.[36] Did the planters enter factory production as well? North Carolina history provides evidence of both patterns.

According to Standard and Griffin, the first successful mill was built in North Carolina in 1814 by a Lincoln County merchant, who ordered spindle machinery from Rhode Island and had the gears constructed locally by his son-in-law. By 1840 the mill produced $21,373 worth of yarn per year and was the center of an industrial community that included a blacksmith shop, a brass factory, a cotton gin, and a shingle factory. The pattern of planter ownership appears equally early, in 1817, in eastern North Carolina. Henry Donaldson, a New England manufacturer who had incorporated several mills in the South by 1830, joined Joel Battle, a wealthy Edgecombe planter who already owned a flour and grist mill and provided $25,000 capital, to establish a mill near Rocky Mount. They hired a trained cotton mill superintendent from Massachusetts and used Battle's slaves for labor. A few years later, Battle's son raised one-half million dollars from neighboring planters to make it the largest mill in the South, but a sudden rise in cotton prices caused them to reinvest in land and slaves instead.[37] This conflict reveals the competition between industrial investment and slaveholding in the Old South and is particularly understandable if Fogel and Engerman are correct that the return from buying slaves was equally or even more profitable than investments in manufacturing. Early mills were threatened by the lack of capital and were often superseded by railroad construction that clearly benefited the planters' export production.

A second boom in mill building occurred in the South from 1845 to 1852, accelerated by the Panic of 1837 and the depression of cotton prices that persisted into the 1840s. Southerners felt that they were disadvantaged by the tariff and the concentration of manufacturing in the North. During this period Virginia's industry grew from 40,000 spindles in 1840 to 54,000 in 1850. North Carolina's grew to 48,000 spindles. Georgia's industry grew most, its production totaling two million dollars in 1850, an increase of 700 percent. New manufacturing centers developed during this period in North Carolina. Two new mills established in Mecklenburg County between 1847 and 1850 aided the growth of Charlotte as a manufacturing and marketing center for surrounding counties. For the first time southern goods began to find their way into the national market. Under the direction of John Motley Morehead, North Carolina held its first manufacturers' convention in 1850 and its first state fair in 1851 to show off its industrial products. Herring writes, "In the flood of articles and pamphlets and speeches on the crisis in the South and its remedies, almost everybody was agreed on two general propositions: that there was an overproduction of cotton, and that any fundamental remedy must include manufacture of cotton by the states that raised it." Another incentive for the development of antebellum cotton manufacturing was the "advantages of providing labor for poor whites who were forced out of the staple raising and *were becoming a social and economic problem*."[38] The boom in mill building ended with the recovery of cotton prices in the early 1850s, when again capital was channeled into agriculture.

The continuity between this antebellum industrial development—which according to Herring's words had slowed by 1853 "but not until considerable advance had been made"—and the rapid industrial growth after the Civil War is important.[39] North Carolina newspapers campaigned in the early 1870s for an industrial reconstruction in response to the ruin of war. General William T. Sherman had burned eight or nine factories in Fayetteville and Cumberland County. General George Stoneman's cavalry hit western North Carolina at Caldwell and Iredell counties. Other mills escaped Union troops, but their machinery wore out during the war years.[40] The South experienced financial chaos after the war. Its currency was of no value. Millions of dollars were lost in public bonds with the cancellation of Confederate and state war debts. It is commonly assumed that capital for postwar development came from the North, but actually the South's industrial thrust after the Civil War was based on local initiative. Northern capital was available only for financing cotton crops needed by New England mills, not for building an industrial South. Capital and firms migrated to the South from New England only in the twentieth century, after the South had established an industrial base and won its competition with the North. Herring writes, "The industrial development of the South has been, in a measure, the result of conscious efforts of Southerners to build an industrial empire."[41] According to J. Carlyle Sitterson, "Not a single person from the Northeast played a decisive role in the building of North Carolina industry in the years 1865–1900."[42] Focusing specifically on the textile industry, Dan Lacy found that no cotton mills were established by northern capital before 1895 in North Carolina and that only a few such mills had been established by 1900.[43] Harry Boyte writes that even as late as 1931 "only 15% of the industry was controlled by 51 large non-Southern firms which had Southern plants."[44]

Who, then, rebuilt the textile industry? Where did they get the cash? For a brief period after the war the world was starved for cotton. Great fortunes could be made growing cotton in the late 1860s. The plantation system was restored through sharecropping and tenancy, and planters soon had cash from cotton sales. Country and small-town merchants were another potential source of capital. They shared in the cotton boom by advancing supplies to planters and farmers for a share in the return of the crop. Unfortunately, the answer to this important question is unclear. Sitterson's important study of postwar industrialists failed to consider carefully their class origins other than to report that the mill builders were not self-made men. Half of the business leaders surveyed were from "upper social and economic status" families, but Sitterson did not specify his criteria for this judgment. He did, however, stress the continuity between the leaders of the antebellum industries and those of the New South.

> In the textile and tobacco industries particularly, there was no sharp break between the prewar and postwar eras. The textile industry of modern North Carolina came directly from the well-established industry of the antebellum period. Not only did many of the owners of the prewar factories continue in control through the War, but they took the lead in founding new factories generally in the central and western counties where the earlier mills had been built to take advantage of the water power of the Piedmont. Of the forty-nine mills in the state in 1880, at least twenty were old ones that had run more or less continually since before the war, fifteen were built by men who had been connected with the prewar mills, and several additional ones were built by men who had married into families of prewar entrepreneurs and had been taken into the business.[45]

Griffin makes the same point, observing that in fact manufacturers came out of the war in better financial shape than did their neighbors.[46] They had built up financial reserves during the war which they used to rebuild their worn-out mills. Griffin and Standard write:

> Despite the precarious existence of mills in the late 1860's and 1870's, there was never a complete breakdown of the industry in the State, and the vast textile expansion after 1880 was built on the foundations that had existed for decades. In the 1880's mills were operating that had been under the same

family management and had had the same families of workers since the 1830's and 1840's. It was this asset—a number of communities with manufacturing traditions and training and enough mills to form a nucleus for further growth—that attracted capital and made the North Carolina Piedmont the textile center of the New South.[47]

From this perspective, the romantic interpretation is wrong in dating the southern textile industry from the 1880s. The cotton mills were *not* "set down suddenly in cotton fields." Perhaps the romantic tradition is also wrong in its claim that the industrial order was a new departure from the world the slaveholders made.

A Test of the Middle-Class Thesis

A definitive test of the middle-class development thesis is impossible in the absence of extensive historical research on the early post–Civil War reconstruction of the southern textile industry. I was able to make a crude, but I believe convincing, test with some fragmentary historical data. Richard Griffin has compiled a complete list of North Carolina cotton mills that operated between 1865 and 1884 and their owners.[48] These were crucial years following the war when the institutional foundations were established for an industrial North Carolina. Capital investments in textile manufacturing increased 60 percent, from $8,140,473 to $13,045,639, during the decade from 1870 to 1880. During the same period the labor force increased 33 percent. Since the number of mills remained approximately the same, this investment represented improvement and expansion of the prewar industrial base. This was a "prelude to the extraordinary expansion during the following two decades," when the number of mills doubled and the labor force more than tripled to over seventy thousand operatives.[49]

Griffin's list includes eighty-eight mills. I used *Branson's North Carolina Business Directory* to identify the owners of these mills. This directory provided a complete inventory of businesses in each county in the state and, more important, it identified "Prominent Farmers" as well. Four editions of the *Directory* were published during the years for which ownership data is available—1869, 1872, 1877–78, and 1884. The first two editions were especially useful because Branson included the number of acres owned by each farmer. A prominent North Carolina historian assured me that the farmers listed in these early editions were indeed planters.[50] (The typical farm sizes classed as "prominent" varied by county. Prominent farmers listed in Richmond County, for instance, averaged 3,000 acres, whereas those of Rockingham County averaged 1,281 acres and those of Guilford County 1,188 acres.) Later editions did not report the number of acres each farmer owned. Consequently, I do not know whether the criteria for determining agrarian prominence remained constant. I doubt that this was the case because later editions showed a larger number of prominent farmers. Whereas the 1869 *Directory* identified roughly twenty-five farmers per county as prominent, the 1884 edition listed as many as two hundred in some counties. Without data on acreage I can say only that farmers listed in the later editions were "prominent agrarians."

Some mill owners could be identified in the 1880s who had appeared in the earliest edition of the *Directory*. In these cases, I am certain that land was the source of their wealth. In other instances I found new names in the 1880s with both industrial and agricultural interests. In those cases I was unable to determine whether the original basis for their wealth was land or industrial profits. The source of wealth was more likely agriculture because of the widespread pattern of heavy reinvestment of mill profits in the textile industry.[51] During this early period of capital accumulation it seems unlikely that industrial profits were invested in agriculture because it yielded declining profits throughout the 1880s. The latter pattern was common in the Mississippi delta region, however, where agriculture was more profitable than in the Upper South and where businessmen emulated the landed elite.[52]

Do these fragmentary data support the claim that cotton

mills were built by the commercial middle class? I think not. After eliminating ten mills for which complete information regarding ownership was missing, I found that eighteen of the seventy-eight mills (23 percent) that operated between 1865 and 1884 were owned by men identified in the 1869 *Directory* as planters. Twenty-six additional mills (another 34 percent) were owned or partly owned by men who can be identified as "prominent agrarians" by the less conservative criteria of subsequent volumes of the *Directory*. That is, over half (57 percent) of the mills operating in North Carolina during this period were owned completely or partly by agrarians. This is a conservative test because the other owners may also have been members of the landholding class but for some reason were not included in the directories, or they may have been sons or relatives of planters. I suspect the latter pattern was rather common. At least eight of the remaining mills were associated with men who shared the same family names with prominent farmers in their counties. (This possible connection raises my estimate to 68 percent of the total.) In reading biographies of mill owners of a later period such as Daniel Tompkins, a prominent cotton mill owner and industrial spokesman in North Carolina around the turn of the century, I frequently found that these men were erroneously referred to as "self-made." Tompkins, for example, was called a typical self-made industrialist of the "Bourbon" period even though he was the college-educated son of a South Carolina planter who had financed his earliest business enterprises. An example of how I coded the data for one county will show why I believe the percentages reported above underestimate the connection between early industrialists and the landed upper class in North Carolina.

Seven mills operated between 1865 and 1884 in cotton-producing Richmond County in the North Carolina Piedmont. One of these was not identified by owner. Another operated only one year—a small mill with only $10,000 capital. Of the remaining five, two mills belonged to planters, each of whom owned three-thousand-acre plantations in 1869—Colonel Charles Malloy and John Leake. Their mills dated from 1867 and 1879, respectively. Two other mills were owned by a Colonel Walter Leake Steele who may or may not have been related to an 1869 planter named R. J. Steele. Another mill was owned by T. B. and J. S. Ledbetter. These two men are not listed as prominent planters in 1869, but several Ledbetters were. The last mill, Midway Mills, chartered in 1881, was identified simply as owned by "Leake, Wall, and McRae"—no first names were given so I eliminated this mill. Although I therefore cannot establish if any of its owners were planters or sons of planters, these three family names were prominent in Richmond County. Among the sixteen planters listed in the 1869 *Directory*, five were Leakes, one was a Wall, and one was a McRae. These three family names were associated with a total of thirty-one thousand acres of land. Steele and Ledbetter account for three more of the family names —making a total of ten of the sixteen prominent farmers. These five families owned nearly forty thousand acres of land in 1869. Yet in my conservative estimate, I identified only two mills in Richmond County as having been owned by planters.

I believe that the majority of North Carolina mill owners who were operating during the period of 1865 to 1884 were prominent planters and agrarians (Type I). Others were members of prominent landed families even though they were not active farmers themselves (Type II). Still others, though a minority, appear to have been upwardly mobile individuals (Type III), many of them merchants. The careers of the following men illustrate these patterns.[53]

> *Type I.* Colonel Thomas M. Holt of Alamance County was the son of Edwin M. Holt, one of the earliest industrialists in the South. Holt was born in 1831 and graduated from the University of North Carolina in 1849. He expanded his father's firm, Granite Mills, at a cost of nearly one-half million dollars. He lived across the Haw River from his mill in his "princely mansion"—"the largest, most elegantly furnished country dwelling in North Carolina" that sat on twelve acres of land. He was also owner of the "famous" Linwood plantation near Lexington that produced wheat, hay, cattle, and sheep. For twelve years he was president of the North Caro-

lina Railroad and a member of the state Board of Agriculture. Holt served in the state senate in 1876, in the United States House of Representatives in 1882, 1884, and 1886, and was governor of North Carolina from 1891 to 1893.

Type II. Walter Leake Steele, from the Richmond County example above, was never identified as a "prominent farmer" in any of Branson's directories but he was a member of a prominent family. Steele was born at Steele's Mills in 1823. His father—who served in the antebellum state house—died when the boy was fifteen, and he was sent to school in Virginia. He attended Randolph Macon and Wake Forest colleges and graduated from the University of North Carolina in 1844. He served in the North Carolina General Assembly in 1846, 1848, 1850, 1852, 1854, and 1858. In 1861 he served as secretary of the state convention that passed the ordinance for secession. He had been elected to the board of directors of the Wilmington, Charlotte, and Rutherford Railroad in 1854, and this railroad connection caused him to be exempted from Civil War service. He was elected to the United States Congress in 1876. After he returned from Congress, he became president of the Pee Dee Cotton Mills. He was also a lawyer and banker.

Type II. William Holt Williamson, who entered the mill business in 1884 at the end of the time period under investigation, was born in Alamance County at the end of the Civil War. He was the grandson of Thomas Williamson, "an extensive planter and a large merchant." His father, also a planter, married a daughter of Edwin Holt (above) and began to manufacture cotton as owner and operator of the Ossipee Cotton Mills. Williamson established and operated the Pilot Cotton Mills at Raleigh, the Hopedale Mills at Burlington, and the Harriet Mills at Henderson. He was also a director and vice-president of the Merchants National Bank at Raleigh.

Type III. John H. Ferree and John M. O'Dell were businessmen whose careers reveal upward mobility. They were both born in Randolph County, a nonplantation county in the west-central Piedmont. Ferree was the son of a Methodist minister. He started out as a clerk in the store of W. C. Ervin, a planter who was in partnership in textile manufacturing with the Holts of Alamance County [Type I], in Morganton.

He prospered as a merchant. After the war, and with several others, he invested in cotton mills. John M. O'Dell was the son of a "sturdy and successful" Randolph County farmer, born in 1831. He clerked for the Cedar Falls Manufacturing Company and eventually bought into the company. He moved to Concord and established a successful wholesale-retail business. He relocated in Greensboro and became a charter member of the National Bank in 1876. He was president of McDonald Mills and the Concord National Bank.

The careers of Type I individuals, who were a majority of the early postwar mill owners, show the direct connection between agricultural and industrial interests in North Carolina. It is significant that an industrial leader like Thomas Holt also had interests in textiles, in railroads, as well as in large-scale agriculture. Some of these men—along with such Type II individuals as Walter Steele, who may have had direct connections with agriculture that my crude methods do not reveal—were also political leaders. Both Holt and Steele, for instance, served in the United States Congress; Steele's political leadership dated back to the 1840s. This evidence suggests that these men were not only builders of the New South but were powerholders in the old order as well. In contrast, John O'Dell, who began his career as a mill clerk, achieved prominence through mobility within the textile industry. Undoubtedly, the career pattern of men like O'Dell became more common with the subsequent expansion of the industry and the migration of mills from the North. Perhaps this later period is what gives the impression of a middle-class revolution. Rapid expansion no doubt created vast opportunities for upward mobility, but it is important to realize that the older, upper-class leaders first established the institutional framework for an industrial economy.

Given literature that suggested the plausibility of the middle-class thesis of development, it is surprising to find that planters and prominent agriculturalists laid the foundation in the two decades after the Civil War for North Carolina's revolution in textile manufacturing. It has been almost dogma among some historians and sociologists that "new men" rebuilt the

South after the old regime of the slaveholders fell. The implicit identification of "modernization" with the rise of the middle class—a generalization from the English pattern of development—has caused scholars to overlook facts, just as the "romantic" interpretation of the textile industry blinded them to the roots of the industrial revolution. Consequently, important links have been obscured between agriculture and industry, between the landed upper class and southern industrialists, and between the world the slaveholders built and the world they rebuilt after their nationalist failure.

The demand for cotton textile manufacturing was a recurring theme throughout the economic history of the Upper South during the antebellum period. As long as investment in cotton growing held a comparative advantage, the industry received little attention, but, when agricultural prices dropped, the demand for manufacturing in the South was renewed. Social, economic, and technological factors after the Civil War rekindled interest in industrialization. The Civil War had, for a time, lessened the region's dependence on northern financiers and manufacturers. The expansion of southern railroads and the development of water power aided in the expansion of internal and external markets. Improvements in the technology of textile manufacturing, especially the perfection of the ring spindle and the automatic loom, permitted the use of unskilled surplus labor.[54] Surplus labor was an ever-present and potentially threatening element in the agrarian order, reflecting the depressed condition of southern agriculture when, after a few good seasons immediately following the war and a brief cotton shortage, the price of cotton began a sharp secular decline. In North Carolina "cotton prices declined from twenty-five cents a pound in 1868 to twelve cents in the 1870's, to nine cents in the 1880's, and to seven cents in the early nineties, finally reaching five cents a pound in 1894."[55] For those planters wealthy enough to take advantage of the opportunity, textile manufacturing, which brought returns as high as 22 percent per annum,[56] surely must have seemed the answer to their own and the region's economic problems.

In an article in the Raleigh *News and Observer* on 28 November 1895, Josephus Daniels reported that North Carolina cotton mills were expected to consume more than half of the state's estimated cotton crop of 450,000 bales. He predicted that at such a rate of increase it would be only "a very few years before North Carolina will manufacture all its own cotton and have to buy from its sister States more in order to keep its mills busy." Thus North Carolina's planter-industrialists supported the demand for cotton, the mainstay of southern agriculture, at the same time that they benefited from its low cost as manufacturers. Add to this the public gratitude mill builders received for providing employment opportunities (at low wages, of course) and it is not hard to understand their commitment to industrialization.

It is unusual, nonetheless, that a landed upper class in a peripheral society would sponsor industrialization. In chapter 2, I asserted that their class interests often cause resistance to change. In some societies, however, landed aristocracies have used their traditional authority to sponsor industrial development. In the following chapters I shall argue that a portion of North Carolina's landed elite brought about such a revolution, achieving at least part of the economic program some had dreamed of as early as 1828 in their pleas to the General Assembly for the encouragement of manufacturing industries in the South.

5. Modernization in the South: North Carolina's Revolution from Above

A recurrent theme among southern writers who interpreted developments in the South for northern readers in the late nineteenth century was that although Civil War and Reconstruction had not destroyed the strong moral fiber of the southern population, they had nonetheless "emancipated the white South from the shackles of an old order that had barred material progress and prosperity."[1] Although fearing the return of "the plantation princes of old time" in the form of greedy commission merchants ("a planting oligarchy of money-lenders") and thus appealing to northern capital for "the establishment of a proper system of credit," Henry Grady nonetheless pictured the New South in 1881 as he hoped it would be—"a prosperous self-respecting race of small farmers, cultivating their own lands, living upon their own resources, controlling their crops until they are sold, and independent alike of usurers and provision brokers." Grady described for readers of *Harper's Magazine* the liquidation of plantations worth from $100,000 to $150,000 before the war at prices ranging from $6,000 to $10,000. He claimed that "never perhaps was there a rural movement, accomplished without revolution or exodus, that equalled in extent and swiftness the partition of the plantations of the ex-slaveholders into small farms."[2] Elsewhere he wrote that "the old plantation is a thing of the past."[3] The poet Sidney Lanier struck a similar note when he claimed in *Scribner's* that "the quiet rise of the small farmer" was "the notable circumstance of the [postwar] period, in comparison with which much noisier events signify nothing."[4]

The writings of New South spokesmen are the origin of myths that found their way into the orthodoxies of latter-day academic historians. These myths include the unprofitability of antebellum plantation agriculture (now challenged by economists) and the postbellum fall of the southern planter.[5] Thus, nearly sixty years later, Paul H. Buck would argue that "the destruction of slavery, the humbling of the planting aristocracy" effected a revolutionary change in the social structure of the South: "The revolution was not slow in materializing. Emancipation of the Negro removed the cornerstone of ante-bellum Southern society. This in itself had far-reaching consequences. The small, rich landowning aristocracy in whose interest so much of Southern energy had been expended was deprived of its privileged position. . . . But most significant, an economy of free labor proved incompatible with the maintenance of great estates. Almost immediately the plantation disintegrated into a system of small holdings."[6]

New South spokesmen apparently were given to exaggeration, often blending description and wish, and were at times self-contradictory. In the same *Harper's Magazine* report, extolling the benefits of agricultural diversification, Henry Grady described the addition in the previous year of over two thousand acres of land to the Capeheart plantation in eastern North Carolina, which originally comprised "several thousand acres."

> This estate is divided into farms of fifty acres each, and rented to tenants. These tenants are bound to plant fifteen acres in cotton, twelve in corn, eight in small crops, and let fifteen lie in grass. They pay one-third of the crop as rent, or one-half if the proprietor furnishes horses and mules. . . . In the center of the estate is a general store managed by the proprietor, at which the tenants have such a line of credit as they are entitled to, of course paying a pretty percentage of profit on the goods they buy. . . . The profits to Dr. Capeheart are large, and show the margin there is in buying land that is loosely farmed, and putting it under intelligent supervision. Of the $52,000 worth of land added to his estates last year, at a valuation of twenty-five dollars per acre, he will realize in rental nine dollars per acre for every acre cultivated, and calculates that in five years at the most the rentals of the land will have paid back what he gave for it.[7]

No doubt the reality of the New South agrarian order is to be found somewhere between the "intelligent supervision" plantation princes were said to have provided and the acclaimed predominance of small farmers that harkened back to Jeffersonian ideas of the South.

Aggregate data, as shown in chapter 4, support the contention that North Carolina was indeed "a state of small farmers." Lefler and Newsome report that the breakup of large plantations is indicated by an increase in the number of farms from 75,203 in 1860 to 225,000 in 1900. The average acreage per farm decreased from 316 acres in 1860 to 101 acres in 1900 and continued to decline to an average of 65 acres in 1925. Much of this breakup, however, merely reflects the shift from the plantation mode to the tenancy system of small holdings, although Lefler and Newsome report "a striking increase in farm ownership as well as in tenancy."[8] There is another way to interpret these data, however.

Table 5.1 reports farm ownership in North Carolina in 1900, the only year in which accurate data on ownership were collected by the United States census. These data reveal that 41 percent of the state's farmers were tenants. Another 33 percent

Table 5.1. North Carolina Farm Ownership in 1900

Total Acreage	Farmers			Farms		
	Number	Percent	Cum. Percent	Number	Percent	Cum. Percent
0	93,008	41.4	41.4	0	0	0
1–99	75,109	33.4	74.8	148,125	65.9	65.9
100–499	53,115	23.6	98.4	72,288	32.1	98.0
500–999	2,612	01.1	99.5	3,275	1.4	99.4
1,000+	793	00.3	100.0	949	0.4	100.0
Total	224,637			224,637		

Source: *Twelfth Census of the United States, 1900*, Vol. 5, pp. 12–13, 314–15. A prototype for this data array presenting data for the southern region is Michael Schwartz, *Radical Protest and Social Structure*, pp. 80–81.

owned less than one hundred acres. Thus nearly 75 percent of the total number of farmers in North Carolina owned or operated farms of less than one hundred acres. The other side of these figures, however, is a concentration of land ownership.

Table 5.2 reports the number, acreage, and value of tenant farms controlled by North Carolina landowners. These data may be compared with the pattern for the entire South reported by Michael Schwartz, whose analysis of ownership provided a model for my presentation.[9] In the South as a whole, 70.4 percent of all tenant holders controlled only one tenant-operated farm each. The comparable figure for North Carolina is 72.2 percent. On the other hand, the small number of southern landholders who controlled five or more tenant-operated farms each (the top 5.8 percent of the southern tenant holders) controlled nearly one-third of all the tenants (31.7 percent). These farms were worth over one-fourth (26.7 percent) of the total farm value in the South. In North Carolina, the landholders who controlled five or more tenant-operated farms each (the top 3.9 percent of the state's tenant holders) controlled approximately one-fifth (19.8 percent) of all the tenants and one-fifth (20.5 percent) of the total value of farm property in the state.

There was also a degree of ownership concentration even within the elite, as shown in Table 5.3. Within the elite group, comprised of only 4 percent of the landowners in North Carolina, a tiny group of sixty-six landowners (2.9 percent of the elite) owned approximately one-tenth (11 percent) of its collective property wealth.

Thus there was a small landowning class in North Carolina in 1900 whose economic power was vastly disproportionate to its size—a class easily obscured by aggregate farm statistics and a class that operated at a statewide level. According to the 1900 census of agriculture, approximately 15 percent of the rental farms in North Carolina were owned by landlords living in other counties.[10] When the fact that 4 percent of North Carolina's landowners controlled the agricultural production of one-fifth of the state's tenants is seen in connection with the fact that nearly half (48 percent) of the state's entire cotton crop in 1899 was produced by tenant labor, one begins to appreciate the

Table 5.2. *Control of Tenants in North Carolina in 1900*

No. of Tenant Farms	No. of Owners	Percent	Cum. Percent	No. of Farms	Percent	Cum. Percent
1	39,822	72.2	72.2	39,822	44.4	44.4
2	8,603	15.6	87.8	17,206	19.2	63.6
3–4	4,425	8.0	95.8	14,712	16.4	80.0
5–9	1,805	3.2	99.0	11,122	12.4	92.4
10–19	371	0.6	99.6	4,696	5.2	97.6
20+	66	0.1	100.0	1,956	2.2	100.0
Total	55,092			89,514		

Source: *Twelfth Census of the United States, 1900,* Vol. 5, pp. 312–13. A prototype for this data array is Schwartz, *Radical Protest,* pp. 82–83.

wealth and power of North Carolina's landed upper class. Landlords were capable of controlling most of the value of tenant production, just as they had done during the slaveholding period through a system of high rents and credit that kept their labor force perpetually indebted.

As I will show in subsequent chapters, for a time the existence of numerically preponderant tenant and yeomen classes limited the political power of the landed upper class, but this did not block the planters' economic program. Many important economic leaders in North Carolina combined plantation agriculture with other economic and industrial pursuits after the Civil War. For example, Robert Henry Ricks,[11] born in 1839, was a "successful and large farmer" in Nash County, who became known as "the pioneer of bright tobacco culture in Eastern North Carolina." In 1889 he became a director in the Rocky Mount Cotton Mills and was elected president in 1899. From 1894 he was a director and vice-president of the huge Washington Cotton Mills in Virginia. Ricks's biographer describes him as a constant Democrat, who had been "zealous to establish

Table 5.2, continued

Acres	Percent	Cum. Percent	Values in Dollars	Percent	Cum. Percent
2,766,410	46.7	46.7	$23,808,512	44.8	44.8
1,082,005	18.3	65.0	9,878,319	18.6	63.4
903,376	15.3	80.3	8,574,134	16.1	79.5
733,975	12.4	92.7	7,101,535	13.4	92.9
303,464	5.1	97.8	2,773,580	5.2	98.1
126,456	2.1	100.0	1,022,507	1.9	100.0
5,915,686			$53,158,587		

on a secure basis the supremacy of the white man in Eastern Carolina."

Robert Rufus Bridges was born in Edgecombe County in 1819 and was graduated from the University of North Carolina in 1841. He passed his law examination and served in the General Assembly in 1844. After this brief public career, he withdrew to law, cotton planting, and banking. According to his biographer, "From a very small patrimony he became one of the largest cotton planters in the State of North Carolina." During the Civil War, Bridges served in the Confederate Congress. He purchased High Schoals property with his brother, a Confederate colonel, and became the second largest iron manufacturer in the Confederacy. After the war he was elected president of the Wilmington and Weldon Railroad. In cooperation with two Baltimore businessmen, he laid the foundations for the great Atlantic Coast Line. He served as general manager and president of this railroad while he continued his cotton planting, merchandising, and turpentine manufacturing.

In the German alliance of wheat and iron interests described

Table 5.3. Concentration within North Carolina's Landholding Elite in 1900

No. of Ten-ant Farms	No. of Owners	Percent	Farms	Percent	Acres	Percent	Value in Dollars	Percent
5–9	1,805	80.5	11,122	62.6	733,975	63.1	$7,101,536	65.2
10–19	371	16.5	4,696	26.4	303,464	26.1	2,773,580	25.5
20+	66	2.9	1,956	11.0	126,456	11.0	1,022,507	9.4
		100.0		100.0		100.0		100.0
Total	2,242		17,774		1,163,895		$10,897,623	

Source: *Twelfth Census of the United States, 1900*, Vol. 5, pp. 312–13. A prototype for this data array is Schwartz, *Radical Protest*, pp. 84–85.

by Barrington Moore as a classical case of "revolution from above," few Junkers were themselves industrialists. In such modernizing revolutions agricultural leaders who initiate modernization typically ally themselves with nascent industrialists. In North Carolina a surprising number of men, such as Robert Ricks and Robert Bridges, combined the two roles in a single career. Other economic leaders, however, were full-time businessmen rather than farmers, but many of these, too, came from prominent plantation-based families. An important example of the latter was Colonel Alexander Boyd Andrews, the son of the leading merchant in Henderson and grandson of John D. Hawkins, whose ten-thousand-acre plantation in Vance County and whose large agricultural holdings in Warren County qualified him as one of the largest planters in North Carolina. Andrews rose from superintendent of the North Carolina Railroad in 1875 to become president of the Richmond and Danville Railroad. Subsequently, he became a vice-president of the $50 million Morgan-owned Southern Railroad. Based in Raleigh, he had interests in several banks, insurance, and manufacturing concerns. With the financial resources of the Morgan empire, he was one of the most visible and powerful figures in North Carolina politics at the turn of the century. Andrews's uncle was Dr. William J. Hawkins, president of the Raleigh and Gaston Railroad, who helped create the Seaboard system, one of the three largest railroads in the Southeast. Hawkins was a director of the Raleigh National Bank and a founder in 1870 of the Citizens' National Bank of Raleigh. The Hawkins family, as noted in chapter 4, had been influential in antebellum politics for decades.

Many sociologists view the family as the principal unit of social stratification.[12] Data on North Carolina families provide even more convincing evidence for a revolution from above than do examples of individual careers. The continuing hegemony of the landed upper class can be seen in families that provided social and economic leadership for several generations, in some instances their prominence extending from the colonial period into the twentieth century. I will illustrate this pattern with five landed families: the Murchisons, the Moreheads, the Pattersons, the Battles, and most prominent of all, the Camerons. During the antebellum period Duncan Murchison was "prominent in the planting and manufacture of cotton" in Cumberland County. Three sons were born at the Holly Hill plantation—John R., David Reid, and Kenneth McKenzie Murchison. John R. Murchison was a Confederate colonel who died in the war. David Reid Murchison was born in 1837 and educated at the University of Virginia. After the war he became a partner with his brother Kenneth and John D. Williams in a cotton brokerage firm with houses in New York, Wilmington, and Fayetteville. In 1880 he purchased a controlling interest in the Central Carolina Railroad. A founder of the Bank of New Hanover, he was connected with "most important business enterprises in Eastern North Carolina." Kenneth Murchison was born in 1831 and was educated at the University of North Carolina. He served as a colonel in the Confederate army. After the war he managed the New York branch of the family firm, maintaining a residence in New York and wintering in North Carolina. With his brother David, he owned the Cane River hunting preserves in western North Carolina, a vast domain that included Mount Mitchell. In 1880 he bought the famous Orton Plantation, which had been the grandest estate in colonial North Carolina, and spent the last fifteen years of his life managing this plantation. His friends frequently compared him with the young Bismarck.

Members of the Morehead family from colonial Virginia served as governors in North Carolina, Tennessee, and Kentucky. John Motley Morehead, who became known as "the Father of Modern North Carolina," was one of the leading industrialists in the antebellum South. He served on the legislature committee of 1828 that drafted the plea for industrialization quoted earlier. Morehead, the son of a Rockingham County slaveholder, was born in 1796. He graduated from the University of North Carolina in 1817 and practiced law in Guilford County. Although he "owned comparatively few slaves"—his wife was a Guilford County Quaker who opposed his heavy investment in slaves—he was the owner of two great plantations at Leaksville, one of which was farmed under his own direction.[13] He was founder and first president of the North Carolina Railroad, stockholder in the Atlantic and North Carolina Railroad, director of the Bank of North Carolina and the Humphrey Cotton Mills. He had commercial interests in what today is named Morehead City in eastern North Carolina, a boat line on the Dan River, a number of sawmills, and numerous other investments. Morehead served as governor of North Carolina from 1841 to 1845 and in the Provisional Congress of the Confederacy. He died in 1866.

James Turner Morehead, the governor's son, was born in 1840. He graduated from the University of North Carolina in 1861 and served in the Confederate cavalry. He manufactured cotton and wool after the war at Spray, North Carolina, in Rockingham County, an industrial community whose population grew to six thousand under his direction. According to *Branson's North Carolina Business Directory*, he owned a three-thousand-acre plantation in that county. James Turner Morehead helped build the North Carolina Midland Railroad and the Cape Fear and Yadkin Valley Railroad. In his laboratory at Spray he was the first person in the United States to produce carbide commercially and to demonstrate the commercial possibilities of the electric arc. He left North Carolina for New York near the turn of the century to further his interests in the chemical industry. He was active in North Carolina politics, having been elected to the state senate as a Conservative Democrat in 1870 and 1872. He was a member of the Constitutional Convention of 1875. According to his biographer, he "exerted a strong influence in establishing the Anglo-Saxons in control of Public Affairs."

Eugene Lindsay Morehead, a younger son of the governor, served as a Confederate lieutenant. He finished college after the war and practiced law in Greensboro with his father's brother, James Morehead, who had served in the United States Congress from 1851 to 1853. Eugene opened the first bank in Durham and held stock in many of that new town's businesses. Colonel

James T. Morehead, Jr., a nephew of the governor, was born in 1838 and graduated from the University of North Carolina in 1858. A colonel in the Confederacy, he served in the state house in 1866 and in the North Carolina Senate in 1872, 1873, 1874, and 1875. He was appointed lieutenant governor in 1875. His brother, Major Joseph Motley Morehead, was a prominent farmer and businessman.

Samuel F. Patterson, born in Virginia in 1799, was one of the most important developers of western North Carolina. His uncle, Major John Finley, urged him to move to Wilkesboro to work in the store of Wagh and Finley. In 1824 he married the daughter of General Edmund Jones, a granddaughter of General William Lenoir of Revolutionary War fame, "and by this connection he became closely associated with some of the leading men of the State." General Lenoir, for whom a North Carolina county is named, was a delegate to the Constitutional Convention of 1788, president of the state senate, an original trustee and president of the Board of Trustees of the University of North Carolina, and a county justice for sixty-two years. Through his influence, Patterson served as a clerk in the House of Commons from 1825 to 1835 and then became chief clerk of the senate. In 1835 he was also elected treasurer of North Carolina and president of the Bank of North Carolina. In 1837 he returned to his business interests in Wilkesboro. In 1840 he was elected president of the Raleigh and Gaston Railroad. His father-in-law died in 1845, and Patterson returned to the Yadkin Valley "to devote the rest of his life to his farming intersts." According to *Branson's North Carolina Business Directory*, his plantation Palmyra consisted of 1,328 acres. His brother-in-law, Edmund W. Jones, owned a 3,332-acre plantation in the same county. Patterson was influential in the formation of Caldwell County and managed the county's internal affairs until Reconstruction. He served in the state senate in 1846 and 1848, in the house in 1854, and again in the senate in 1864. He was also a major general in the state militia.

Rufus Lenoir Patterson, Samuel's son, was born in 1830 and graduated from the University of North Carolina in 1851. He lived for a while at Palmyra but, "not being enamored of farming," he moved to Greensboro and went into banking with his wife's uncle. His wife was a daughter of former Governor Morehead. Aided by his father, he bought a cotton mill in Salem. He served as chairman of the Forsyth County court and a mayor of Salem. He was also member of the state secession convention. Patterson's wife died during the Civil War, and he sold his Salem property and managed the family's cotton mill at Patterson, North Carolina. In 1864 he married Mary Fries, the daughter of Francis Fries, the Salem farmer merchant-industrialist whose family established the Wachovia banking empire. The Pattersons had six children. Two became cotton manufacturers, one a New York cotton commissioner, one a newspaperman, one a physics professor, and one the third vice-president of the American Tobacco Company. After the war, Patterson shifted his loyalty to the Republican party. He was a director of the Western North Carolina Railroad and of the North Carolina Railroad and treasurer of the Northwestern North Carolina Railroad. At the urging of his friend, President Kemp Battle, he was appointed to the University of North Carolina Board of Trustees.

Samuel Legerwood Patterson, born in 1850, was a younger son of Samuel F. Patterson. He graduated from the University of North Carolina and worked for a while after the war as a clerk in his brother's cotton mill in Salem. He preferred agriculture, however, and went back to manage the family farm. A Democrat, he served in the state house in 1891 and the senate in 1893. He served as North Carolina commissioner of agriculture from 1893 until he was ousted by the Populists in 1896. He was reelected to the house in 1899 during the Democrats' white supremacy campaign and was subsequently reappointed commissioner of agriculture. He became the first elected commissioner in 1900 during the administration of Charles B. Aycock.

Rufus Patterson, Jr., was born in 1872. After graduating from the University of North Carolina he worked with William Kerr of Concord in bag manufacturing. He moved to Durham and became involved in the Golden Belt Manufacturing Company, where he designed bags for the tobacco industry. By the age of twenty-five he had invented a successful machine for weighing, packing, and labeling tobacco. He was made a director of the American Tobacco Company by age thirty. Later he was president of the International Cigar Machinery Company, valued at $10 million, and of several other companies. He married a granddaughter of former Governor Morehead.

The Battle family of eastern North Carolina, one of the most distinguished families in the state, produced many social and economic leaders. The earliest known member of the Battle family in America bought land in Virginia in 1662. Elisha Battle, born in 1723, moved to North Carolina and established the Cool Springs Plantation—the foundation for family wealth that persisted into the twentieth century—five miles from Rocky Mount. Elisha Battle became "one of the most substantial men of his county." He was a justice of the peace and Tarboro commissioner. He represented Edgecombe County in the colonial General Assembly for twenty years and was a delegate to the Constitutional Convention.

James Smith Battle, the grandson of Elisha Battle, was born in 1789. He graduated from the University of North Carolina in 1800. A lifelong cotton planter, he owned about five hundred slaves and added thousands of acres to the Cool Springs Plantation. According to his biographer, "Although he became the purchaser, in 1848, of the Rocky Mount Mills, one of the earliest cotton factories in the State, built by his cousin, Joel Battle, . . . he could not be diverted into manufacturing, but confided the actual management to his son William." Only once was he distracted from agriculture. "When the Wilmington and Raleigh, afterward Wilmington and Weldon Railroad, was chartered in 1838, his public spirit prompted him to become one of its most munificent stockholders. He then built by contract, chiefly with his own slaves, many miles of the road."[14] Battle served for years as an Edgecombe County justice of the peace. He is claimed to have been loved by his slaves, one of whom was granted the "privilege" of being buried at his feet. His son, Kemp P. Battle, described his paternalistic sense of responsibility as follows:

He required and obtained from his slaves obedience and industry, and gave in return everything needed for health and happiness. Every family had its canoe and fishing grounds. Opossums, raccoons, and hares were abundant in the woods and fields along the river; dancing, singing, a banjo playing enlivened "the quarters" at night. Unlimited fuel was supplied and an abundance of food and clothing. The best of physicians were employed for the sick and medicines provided. Families were never separated; cruel punishments were never inflicted. In fact, it is to be doubted if a happier set of laborers could have been found in the world.[15]

William Smith Battle, James's son, was born in 1823; he graduated from the University of North Carolina in 1844. Like his father, he planted cotton as his main money crop in Edgecombe County. He was manager and part owner of a Rocky Mount flour and grist mill and a cotton mill. Federal cavalry burned these mills during the Civil War but Battle soon rebuilt both the mill and factory. A member of the secession convention, "he . . . supported all measures recognizing the right of secession and providing for carrying on the War with the utmost vigor."

William Horn Battle, born in 1802, was the son of Joel Battle, who built one of the first mills in the state, and the great-grandson of Elisha Battle. He graduated from the University of North Carolina in 1820 and was admitted to the bar in 1825. He served briefly in the state house and became a member of the Superior Court in 1840. In 1852 he was appointed to the North Carolina Supreme Court. A law professor at the University of North Carolina, he was the sole reviser following Reconstruction of the statutes of the state in 1872. He was elected president of the Raleigh National Bank in 1875. He also served on the national committee of the Episcopal church. One of Battle's sons became a cotton planter. His other sons were Richard H. Battle and Kemp Plummer Battle.

Richard Battle was born in 1835 and graduated from the University of North Carolina in 1854. He practiced law in Wadesboro and had numerous business interests in Raleigh. He served as a director of the Citizens' National Bank of Raleigh, the Raleigh Cotton Mills, the Neuse River Cotton Mills, and was president of the North Carolina Home Insurance Agency. Battle was chairman of the State Democratic Executive Committee from 1884 to 1888. Richard's brother, Kemp Plummer Battle, was born in 1831, on his father's farm in Franklin County. Kemp Battle graduated from the University of North Carolina in 1849. He practiced law in Raleigh until 1876. In 1857 he was made a director of the Bank of North Carolina. He served as president of the Chatham Railroad Company, 1861–66, president of the State Agricultural Society, 1867–70, and president of the North Carolina State Life Insurance Company. In 1876, Battle became president of the University of North Carolina.

Thomas H. Battle, born in 1860, was a son of Kemp Battle. He graduated from the University of North Carolina in 1880. In 1885 he was made a director of the Rocky Mount Cotton Mills and president two years later. He increased the number of spindles in this old mill from three thousand to twenty-six thousand and established "an enviable reputation as a mill manager." A Democrat, he was elected mayor of Rocky Mount in 1886. He played a "prominent" role in school development and organized the Rocky Mount Graded School in 1901. In 1889 he established the Bank of Rocky Mount and became its president. He was also president of the Rocky Mount Saving and Trust Company and the Rocky Mount Building and Loan Association. He was one of the organizers and first president of the North Carolina Bankers Association.

Kemp Battle's other son was Herbert B. Battle, born in Chapel Hill in 1862 and graduated from the University of North Carolina in 1881. Herbert was the state chemist and director of the North Carolina Agricultural Experiment Station. In 1897 he organized the Southern Chemical Company in Winston-Salem and he was associated, along with Daniel Tompkins, with the Southern Cotton Oil Company. He married the daughter of Major James W. Wilson, president of the Western North Carolina Railroad and chairman of the North Carolina Railroad Commission.

Samuel Westray Battle, born in 1854 in Nash County, was the son of William Smith Battle and the grandson of James Smith Battle. Samuel graduated from the University of Virginia and received his M.D. from a medical college in New York. He was a United States Navy surgeon and married an admiral's daughter. When he retired from the navy in 1885 he moved to Asheville, North Carolina, which he promoted nationally as a health resort. He was vice-president of an Asheville streetcar system and he invested in furniture and woodworking plants.

Jacob Battle, born in 1852, was the son of Captain Turner Westray Battle, a planter. He graduated from the University of Virginia in 1872. He practiced law in Rocky Mount and served in the state senate in 1893.

George Gordon Battle, a younger son of Captain Turner Battle, was born in 1868 on the Cool Springs Plantation. His mother, the daughter of a United States Supreme Court justice, was a member of the Randolph family of Virginia. George graduated from the University of Virginia in 1889 and Columbia Law School in 1890. He served from 1892 to 1897 as assistant district attorney from New York. When his biography was written, he was practicing law in New York City and spending his summers on the 150-year-old plantation.

The Cameron family of Orange County was probably the wealthiest family in North Carolina during the decades surrounding the Civil War. The career of this one family alone is almost enough to demonstrate my claim that the small landed upper class laid the institutional framework for modern North Carolina. The story of the Cameron family, according to one of its biographers, "is the story of two families, the Bennehans and the Camerons, joining in the early 19th century and making one family so strong that neither the Civil War nor Reconstruction could shake it loose from its foundations or damage it in any serious way."[16] Ironically, I learned of the Camerons while browsing in a book on architecture, rather than through the state histories that focus more on such social actors as office-holders who figured more in the foreground of political life. The Camerons, nonetheless, were celebrated by Thomas Dixon, a close family friend, whose novel *The Clansman* focused on a principal aristocratic family called the Camerons. The film *Birth of a Nation*, based on Dixon's novel, was filmed partly at Fairntosh, the Cameron plantation.

Richard Bennehan moved from Virginia to North Carolina in 1768. He became a business partner with William Johnston, a Scottish planter of great wealth and influence in the colony. (Johnston was the nephew of a colonial governor and a financial agent of the Transylvania Company; he dispatched one of his employees, Daniel Boone, to explore the company's vast lands in Tennessee and Kentucky.) In 1776, Bennehan purchased a large tract of 893 acres, which formed the nucleus of his plantation, Stagville. He married into one of the leading planter families in the state. Records show that in 1790 he was the largest slaveholder in Orange County (ninety slaves) and the second largest landowner (2,355 acres). By 1802, Bennehan owned 4,803 acres.

Duncan Cameron (1776–1853) was the son of the Reverend John Cameron, who came to Virginia from Scotland in 1770 and married Annie Owen Nash, who was a niece of Abner Nash, a colonial governor of North Carolina, and of General Francis Nash. Duncan, his oldest son, settled in Hillsboro in Orange County in 1797 and established a law career. He married Rebecca Bennehan at the Stagville Plantation in 1803 and was deeded the Brick House Plantation by his father-in-law, Richard Bennehan. Cameron became a Superior Court judge in 1814. He was president of the State Bank of North Carolina, a University of North Carolina trustee, clerk of the state Supreme Court, and a member of the state Board of Internal Improvements. He devoted the last twenty years of his life to his beautiful plantation, Fairntosh, and also maintained a twenty-acre residence on Hillsboro Street in Raleigh. Fairntosh "contributed to a way of life and an economy as well balanced and complete as that of the medieval lord." According to one of his biographers, Samuel Ashe, "His own looms converted his wool and cotton into clothing for his slaves, and his shoemakers, carpenters, blacksmiths, and other artisans combined to make the plantation a development of practical industry that was no less profitable than interesting."[17] (A visit to Fairntosh, near Durham, gives one a sense of how the self-sufficiency of the plantation, the principal unit of social organization in the South, hindered the development of southern communities.)

Duncan Cameron had eight children, but only two survived to inherit his wealth. Only one of his daughters married, she to the wealthy Wake County planter George Mordecai, who succeeded Duncan Cameron as president of the State Bank (according to Branson's *Directory*, Mordecai's plantation was valued at $85,500). Paul Carrington Cameron, born at Stagville in 1808, inherited an "immense fortune" in 1853. He attended the University of North Carolina for two years and graduated from Washington College in Connecticut in 1829. In 1832 he married Anne Ruffin, the daughter of Thomas Ruffin, chief justice of the North Carolina Supreme Court. Owner of at least thirty thousand acres by the time of the Civil War, Paul Cameron was "unquestionably the richest man in North Carolina."[18] His four plantations, Snow Hill, Brick House, Stagville, and Fairntosh— along with adjoining smaller plantations and farms—extended over what is today Durham, Granville, and Wake counties. His ownership of more than nineteen hundred slaves qualified him as one of the largest slaveholders in the entire South.[19] Charles Richard Sanders writes, "The wealthiest man in the State at the beginning of the War, he was still the wealthiest, despite the loss of his slaves at the end of it."[20]

According to Sanders, Paul Cameron "was conservative in his attitude toward social change but progressive in terms of whatever had to do with improimg the material accommodation of life—land, livestock, rivers, canals, railroads, forests, building, and industrial processes." He was "perhaps the supreme example of the benign enlightened Southern planter, citizen, and builder of institutions of his day, who was guided, not by the principles of equality but by the kind of humanized paternalism that Carlyle advocated."[21]

True to the pattern of a revolution from above, Cameron's chief interest was agriculture. "He saw in agriculture the great mainspring of commerce, of prosperity and social happiness, and the foundation upon which was laid the great superstructure of human advancement and enlightenment."[22] But Cameron was also a banker and industrialist. He promoted the building of the North Carolina Railroad and was a director of the Raleigh and Gaston Railroad and the Raleigh and Augusta Air Line. He owned stock in two Raleigh banks, the Citizens' and the Raleigh National, and in textile mills in Rockingham, Rocky Mount, and Augusta, Georgia. Cameron was somewhat active in politics. He served in the state senate in 1856, and he chaired the North Carolina delegation to the Democratic convention of 1876.

Paul Cameron's papers include an unpublished twenty-six-page open letter to friends entitled "A Peep into the Old Dominion," written in 1868 after a tour through Virginia with his friend General Wade Hampton of South Carolina that ended at Lexington, Virginia, with a visit to Robert E. Lee on the occasion of Hampton's commencement address to Washington College. In this long letter—written when Henry Grady, the New South's most familiar spokesman, was only eighteen and two decades away from his famed New South speech of 1886 to the New England Society—North Carolina's largest planter discussed not only the problems of black emancipation and southern agriculture, but described his dream of an industrial South, mighty and independent:

> Everywhere in Virginia the farmers are providing themselves with species of labor saving machinery, especially the Reaper-Mower and Storage [illegible word]. Many of the Railroad warehouses were crowded with every tool that a farmer needs. Much the larger part had been manufactured in Baltimore. It will not be long before the city of Richmond will take the lead not only in this but as the great Manufacturing City of the South. From its forges and furnaces came the Crimson and Shell of four long years of strife—and it can soon provide us with all that we need from a horseshoe to a reaper or from a fishhook to an ocean of iron clad steamers. Not until the South shall hammer and plain, stitch and grind

and bring the plow, loom, and anvil close to each other will it become self-dependent and *independent*. This is our road to wealth and consequence. Richmond has all the elements with associated wealth and enterprise to become alike a Birmingham and a Manchester.[23]

One finds here, in Cameron's image of the future, a vital link between the Old South and the New.

When Paul Cameron died, properties in his estate included a 10-acre family home in Raleigh, 25 acres near St. Mary's College in Raleigh, 140 acres in West Raleigh, 130 acres near the state fairgrounds, four city lots, assorted properties in Graham County, Person County, and Charlotte, 100,000 acres in Buncombe, Henderson, and Transylvania counties that were later incorporated into the Biltmore estate, 2,240 acres near Memphis, Tennessee, 1,500 acres in a Florida phosphate belt, 100 shares of a Florida orange grove, and, finally, Fairntosh, which by then consisted of thirteen contiguous plantations.[24]

Paul Cameron's only son who survived to adulthood received the bulk of the Cameron estate. Bennehan Cameron (1854–1925) continued the work of his father, grandfather, and great-grandfather. He attended Eastman Business College in Poughkeepsie, New York, and graduated from Virginia Military Institute in 1875. He married the daughter of Peter Mayo, a large farmer and renowned manufacturer in Richmond, Virginia. He studied law, but devoted his life instead to agriculture. He served many terms as director and president of the State Agricultural Society. He also served as vice-president of the Southern Cotton Growers' Protective Association and as vice-president and president of the Farmers' Congress of America. Like his father, Bennehan Cameron was also "greatly interested in finance and industry." He was a director of the Morehead Banking Company and with Eugene Morehead helped to organize the First National Bank of Durham. He served as a director and, for a while, as president of the Rocky Mount Cotton Mills, which the Battle family had established. Other investments in textile manufacturing included mills in Richmond and Nash counties, the Great Falls Manufacturing Company, and a mill in Augusta, Georgia.

As a planter-industrialist Cameron was particularly interested in the South's transportation problems. He was involved in the building of the Caraleigh Railroad Branch, the Union Depot in Raleigh, the Oxford and Clarksville Railroad, the Lynchburg and Durham Railroad, the Durham and Northern Railroad, the Oxford and Dickerson Railroad, and the Oxford and Coast Line railroad. He served as a director of the partially state-owned North Carolina Railroad for thirty-five years. As a representative of its private stockholders, he played "a leading part in leasing it to the Southern Railroad" for ninety-nine years in 1895, an act of cooperation with the Morgan financial empire that outraged the North Carolina Populists. Finally, according to biographers, his "greatest work" was his role in the creation of the vast Seaboard Air Line System, one of the South's three principal railroads. He served as president of the railroad from 1911 to 1913.

Cameron's interest in transportation was not confined to railroads. He was an organizer and director of the Quebec–Miami International Highway plan, the head of the Bankhead Highway Association that sought to connect the southern states with better roads, and a director of the American Automobile Association. In 1915, as a member of the state House of Representatives, he introduced a bill to create the North Carolina Highway Commission and to issue $50 million in bonds to pay for highway improvements in the state.

Cameron was active in politics and was appointed to various official positions by governors Zebulon Vance, Thomas Jarvis, Alfred Scales, Daniel Fowle, Thomas Holt, and Elias Carr. He was elected to the North Carolina House of Representatives in 1915 and 1919 and to the North Carolina Senate in 1921.

The history of the Cameron family contradicts the middle-class development thesis and the interpretation advanced by C. Vann Woodward and others of the origins of the New South. Sanders writes, "Conspicuous in the story of the Camerons and their progenitors is a pattern which has persisted for at least five generations. It is a striking fact that neither the institution of slavery nor the abolition of it was able to destroy or even seriously change this pattern."[25]

Several observations can be made about the individuals and families described above. Foremost is the fact that these were not isolated individuals but members of a social class bound together through their common interests in plantation agriculture as well as by a web of social relationships. The family was one of these social bonds. "Right" marriages established some of these men—Samuel Patterson, for instance, married into the Lenoirs and Duncan Cameron into the Bennehans—and subsequent marriages strengthened their family connections. Thus the Patterson family was united with the Moreheads, the Camerons with the Ruffins, the Battles with the Randolphs of Virginia. The Battles and the Moreheads were North Carolina branches of larger families that originated in colonial Virginia. Although I confined my research to North Carolina, it would be interesting to know the extent to which intermarriage related landed families throughout the whole southern region.

In addition to family connections, these people were united by business interests. They worked together on the same development projects, and they served together as directors of the same railroads, textile mills, banks, and businesses. Further, they associated through such other institutional structures as the Democratic party, the Confederate army, and, perhaps foremost, the University of North Carolina. Most of these individuals were students at the University of North Carolina, a few served as professors, one as president, and several as university trustees.

The economic and social basis for this upper class was land ownership. Agriculture produced wealth that was used in diverse ways, including industry. The hegemony of these slaveholders survived the Civil War and emancipation, and they laid foundations for a new North Carolina after the war. These agriculturalists provided leadership in banking, insurance, railroad building, cotton mills, and other enterprises. Sometimes the same individuals actively pursued both agricultural and industrial interests. An example is Bennehan Cameron, who served as president of the State Agricultural Society and of the Farmers' Congress of America and also as a director of railroads, banks, and cotton mills. In other instances a division of activities occurred within the family as, for example, in the Patterson family. Rufus Lenoir Patterson managed the family cotton mills while his brother, Samuel Legerwood Patterson, ran the farm and served as state commissioner of agriculture.

The social philosophy of this class reflected its agrarian moorings. Although sociologists often describe prejudice as a lower-class personality trait, it was actually a cultural construct of the landed upper class. The labor needs of the plantation were reflected in a white supremacist ideology. Thus Robert Henry Ricks was "zealous to establish on a secure basis the supremacy of the white man in Eastern North Carolina," and James Turner Morehead "exerted a strong influence in the establishment of Anglo-Saxons in control of public affairs." Many of these men supported secession as the last recourse in the defense of the southern slaveholding system. In the name of social responsibility their dominance was legitimated by an ethic of paternalism. In the following chapter I shall examine how they extended paternalistic dominance from the cotton field into the cotton factory, one of the most striking consequences of their sponsorship of southern industry.

A number of important questions about this class remain. The data show that these landholders were politically powerful before and after the Civil War. They served as governors and as advisers to governors, as state commissioners, mayors, Democratic party leaders, judges, justices of the peace, county commissioners, and members of the North Carolina General Assembly and the United States Congress. The last quarter of the nineteenth century was a period of great instability in southern politics. In subsequent chapters I shall explore the relationship between this group and important occurrences in North Carolina politics, including the Populist revolt and the reform movement at the turn of the century.

Biographical data also show that the economic interests of

these families and individuals were statewide and regionwide. The Moreheads owned properties on the coast; the Camerons and the Murchisons owned vast territories in the mountains. Equally important were the ties they had to metropolises outside the South. The Murchisons, for example, operated a New York branch of the family cotton business. James T. Morehead moved to New York to further his interests in chemical production, and George Gordon Battle went there to practice law. More important, however, was the relationship between North Carolina's landed upper class and northern finance capitalism.

Southern historians such as Paul Buck have described the gradual reconciliation of North and South in the decades after the Civil War, a reconciliation achieved by the Compromise of 1877 that ended Reconstruction and ensured the restoration of white rule in the South.[26] Given this one condition of white supremacy, southerners cooperated with northern capitalists on a number of social and economic development projects. For example, North Carolina's education reformers Walter Hines Page, Charles D. McIver, and Edwin A. Alderman sat with such northern industrialists and financiers as George Peabody and John D. Rockefeller, Jr., on the General Education Board.[27] Cooperation in making war was another source of elite integration. Southerners valiantly rose to defend and extend America's economic empire in the Spanish-American War. More than half the South's cotton was sold internationally. The region's stake in the export of cotton cloth, at least some of which went to the Philippines, was greater than that of the Northeast. South Carolina alone "exported close to one-half of all the cotton cloth reported to the census as having been dispatched to foreign countries."[28] I used Paul Carrington Cameron's visit to Robert E. Lee and his subsequent remarks on industrialization to symbolize the commitment of the South's agrarian leaders to a new direction after the war. The presentation by Bennehan Cameron, his son, of a fine stallion to Lee's nephew, Fitzhugh Lee, for the Cuban campaign, may be seen as a symbol of the New South's integration into America's international political and economic role.

The cooperation between Southern agrarian leaders and northern financiers for railroad development was even more important in effecting sectional reconciliation. Because of economic and political instability in the region in the years following the Civil War, railroad building was the southern investment most favored by northern capitalists. "If the improvement of the railroad facilities of the South was primarily the work of Southern men," writes Buck, "the money which financed it came from the North."[29] American railroads generally are considered to have been economically insecure after the Civil War. George Edwards reports that "in 1876 39 percent of all the railroad bonds [in the United States] were in default, while in 1879, 65 roads with capitalization of $234,000,000 were sold under foreclosure."[30] The reason typically given for the entry of northern bankers such as J. P. Morgan into railroad management and consolidation in this period was to protect their loans and investments "from the havoc of competitive anarchy."[31] They certainly did achieve this.

According to Buck, the South's ten thousand or so miles of railroad were either destroyed or badly worn at the end of the Civil War. By 1873, however, the region had rebuilt these and added an additional eight thousand miles so that "by 1880 the South had a modern railroad system of twenty thousand miles which gave it better economic unity than it had ever previously possessed."[32] North Carolina railroad building better than kept pace with this rate. Its mileage more than doubled from 1880 to three thousand miles in 1890.[33] Three great interstate systems, the Southern Railway Company, the Atlantic Coast Line Railroad, and the Seaboard Air Line Railway, consolidated and dominated the state's railroad traffic by 1900.[34]

Bennehan Cameron's role in leasing the North Carolina Railroad to the Southern and his leadership in the creation of the Seaboard system suggests the partnership between northern capitalists and the state's landed upper class. The latter benefited from improved transportation but lacked the necessary means to carry out its expansion. In contrast to this interpretation, C. Vann Woodward's analysis of railroad building and economic development in the New South suggests a prostrate postwar South helpless to defend itself against the invasion of northern capital: "As the old century drew to a close and the new century progressed through the first decade, the penetration of the South by Northeastern capital continued at an accelerated pace. The Morgans, Mellons, and Rockefellers sent their agents to take charge of the region's railroads, mines, furnaces, and financial corporations, and eventually many of its distributive institutions."[35] Woodward adds that "like republics below the Rio Grande the South was limited largely to the role of a producer of raw materials, a tributary of industrial powers, an economy dominated by absentee owners."[36] This colonial interpretation underestimates the active role of the South's economic and political leaders. None of North Carolina's early postbellum textile mills were built by northern capital. Nonetheless, Woodward points to one of the dilemmas of the South's conservative modernization. North Carolina's agricultural crops and manufactured products were valuable only if they could be shipped to external markets because the state's low agricultural and industrial wages limited its domestic market. The dependence of planter-industrialists on northern capital for railroad construction, however, no doubt compromised the extent of regional independence that Paul Carrington Cameron and others envisioned in 1868. As a class, however, and as railroad stockholders, the planters prospered nonetheless. More important, however, as industrialists, independent of northern capital, they thrived.

6. Labor Relations and Ideology in the New South: Consequences of North Carolina's Revolution from Above

The discovery that industrialization in North Carolina was sponsored by the landed elite is surprising, as I have noted, because landed upper classes in plantation societies, including the Deep South of the United States, typically oppose such change. According to Barrington Moore, however, "The notion that a violent popular revolution is somewhat necessary in order to sweep away 'feudal' obstacles to industrialization is pure nonsense as the course of German and Japanese history demonstrates." Traditional landed elites have occasionally transformed their societies by sponsoring industrial development, a pattern Moore calls "conservative modernization" through "revolution from above." This situation as a rule has proved highly "unfavorable to the growth of free institutions."[1]

In Germany and Japan industrialization was led by agrarian elites. Eastern Europe was incorporated into the world market system as a grain-exporting region in the sixteenth century. Indigenous German nobilities reintroduced serfdom on big landholdings in the eastern principalities in order to expropriate greater quantities of grain for export from the formerly free peasantry. Japanese rulers preserved traditional peasant society but exploited it more intensely for commercial purposes.[2] Both agricultural systems, like that in the American South, were highly labor-repressive. According to Moore, "Both the system of maintaining peasant society intact but squeezing more out of it and the use of servile or semiservile labor on large units of cultivation require strong political methods to extract the surplus, keep the labor force in place, and in general make the system work."[3] In later centuries, when international military pressure encouraged these elites to industrialize, this same authoritarianism was used to develop industry and to repress individual freedom. The roots of contemporary Japanese labor relations and industrial ideology are to be found in this manner of modernization. Robert Cole writes of the Japanese experience:

> From the Meiji period onwards the ruling class sought to make Japan strong, first in the face of Western threats and then to embark on its imperialist adventure. This required a policy of rapid industrialization for which the ruling class closely allied itself with major industrial enterprises. It is not surprising that after the first great liberalizing reforms of the Meiji Reformation, the ruling class gradually put its stamp of approval on traditional values and practices designed to boost the authority of employers in the rapidly developing industrial firms. This enabled production to continue uninterrupted by work stoppages and without the payment of high wages which would have diverted capital from still greater efforts at industrialization.[4]

Similarly, the stamp of traditional approval was put on German industry by agrarian leaders, the Junkers.

The first stage in the development of modern Germany was the growth of the strong Prussian state. The Prussian nobility expanded its holdings at the expense of the peasantry, which was reduced to serfdom, at the same time that it weakened urban merchants by bypassing them with its exports. The Hohenzollern monarchs subsequently subdued the nobility and prevented parliamentarianism by playing off classes against each other. "The result in the seventeenth and eighteenth centuries," according to Moore, "was the 'Sparta of the North,' a militarized fusion of royal bureaucracy and landed aristocracy."[5]

A second stage in German development occurred in the late nineteenth century with the alliance of the dominant landed class of the East and the weak industrial classes of the West. After an abortive liberal revolution in 1848, the Prussian monarchy led the other German states in a conservative counterrevolution that resulted eventually in the formation of a German

Empire that excluded Austria and was dominated by Prussia. Otto von Bismarck, prime minister of Prussia, became the empire's first chancellor in 1871. Bismarck, the son of a Junker landlord, was born on a manorial estate in Brandenburg that had been in the family's possession since the fourteenth century.[6] As chancellor he was determined to maintain the predominance of the Junker class, although the agrarian order was precarious. Agriculture was badly depressed in Europe in the 1870s, but had been bad for some time. According to Theodore S. Hamerow, "The burden of indebtedness of the Prussian aristocracy doubled between 1805 and 1845. Faced with the threat of bankruptcy, the nobility had recourse to entailment as a weapon against grasping creditors, but even this device proved inadequate for the purpose of economic security. Land continued to change hands so rapidly that by 1885 only 13 percent of the latifundia of East Prussia had been in the possession of the same family for more than fifty years."[7] The situation was even worse, of course, for peasants. They were free again, but—like their American counterparts in the 1870s, emancipated southern slaves—they lacked economic resources to defend their political status.

In a brilliant political move that reversed Germany's free-trade policies, Bismarck secured the loyalty of German industrialists in the West and simultaneously preserved the political ascendancy of the Junker class by preventing the breakup of the big estates.[8] He imposed heavy protective tariffs on both manufactured and agricultural goods. This move toward partial economic closure aided German industry, protected Junker producers against cheap Russian and American grain, and encouraged a strong nationalism.[9] Industrial development was also aided by the creation of a common currency, a central bank, a commercial code, and, most important, a paternalistic system of social security measures compatible with conservative noblesse oblige. The latter in particular helped to assure the loyalty of the industrial working class and to coopt the socialist threat.

In both Germany and Japan the threat of foreign dangers kept up the aristocracy's commitment to industrial development, especially as it involved the building of a war machine. In both instances, according to Moore, the state "aided industrial construction in several important ways. It served as an engine of primary capitalist accumulation, gathering resources and directing them toward the building of an industrial plant." The state was also able to "see to it that the lower classes who pay the costs under all forms of modernization do not make too much trouble."[10] This contrasts with the laissez-faire system of England and France, where the commercial bourgeoisie extended the range of individual liberty because they opposed traditional feudal constraints on commerce. As Reinhard Bendix has shown, the result was the gradual extension of citizenship rights to the common man.[11] Such an extension of liberty has not occurred where authoritarian regimes seek both to encourage industry and to preserve the traditional agrarian social structure, the source of their own wealth and power. In such instances, the state is at the same time an instrument of modernization and of repression.

Earlier I noted that the comparative study of social stratification requires that "the emergence, consolidation, and political roles of classes and status groups must be appreciated as elements of" the worldwide capitalist market system.[12] Germany and the American South occupied comparable niches in the world market system in the nineteenth century. Both societies exploited servile labor to produce agricultural commodities, wheat and cotton, for export. Labor-repressive agricultural policies required authoritarian measures for social control, and the landowning classes of both societies developed antibourgeois sentiments and aristocratic pretensions despite their involvement in the capitalist system. I believe that the landed upper classes in both societies responded similarly to external pressures—in Germany, to foreign threats from Austria and France and, in the American South, to northern restraints on geographical expansion of the slave system—with nationalism, militarism, and industrialization.[13] The South lost its nationalistic struggle; thus its subsequent modernization was not altogether comparable with Germany's. Most important, at least during Reconstruction, the landed upper class in the South lost control of the state although in later years the American federal system provided some latitude to southern elites. My research on the social origins of North Carolina industry suggests that despite constraints, the landholding class used its traditional social authority to carry out an industrial war in response to political defeat. The following excerpt from an editorial that appeared in the Raleigh *News and Observer* on 9 November 1880 suggests something of the flavor of this response. "We have been defeated in the national contest. . . . What, then, is our duty? It is to go to work earnestly to build up North Carolina. Nothing is to be gained by regrets. . . . Out of our political defeat we must work . . . a glorious material and industrial triumph. We must have less politics and more work, fewer stump speakers and more stump pullers, less tinsel and show and boast, and more hard earnest work. . . . Work for the material and educational advantages of North Carolina, and in this and not in politics, will be found her refuge and her strength." Despite obvious political differences involving the role of the state in industrialization, similar outcomes of conservative modernization in North Carolina, Germany, and Japan can be seen in their comparable patterns of labor relations and ideology.

"Tradition," according to Bendix, refers to the legacy of pre-industrial values and social relationships that persists in industrial societies.[14] Societies vary in the extent to which traditional ways of thinking and relating are superseded by new ways with the advance of industry. In the South, under the leadership of the landed class, textile manufacturing was incorporated into the traditional social structure when the paternalistic ethos of the plantation was extended into mill villages. Descriptions of labor relations in the North Carolina textile industry—including Boyte's "The Textile Industry: Keel of Southern Industrialization," Gilman's *Human Relations in the Industrial Southeast*, McLaurin's *Paternalism and Protest*, George Mitchell and Broadus Mitchell's *Industrial Revolution in the South*, and Pope's *Millhands and Preachers*—all suggest an industrial pattern distinctive to southern cotton manufacturing.[15] The incorporation of mill villages in rural society in the South, under the auspices of agrarian leaders, seems to have resulted in the creation of communities with strong social cohesion and in a work force with blunted occupational consciousness.

After the Civil War, a wasted South had to be rebuilt. According to the standard interpretation by historians of this epoch, the Old South was not reconstructed but instead a "new middle-class society" was established. Its recruits, "in spirit as well as in its outer aspect," strikingly resembled "the same [middle] class in Midwestern and Northeastern cities."[16] While undoubtedly the rapid postbellum growth of industry heightened middle-class prestige and mobility as management opportunities were expanded, this interpretation obscures the real social foundations and subsequent class relations of the New South.

The hallmark of conservative modernization is preservation of traditional agrarian social relations. In the South the first priority after the war was the reconstruction of the rural social structure. After a brief period of disorganization, despite formal emancipation of the labor force, the plantation system was reorganized through sharecropping and tenant farming. Social and economic reforms promised during the period of Radical Reconstruction were aborted and the civil and political rights of freedmen were limited, first by physical force and terror, and at the end of the century by law. In North Carolina, at least, old slaveholders returned to power.

Antebellum industrialists survived the war in relatively good financial shape. These men rebuilt and expanded their factories. Briefly, in the late 1860s, cotton prices were high because northeastern and English textile manufacturers had been short of cotton fiber. These sales were an important temporary source of capital for the region. In the 1870s cotton prices dropped, and marginal farmers suffered. The great textile mill crusade in the last quarter of the nineteenth century, resting on antebellum foundations and sponsored by agrarians, promised employment opportunities for marginal farmers and their families in the Carolina Piedmont and thus promised to reduce potential unrest. Postwar industrialization became an important form of rural social control, functioning just as it had in the antebellum period during times of agricultural depression.[17]

During the antebellum period, Genovese writes, "the master-slave relationship [had] permeated Southern life and influenced relationships among free men." Among these were the semipaternalistic relationships between the planter class and the more numerous yeomen farmers. "The plantation offered virtually the only market for the small non-staple producing farmers and provided the center of necessary services for small cotton growers. Thus, the paternalism of planters toward their slaves was reinforced by the semipaternal relationships between the planters and their neighbors."[18] This paternalistic relationship was intensified after the war when poor white farmers became millhands. Their loyalty to the planter-industrialist was assured by the racial exclusivity of the mill village. After emancipation, factory jobs were for whites only. "The poor whites under slavery had been excluded, while slaves were cherished. Now the disinherited were read into the will. They had been starved, now they were subsidized. They had been unnecessary, now they were all-important. The bond of sympathy between whites of both classes was cemented against the common enemy, the Negro. The factory owner, by tradition, through economic mastery, and as a racial champion, went unquestioned."[19]

My discovery that members of North Carolina's small landed class led in rebuilding and expanding the textile industry gives new credence to W. J. Cash's argument in *The Mind of the South*—an interpretation of the region that has been both maligned and celebrated but is more consistent than any other I have read with the theme of conservative modernization I am developing here—that the plantation was the model for social relations in the mill villages: "One curious consideration we need to bring into the reckoning is that Progress was being accomplished so completely within the framework of the past that the plantation remained the single great basic social and economic pattern in the South—as much in industry as on the land. For when we sound the matter, that is exactly what the

Southern factory almost invariably was: a plantation, essentially indistinguishable in organization from the familiar plantation of the cotton fields."[20]

In *The Industrial Revolution in the South*, George and Broadus Mitchell contradict an earlier claim made by Broadus Mitchell— a claim upon which Woodward's account of the textile history rests—that southern mills were built by "new men." They observe that the "industrial leaders in the South in the opening decades were of a different stripe from most of the cotton manufacturers, mine owners, and iron masters who figured in the English Industrial Revolution. The former were gentlemen, the latter were small men who struck it lucky." The social implications they deduced were similar to the observations made by Cash:

> The pioneers in the industry were generally gentlemen. Not operatives or mechanics as in England, they did not see themselves as seizing mean advantage. Many had been slave-owners, they took authority by habit, they were accustomed to being looked up to, and they were moved by the spirit of noblesse oblige. The duty that they had acknowledged to their house servants and field hands in the quarters to treat them with consideration, to be responsible for the supply of their wants and answerable for all their actions, was now transferred, with the fervor of a new dedication, to the inhabitants of their mill villages. The manorial lord of the early middle ages, as owner, had been also judge, teacher, monitor, all but priest and certainly champion. The same was true of the old Southern planter so that he, and those who shared his tradition, carried their accustomed methods over into the new calling. The factories were nursing mothers to the operatives, furnishing quite as much directly in goods and services as they bestowed in wages.[21]

Mill village paternalism at first developed naturally out of planter-industrialists' traditional sense of social responsibility; their dealings with white operatives were guided by the old grammar of master-slave relations. Out of necessity as well, mill owners built villages and provided services for their physically isolated workers because early mills were often located in remote areas where the force of Piedmont streams could be harnessed.[22] Later, when other energy sources were available, the practice persisted in villages built on the fringes of Piedmont cities like Charlotte and Greensboro. "What at first," according to the Mitchells, "had been a necessity of mill building, and a perfectly natural expression of the traditional responsibility of the master for his dependents, now became, on the part of many, a studied tactical pose."[23] Over time a system of professional welfare work that routinized the charisma of the pioneer planter-industrialists aided in the social control of the work force and the rationalization of production. The system was grounded in agrarian tradition.

Along with jobs, mill owners provided housing, stores, churches and clergy, schools and teachers, recreational and social services. McLaurin aptly calls this complex the "industrial plantation."

> In short, the mill village was an almost completely paternalistic system. Management controlled outright when, where, for how long, and for what wages the operatives worked. It exerted a substantial influence over where the operatives lived, shopped, studied, played, and worshipped. In addition, management thoroughly policed the village, making sure the threats to the operatives' morality—liquor, prostitution, and labor organizers—were kept at a safe distance. Within some villages, management even went so far as to suppress local politics so that "no mayorality elections, aldermanic squabbles" or ward politics "kept the people in ferment." State and national politics, which could not be prevented, were carefully watched. Management in such villages placed inspectors at the ballot box to see that each operative voted the right way. If an operative failed to vote for the management's convictions, "he would bring down a lot of trouble upon himself." In such a tightly organized and controlled environment, any unionization attempts were necessarily predisposed to failure.[24]

Mill owners in New England were also forced to provide many services for their workers since they, too, had built industrial villages in rural areas, but apparently they were much more distant, socially and geographically, from their workers than were their southern counterparts. Cochran and Miller describe a group of Boston industrialists who controlled 20 percent of the nation's cotton spindles by 1850 as follows: "Living sumptuously on Beacon Hill, admired by their neighbors for their philanthropy and their patronage of art and culture, these men traded in State Street while overseers ran their factories, managers directed their railroads, agents sold their water power and real estate. They were absentee landlords in the most complete sense. Uncontaminated by the disease of the factory town, they were also protected from hearing the complaints of their workers of suffering mental depression from dismal and squalid surroundings."[25] Southern industrial paternalism has its parallel not in New England but in Japan.

Still today in Japanese industry, paternalism encompasses such practices as the provision of "recreational facilities, health facilities, company housing, cafeteria and lunch subsidies, company discount stores, job training and retraining of employees, saving institutions, and permanent employment."[26] Comparative survey research on Japanese and American work attitudes reveals that the two work cultures vary dramatically in terms of the extent to which the Japanese company is involved in the total life of its work force.[27] Students of Japanese society view "the strength of tradition as part of the explanation for Japan's success in industrialization and for the absence of strong revolutionary currents."[28] Robert Cole's account of Japanese industrial development suggests parallels in the structure and functioning of industry in Japan and that of North Carolina.

> Throughout Japan's industrialization the web of reciprocal obligations has been a powerful control device committing workers to factory life and making them conform to company discipline. Superior-subordinate relationships, in particular, obligated the superior to paternalistic care of his charge and

the subordinate to repay with loyalty and hard work. Economic insecurity in the city resulting from inadequate social welfare measures and vast underemployment in the country reinforced and tightened the web. The mutual interdependence in the factory, where individual will of necessity was subordinated to group efforts for survival, fits well the varying patterns of cooperation and stratification that had been established over the centuries in innumerable Japanese villages. Judging by the absence of strong revolutionary currents and the failure of workers to organize themselves as an effective social or political force, the structure of authority as it rests on this web was remarkably absorbant of successive shock waves emanating from the introduction of modern technology. Concessions and compromises in interpersonal relationships required by involvement in the web are key elements in understanding the irrelevancy of Marxist expectations of revolutionary social change in the course of Japanese industrialization.[29]

Japanese firms are typically compared to the family. According to Cole, workers refer to their company as *uchi*, which connotes "our family circle." The patron-client relationship—in Japanese, *oyabun-kobun*, which translates literally as "parent-child"—is the model for the relationship between management and workers. According to Cole, "The firm's assumption of wide responsibilities fits well with the values of the *shuju* (lord and vassal) relationship of the feudal period; and it is likely these values worked toward acceptance of the role." The historical link with the *shuju* relationship was the Japanese labor contractor, whose services to rural clients obligated the latter as subordinates. Employment was viewed as a personal favor, the benefits of which workers were obliged to repay with hard work and loyalty. Once on the job, the "rule [was] strict adherence to the authority of a paternalistic employer."[30] Even foremen enjoyed a familylike relation to workers. They served in loco parentis and were consulted on personal as well as work matters.

Personalistic recruitment and paternalistic favors obligated the southern millhand just as surely as they did his Japanese counterpart. Entrepreneurs "were most eager to know their employees individually and to guard their moral character."[31] In the early years of the postwar period, there was an interpenetration of southern agriculture and industry. Traditional rural relationships were upheld as planter-industrialists and farmer-millhands alike fluctuated between cotton cultivation and cotton manufacture. Although systematic research is unavailable on this important matter, early observers such as the Mitchells acknowledged vital links between southern industry and agriculture. They suggest that this was the case since the labor force —and the industrialists—were drawn from farming and the principal manufactured product, cotton, was grown locally. They report a "forward and backward flow between farm and factory."

> In the intervals between profit in agriculture through high price and profit in manufacture from the same cause, operatives accustomed to raising the staple have left the spindle for the plow, relieving impending unemployment and steadying price levels. In some instances, as at Kannapolis, North Carolina, there has even developed a regular seasonal flux. This ready cordiality between industry and agriculture had many conscious manifestations. So far from distrusting manufactures, important planters led movements to set up factories in their fields, some mill companies raised their own cotton and processed it without baling, while others purchased large tracts of land with a view to such a possibility.[32]

The personalistic orientation of southern mill owners and the origin of this trait in traditional agrarian relations is revealed in the following excerpt from a biographical sketch of Mark Morgan.

Morgan, born in 1837, was a manufacturer, banker, legislator, and planter. The death of his father forced him to work in mills from the age of seven. He acquired mechanical skills that proved valuable after the Civil War when he helped rebuild mills for Colonel Thomas Holt and Colonel Charles Malloy. The latter took him in as a partner, and eventually he became president of three mills and a founder and director of the First National Bank of Laurinburg, North Carolina. According to his biographer, "But for his greater reputation as a manufacturer he would be widely and favorably known as a prominent farmer of the State." Morgan recruited labor for his mills with the same personal attention he gave to his farm.

> The surrounding country is very productive in cotton, which was bringing a high price at that time. The work in cotton fields was more attractive to most laboring people, who were hard to get into cotton mills. Mr. Morgan walked through the surrounding country personally soliciting the services of such laborers as were properly open to such proposals, and by his *personal contact* with prospective laborers protecting the character of the mill settlement by not taking people whose appearance seemed to indicate criminal tendencies. In truth, while such personal solicitation has long since passed, *he has always endeavored to protect the character of his people* by excluding the vicious, so much so that it was a matter of pride often referred to by his more experienced hands that they were with Mr. Morgan so long. *Nor is this confined to his mill operatives, but applied to his farm laborers and tenants as well.* Often they state that they intend to remain with Mr. Morgan so long as they live, if he will keep them so long.[33]

All observers of the textile industry comment on this distinctive personal style. Gilman suggests that mill owners were warm and friendly, whereas line supervisors were distant and impersonal. "This tendency to absolve top management of responsibility for the out-of-line activities of supervisors and to consider the latter as indicative of personality quirks of individuals rather than as representative of company policy is still characteristic of southern textile work forces."[34] Cash depicts the same personal relationship between owners and workers that Morgan's biographer undoubtedly exaggerates.[35]

> The master of the mill stood to his workmen as the immediate representative of the upper classes, of course. And it was an inherent part of his paternalistic approach, a natural corollary of the bringing over of the plantation system, that, as I have before suggested, the old easy personal relations should have been brought over too. The baron knew these workmen fa-

miliarly as Bill and Sam and George and Dick, or as Lil and
Sal and Jane and Lucy. More, he knew their pedigrees and
their histories. More still, with that innocent love of personal
detail native to southerners, he kept himself posted as to
their lives as they were living under his wing.[36]

Industrial paternalism and the successful accommodation
of industrial development to traditional relations are effective
means of cultural control. In Japan, "the combined existence of
pre-industrial values and practices made management choices
of these policies and worker acceptance of them more likely.
However, the very existence of this role over the years deprived
workers of their initiative and made them subordinate to company policy."[37] Similarly, in North Carolina, mill owners' control "functioned effectively to destroy any autonomous social
space, and institutions which the working class could claim as
their own—in which independent leadership could emerge and
develop, in which popular traditions could be sustained, or
in which workers could compare and analyze their experience
as working people."[38] Exactly how this occurred, however, is
unclear.

Many writers have speculated on why unionization drives
have been so unsuccessful in the southern textile industry. North
Carolina's industrial work force remains the least unionized in
America. Writers have readily attributed this failure to the geographical isolation of mill villages and to workers' dependency
on the owners, to the homogeneity of the work force, and to
workers' fear of job competition with blacks.[39] The radically different history of similarly isolated and paternalistic coal towns
in the Southern Appalachians, however, which produced great
labor militancy and industrial conflict, shows that the matter
is not so simple. There industrial communities were built by
entrepreneurs foreign to the region. Although they were highly
paternalistic, these communities were not outgrowths of traditional social relations as were the mill towns.[40] Some of the
nation's most violent labor struggles took place in such southern
mountain communities as Logan County, West Virginia, and

"Bloody" Harlan County, Kentucky.[41] Unlike the coal operators, whose control tactics included the hiring of Chicago gun thugs to police dissident mining camps, the planter-industrialists of the Carolinas possessed traditional sources of authority with which they could secure the loyalty of operatives. They may have had even greater incentives to control labor tightly. The southern mills' principal competitive advantage in production over northern mills was cheap labor; high intraregional shipping costs somewhat negated their proximity to cotton cultivation. Wages had to be kept low. On the average, wages were 40 percent lower in the South than in New England. Work days were 24 percent longer.[42] Although interregional competition among coal operators also forced great pressure against wages in the mountains, the location of the coal industry in the South was partly a response to the discovery of rich coal deposits and not simply the availability of reserve labor.[43]

The prestige of employers, the paternalistic language of their demands for loyalty, and their incentives for labor control are not sufficient to account for the fact that working-class consciousness and militancy have been at best spasmodic in North Carolina. We must also understand the development of working-class institutions in the South, but, just as the history of the textile industry is sketchy, little systematic research has been done on working-class culture. It is not clear, for example, whether anything like a traditional craft community emerged among textile workers in the antebellum industry or what their response might have been to postbellum industrial expansion. Much of the industrial conflict in the United States at the turn of the century, as documented in community studies such as the Lynds' *Middletown*, occurred as a result of factory owners' efforts to reduce their dependence on skilled workers.[44] They did so by the introduction of technology that lowered the skill levels of factory work and transferred greater control of the work process to management.[45]

The postbellum expansion of textile manufacturing in the South was facilitated by new technology that permitted the employment of unskilled labor, including children.[46] The brief flurry of agitation led by the Knights of Labor in North Carolina during the 1890s, especially in older mill communities such as the Haw River section of the Carolina Piedmont,[47] may have been partly a response to this. Older workers perhaps fought to defend their job control because skill levels were being degraded by technology, although this is only speculation.[48] The large labor reserve produced by agricultural depression undoubtedly weakened any such attempts. Since the average monthly wage in 1899 for male farm laborers in North Carolina was only $8.91, even the average daily wage in 1893 of $.69 for unskilled men in cotton mills must have been attractive to financially desperate tenants.[49] This was especially true because wives and children also could work, though at lower wages, and because mill owners provided many desirable services. For the most part, grievances were privatized.

In one of the few historical surveys of North Carolina workers, Harry Douty reports that from 1880 to 1930 labor turnover in the textile industry was an index of social protest against wages, hours, and working conditions. He reports a history of industrial nomads "wandering from mill to mill in search of something better than they had known."[50] The search for a kinder patron as a form of private protest surely reinforced the personalistic style of labor relations in the industry. The few extensive strikes that did take place in North Carolina, such as in Gastonia in the 1930s, seem to have "occurred where the 'social space' between management and workers had widened the most."[51] Usually these were absentee-owned mills. There is evidence that paternalism declined in the 1930s when management sought to further rationalize the textile industry. Speaking of this generation of manufacturers, the Mitchells wrote: "In fact, they are industrialists, businessmen, capitalists, and congratulate themselves upon supporting these characters. They are not subject to the restraints of their fathers. They do not have an emotional attitude toward their workers. They are not burdened with a sense of *noblesse oblige*. They are not aristocrats, but bourgeois. They are class-conscious and money-wise."[52] Given the industry's relation to rural social structure, it would be interesting to test whether a model of peasant movements rather than industrial conflict best predict textile strike patterns. Peasant movements typically are not motivated by a desire for improvements. Rather, they are hostile reactions to the loss of traditional privileges. We may indeed find that "when southern labor stirs"[53] most often, in the early textile industry, it was in an effort to restore the balance of rights and duties and to defend the style of personal relations in the mills that workers had been taught to expect in the early postbellum period. This makes some sense, at least, of Liston Pope's observation that "lower wages appear not to have been crucial" to the famous strike at the Loray mills in Gastonia, "nor was the fact of a stretch-out in itself of supreme importance." Rather, he says, "so far as internal mill policies were concerned, the impersonal and arbitrary methods of the superintendent appear to have been the most significant factors underlying the strike."[54]

In addition to employers' personalistic style, other techniques have ensured labor discipline and reinforced social control in mill villages. Besides their use of paternalism, textile manufacturers have threatened to hire blacks instead of whites and, as a last resort, they have used state force to control labor and prevent unionization. Experts consider North Carolina's labor laws to be among the most restrictive in the country.[55] Although the use of state police has occasionally been decisive in managing strikes, as in Gastonia in the late 1920s or in Henderson in the 1950s,[56] generally fear has been the most effective way to curb labor independence. Racial fears, especially, have inhibited southern workers from challenging management's authority.

McLaurin reports that in the 1890s "management was able to play the role of [labor's] protector against the blacks while, at the same time, using the blacks as a threat to keep wages depressed and hours of labor unchanged." At the height of organizing drives during this period a Greensboro newspaper warned operatives that "the colored man is now knocking at the door of cotton mills asking for work at lower wages than white men could think of." In testimony to the Industrial Commission of 1900, John Coffin, vice-president of the Southern Industrial Convention, bluntly acknowledged the strategic value of such intimidation in controlling workers. According to McLaurin, "When asked if he was holding up the Negro as a threat, not just to prevent unjust demands by the whites, but to force whites to accept any terms offered, Coffin's reply was brief and to the point. 'The employer must have something to hold over union organizations, or just turn his business over to the union and let them run it.'"[57]

The legacy of such practices is still to be seen in North Carolina. Presently the state ranks second among the fifty states in the percentage of its work force in industry, yet it ranks fiftieth for its low industrial wages and fiftieth for its level of unionization as noted. Both the success and the failure of North Carolina's conservative modernization are apparent in these facts. Industrialization has been rapid, extensive, and inequitable. The extent to which this results from the continuity between textile manufacturing and agrarian social patterns can be shown by some contrasts provided by North Carolina's tobacco industry.

A Different Ethos along Tobacco Road

Members of North Carolina's landed upper class provided postwar leadership in textile manufacturing, banking, insurance, railroad building, and other large business enterprises. Tobacco manufacturing, along with furniture manufacturing,[58] was an important exception to this pattern. Its industrial leaders were indeed "new men." Washington Duke owned three hundred acres of land, two army mules, and fifty cents in cash after the war. He farmed and manufactured tobacco with his sons on his farm. At one point, out of desperation, he sold his farm to a neighbor on credit and worked on it for wages. The other early manufacturers in Durham who merged with the Dukes to establish the American Tobacco Company were also upwardly mobile "new men." W. T. Blackwell, with only a common school education, started out in the tobacco business as a broker and trader, peddling tobacco from a wagon until the end of the war. Julian S. Carr was the son of a Chapel Hill grocer. Richard H. Wright was orphaned at age fourteen and began work as an apprentice in a general store for $50 per year and board. George W. Watts was the son of a prosperous Baltimore wholesale dealer. R. J. Reynolds, who built a factory in Winston, was the only exception. His father, also a tobacco merchant and manufacturer, was a wealthy Virginia planter.

The absence of large landowners from the development of the tobacco industry can be explained by planters' lack of experience both with growing tobacco and with its preparation and manufacture. In nineteenth-century North Carolina tobacco was grown primarily by small farmers. Unlike Virginia, where tobacco was the principal plantation crop, in North Carolina, tobacco was typically cultivated by yeomen. Although a few wealthy planters such as Bennehan Cameron's close friend, John S. Cunningham, acquired reputations as large growers, "in the early years of the post-bellum period small holdings were . . . the general rule."[59] Most tobacco was grown on farms ranging from fifty to two hundred acres. Since the production of plug and smoking tobacco initially required simple equipment, tobacco manufacturing developed as a craft industry conducted by yeomen farmers and artisans. Prior to development of mass-production techniques, its manufacture required little capital. Like early furniture manufacturing in the mountains, tobacco processing was an important investment opportunity for small businessmen, unlike textile manufacturing and railroad building that were much greater undertakings.[60] Washington Duke's first tobacco factory was a sixteen-by-eighteen-foot log house where he prepared leaf tobacco during the winter. With two of his sons, Benjamin Newton and James Buchanan, he expanded this domestic craft into one of the largest industrial enterprises in the world at the time.

The invention of cigarette-making machinery in the 1880s provided new technology for mass production that radically changed the tobacco industry. Among the first to take advantage of such technology, the Dukes and their associates in Durham built the largest business organization in the South. By 1904 the American Tobacco Company was capitalized at $300 million.[61] In distinct contrast to the highly competitive textile industry, which consisted of a large number of small producers, the American Tobacco Company grew to exemplify the bureaucratically organized monopolies Alfred Chandler has described as coming to dominate American business in the period from 1870 to 1900. Like other big businesses of the period that manufactured consumer goods from farm products for sale nationally in urban markets, the Dukes combined and centralized raw material purchase, mass production, distribution, and finance functions in a single, vertically integrated business structure.[62] When supply overran demand, the Dukes developed modern marketing techniques, including mass advertising campaigns. They created a national and then a worldwide selling organization. They captured 95 percent of the total American cigarette market in the 1890s.[63] Cigarettes manufactured in North Carolina soon became one of the nation's first name-brand products. Since they manufactured a finished product for a rapidly expanding national market, tobacco manufacturers, unlike the planter-industrialists in the textile sector, broke out of North Carolina's otherwise dependent economy.

In *Southern Industry and Regional Development*, Harriet Herring demonstrated that in contrast to cotton manufacturing, the tobacco industry experienced a proportionately high value added by manufacturing (relative to the worth of its raw materials) and that it contributed a large multiplier effect to regional growth. "Cigarette manufacture," she noted, "is one of the few industries in the South which completes the process of manufacture for the ultimate consumer instead of a few of the early, least skilled, least profitable stages."[64] By 1940 cigarette manufacturing furnished a principal market for more than a quarter of a million farmers, and its processing created high-wage employment opportunities for thousands of workers. Its demand for buildings and machinery, its accessory industries such as tin foil and paper, and its large advertising expenditures all created secondary growth. Finally, a large proportion of the industry's high profits were reinvested in the region. Tobacco money contributed to the expansion of banks, railroad construction, textile growth, and most important, the development of hydroelectric power in North Carolina.[65]

Because they have not understood the social origins of southern industry, historians have not perceived the fact that tobacco manufacturing conflicted in many ways with the rest of North Carolina's political economy. Social relations in the tobacco industry deviated from the traditional pattern of southern labor relations. Its leaders were new men with a new product. They had no class interests in preserving the agrarian social order. Unlike the early textile manufacturers, they were not landowners. They paid high wages and employed blacks, two violations of the state's industrial practices. In contrast with mill village paternalism, they built no industrial communities and accepted unionization when it came. A different community ethos came to characterize the towns along tobacco road.

Initially wages were quite low in the tobacco industry, at first lower than wages in textile manufacturing. In 1880 the average annual wage in all tobacco manufacturing industries was only $101 while annual textile wages averaged $132. By 1900, however, wages in the two industries were equivalent. Although the American Tobacco Company originally pursued a "ruthless labor policy," mechanization and marketing success eventually permitted substantial wage increases. Wages in the tobacco industry increased during the World War I boom by 222 percent compared with only 148 percent in textiles. By 1929 the work day in cigarette factories had decreased and wages were much higher than in cotton manufacturing.[66] Eventually, the tobacco industry was forced to accept unionization.

The great wage disparity between tobacco and textile manufacturing can be traced in part to differences in industrial structure. In contrast to the competition between southern and northern textile firms, the American Tobacco Company competed through advertising wars rather than price wars. Tobacco manufacturers "aimed at increasing the volume exchanged not by reducing the price for a given product but by inducing consumers to take more of the product at a given price."[67] This strategy, plus the high monetary value of workers' productivity, permitted high wages. Rice reports that in the 1930s the cigarette industry maintained the highest net profit per employee in America.[68]

If industrial structure accounts for the wage differential between tobacco and textiles, the same cannot be said of the industries' comparative racial practices. For all practical purposes, southern textile manufacturers kept the cotton industry lily-white. In 1930 there were only 477 black textile operatives in North Carolina out of a work force of 100,000.[69] Liston Pope and Hylan Lewis both have commented on the strict segregation in southern mill towns.[70] In *Blackways of Kent*, Lewis reported that only about 25 blacks were employed in the mills he studied and that these worked exclusively as maintenance persons or janitors.

In sharp contrast, the tobacco industry always employed a high proportion of black workers. In 1930 almost 2,500 of the 3,865 tobacco operatives in North Carolina were black, as were 4,166 of the 4,966 male laborers. Blacks comprised an even higher portion of the female work force. Of 9,904 female tobacco operatives, 7,143 were black, as were 1,291 of the 1,831 female laborers. This cannot be explained as the exploitation of black labor in disagreeable, low-income jobs since "the tobacco worker, both white and colored, in general [was] envied by fellow workers in other southern industries, and the wages far exceed[ed] those of many white collar workers, teachers and professionals."[71]

The Dukes and the other tobacco manufacturers were not members of North Carolina's landed upper class. Unlike the planter-industrialists, they did not have as much at stake in preserving the racial caste system upon which the agrarian order was based. Benjamin Duke owned a farm in North Carolina, along with his mansions in Durham and New York City, but it was not the source of his wealth and power. When Duke sold his North Carolina farm he noted that "I am glad it is off our hands."[72]

Durham tobacco manufacturers not only employed blacks in their factories—they broke the South's racial code even further by employing blacks in textile mills. Though Julian Carr was a white supremacist, he encouraged black economic participation in cotton manufacturing in accord with the philosophy of Booker T. Washington. "Inviting Negroes to help the South overtake the economy of the North, he established a 'Jim Crow' cotton mill to provide employment for blacks outside the established lily-white mills. Carr's Negro mill could be seen entirely as a tactic to exploit cheap Negro labor, but he just as eagerly lent his support to a Negro-owned cotton mill begun in 1898 by W. C. Coleman, a black businessman in Concord, North Carolina."[73] Washington and Benjamin Duke loaned money to Coleman's mill, but it failed in 1904. Robert Durden points out that their involvement in black businesses was "both incidental and, in the last analysis, kept on a cool, businesslike basis," but, as Durden stresses, "even that kind of relationship was in stark contrast to the harshly discriminatory policies of disfranchisement and segregation of blacks that the Southern Democrats championed so successfully in those same early years of the twentieth century."[74]

The existence of a landless black working class in tobacco cities of the North Carolina Piedmont like Durham created a market for black businesses and sustained a black middle class. The North Carolina Mutual Insurance Company, founded by John Merrick, grew to become the "world's largest Negro business." It, too, had the financial support of the Dukes and of George Watts.[75] In fact, black businesses did so well in the relatively permissive atmosphere of Durham that the new city acquired a special reputation in the South. Booker T. Washington reported that in Durham he found "the sanest attitude of the white people toward the blacks."[76] The black sociologist E. Franklin Frazier described Durham in the 1920s as the "capital of the black middle class. . . . Durham offers none of the color and creative life we find among Negroes in New York City. It is a city of fine homes, exquisite churches, and middle class respectability. It is not the place where men write and dream; but a place where black men calculate and work. No longer can men say that the Negro is lazy and shiftless and a consumer. He has gone to work. He is a producer. He is respectable. He has a middle class."[77]

In an analysis of black political participation in Durham from 1933 to 1958, Robert Cannon reports a "degree of success that was difficult for blacks in other Southern communities to duplicate."[78] One can sense something of the vitality and independence of this urban black culture in the upbeat music performed in the tobacco manufacturing centers and especially in Durham. Blues performers like Blind Boy Fuller, Sonny Terry, and Brownie McGee created a musical style, known as "Bull Durham Blues," that reflected the hopes and disappointments of the urban black working class. Its sound was a departure from the usual melancholy of rural southern blues.

> Unlike the sultry, mournful music of the Mississippi Delta, the Piedmont country blues is enthusiastic foot-tapping music. Despite slow bluesy moments, it is distinguished by a ragtime energy accentuated by the rhythmic rapping of a washboard and punctuated by the whoops and calls of the harmonica. The men who made the Piedmont blues attained an astonishing level of technical virtuosity while engaging in a debilitating struggle for survival. Their music pulsates with all the hopeful feelings and painful memories of a generation of blacks living in the industrialized southern Piedmont.[79]

I do not wish to portray the situation in Durham as better for working-class or middle-class blacks than it was. Rather, I suggest that the political economy of tobacco manufacturing generated a social structure that was quite different from that of planter-dominated textile towns. In mill villages such as "Kent" there was "no Kent Negro economy, nor [was] there a significant elaboration of economic activities with specific reference to the needs or demands of the Negro community."[80] Mill villages permitted the development of far less cultural autonomy for the working class than did tobacco centers. The very fact of black musicians performing on the corners of Pettigrew Street nearest the factories in Durham, as well as the fact of black businesses, taverns, and churches, indicates a social basis for the emergence of independent and solidary ethnic and class communities impossible elsewhere in the Carolinas. Politically, as well, tobacco manufacturing broke with southern tradition. Historians have overlooked potential political antagonisms between tobacco manufacturers and the landed upper class. The Dukes, for example, though among the richest individuals in the state, were political outsiders. James and Benjamin Duke were both Republicans. Recent research in the papers of the Populist leader Marion Butler has disclosed the fascinating fact that Benjamin Duke financed Butler and his newspaper the *Caucasian*, the Populists' political voice, during the Populist revolt.[81] Perhaps Duke was merely buying favors in anticipation of a Populist political victory, but I suspect that there was more to it. My research on state politics divulged hints of a stance among tobacco industrialists that was at odds with North Carolina's politics of development. Benjamin Duke was not the only tobacco man with Populist connections. Julian Carr, who ran unsuccessfully as a "liberal" against party leader Furnifold M. Simmons in the 1906 Democratic senatorial primary, was the father-in-law of W. A. Gutherie, the 1896 Populist candidate for governor. Gutherie was an American Tobacco Company lawyer. W. T. Blackwell was the son-in-law of W. J. Exum, the 1892 Populist candidate for governor. The implications of such family connections deserve further study.

There is also evidence, unexplored by historians, that the tobacco industry was looked upon rather ambivalently in North Carolina. Lefler and Newsome report that the textile industry was viewed as a "public, patriotic enterprise and manufacturers were considered philanthropists and public benefactors," but that tobacco manufacturing "was regarded as a strictly private enterprise."[82] It would be interesting to explore further why this was so. It is also interesting that North Carolina's Corporation Commission—created in 1899 by the Democrats—ignored the textile industry, dropped charges against the railroads, and instead attacked the American Tobacco Company.[83] Further research into these questions should eventually contribute to a fuller understanding of the political economy of the New South.

Understanding the New South's Creed

Planter leadership in cotton manufacturing affected the textile industry's ideological justifications as well as its labor relations. Just as the labor practices of cotton manufacturing set the standards for southern industrial relations, despite alternative practices in such other industries as coal mining and tobacco manufacture, the textile industry was also the predominant influence on the construction of postbellum southern ideology. In this realm, too, postwar North Carolina developed similarly to other societies that were transformed by conservative modernization.

The social function of ideology is the same in all societies: the legitimization of an elite's privileges and the control of subordinates. As Rousseau said in the *Social Contract*, "The strongest is never strong enough to be always master, unless he transforms his strength into right, and obedience into duty." In his comparative study of the "ideologies of management in the course of industrialization," Reinhard Bendix has shown that understanding ideology "may be a symptom of changing class relations and hence a clue to an understanding of industrial societies." "For, if comparable groups in different societies confront and over time resolve a common problem," he notes, "then a comparative analysis of their divergent resolutions will reveal the divergence of social structures in a process of change."[84]

In Germany under the authoritarian Junkers, "hierarchy, discipline, and obedience" were values in their own right.[85] In Japan, during the period of rapid industrialization, "new organizational forms and practices were legitimated by traditional values stressing internal harmony, loyalty, and paternalism."[86] Similarly, in the New South, "the program of paternalism, education, regulated franchise and increasing segregation was advanced. . . . Thus it was that one-partyism, white supremacy, patriotism, morality in government, and the industrial revolution were all part of one program."[87] In each of these societies, values espoused during the period of rapid industrialization differed from typical bourgeois legitimations.

Industrial ideologies figure in the effort to make the development of industry socially acceptable, both to traditional authorities and to the masses. According to Bendix, "Where industrialization is the work of a rising entrepreneurial class, that class is likely to seek social recognition from the ruling groups at the same time that its ideas and economic activities challenge the traditions of the ruling groups at many points."[88] This was the case in England and France, where the influence of the commercial middle class threatened the "benevolent authoritarianism" of traditional rule. The ideological result was a declaration of the rights of man. C. MacPherson calls this image of man the ethos of "possessive individualism," noting that from such a perspective "society becomes a lot of free individuals related to each other as proprietors of their own capacities and of what they have acquired by their exercise." Ideologically, "society consists of relations of exchange between proprietors."[89] In bourgeois society, the rights of property and the impersonal forces of the market were legitimated. According to Bendix,

> In the West, and especially in the United States, authority in industry is justified explicitly on the ground that the man who already enjoys the good things in life has earned them and is entitled to the privileges which they confer. Hence, the employer's authority as well as his earnings and privileges are the rewards of past and present exertions. For the people at large such rewards are promises held out for the future and little effort is made to disguise the heavy burden of labor. Most attempts to increase the present satisfactions of work consist rather in promises of future rewards and in benefits and appeals which have the character of additional incentives offered by the employer.[90]

Industrial ideology in the South and its relationship to the class structure have not received satisfactory treatment, partly because historians have not grasped the continuity between the landed upper class and industrial leadership. Paul Gaston, an authority on the "New South creed," admits that "today we are likely to agree that [historians] have yet to produce the 'all-around view' with which our guild can be permanently satisfied."[91] Partly this is true because of apparent internal contradictions in the South's industrial philosophy. McLaurin, for instance, reports elements of both paternalism and Social Darwinism in postbellum thought.[92] Cultural developments are related to economic and social practices, yet they have a life of their own. The South has always shared the ideological currents of the nation as a whole. Thus there are similarities between the ideas of industrialists in the South and those of their peers throughout the rest of the nation. C. Vann Woodward claims that southern industrialists "were preaching laissez-faire capitalism, freed of all traditional restraints, together with a new philosophy and way of life and a new scale of values." He suggests that North Carolina mill builder and newspaper owner Daniel Tompkins, for instance, shared the world view of other nineteenth-century American entrepreneurs. "Like Carnegie, a reader of Herbert Spencer, Tompkins believed that 'the survival of the fittest is, has been, and will always be the law of progress.' In his papers he fought child-labor legislation and sought to save 'Democracy from Communistic Populism' and capitalistic enterprise from governmental regulation of any sort."[93] Actually Social Darwinism and paternalism are not incompatible when the former is a justification for white supremacy and the latter is taken as both a sign and an obligation of racial superiority.

In *The New South Creed*, Paul Gaston has struggled with the apparent contradiction in southern ideology between the cult of the Lost Cause and the metaphor of the New South. According to Gaston, romantic images of the Old South and the Lost Cause pictured "the old regime as a society dominated by a beneficent plantation tradition, sustained by a unique code of honor, and peopled by happy, amusing slaves at one end of the social spectrum and beautiful maidens and chivalric gentlemen at the other—with little in between." At the same time, however, the New South lexicon "bespoke harmonious reconciliation of sectional differences, racial peace, and a new economic and social order based on industry and scientific, diversified agriculture—all of which would lead, eventually, to the South's dominance in the reunited nation."[94] Often the same writers employed both images. Thus Daniel Tompkins attacked the economic logic of slavery in his pleas for the spread of textile manufacturing at the same time that he "defended the humanity of the [slaveholding] system and wrote idyllic pictures of 'Life in the Old South.' "[95]

Gaston attempts to resolve this paradox by arguing that the Lost Cause cult and the New South creed were actually mutually supportive myths. He concludes that romantic images of the Old South were not used to argue against southern industry but instead functioned in the South to give the region "a vitally necessary sense of greatness to assuage the bitter wounds of defeat." At the same time, the myth functioned in the North to promote an image of racial harmony. "By convincing Northern readers that relations between the races were kindly and mutually beneficial," Gaston argues, "a principal obstacle in the way of sectional harmony was removed."[96]

Gaston's thesis that the New South creed functioned primarily to promote sectional reconciliation is an important insight into southern ideology but not a totally adequate explanation. Romantic images of the paternalistic slaveholders' regime and of southern industrial development are not at all contradictory in view of the fact that planters sponsored southern manufacturing. Certainly Paul Carrington Cameron saw no contradictions between the two systems in 1868 nor had Old South slaveholder William Gregg.[97] By failing to explore the class origins of southern industry, Gaston mistakes the social roots of New South ideology. He interprets the journalists who spoke for industry, such as Henry Grady of the Atlanta *Constitution*, or Henry Watterson of the Louisville *Courier-Journal*, in the same way that he interprets industrialists such as Daniel Tompkins.

Grady, the son of an Atlanta merchant, was a member of the South's small urban middle class. Tompkins, a prominent southern industrialist, was the son of a wealthy South Carolina planter. One of Tompkins's grandfathers, a first cousin of John C. Calhoun, was a well-to-do South Carolina planter who briefly owned a cotton mill near Spartanburg. His other grandfather was a North Carolina planter. Along with his cotton mills,

Tompkins owned an important newspaper, the Charlotte *Observer*. Unlike Grady, however, who was economically dependent on his career as an editor, Tompkins reported that "the only thing I wanted the paper for was to preach the doctrine of industrial development and the reasons for it."[98] By treating these two men the same, Gaston fails to differentiate middle-class spokesmen for southern industry from the actual builders of New South industry. Hence he fails to grasp the traditional agrarian roots of the New South movement.

Thus, despite what superficially appear to be contradictions in postbellum southern thought and despite elements borrowed from northern business philosophy, there was a distinctive quality to southern ideology. The organizational image for social relations in much of American industry outside the South was the impersonal market. Possessive individualism was valued. The southern textile industry, by contrast, stressed communal values. Its image for social relationships in mill villages was not the market but the paternalistic family. Oversimplifying, perhaps, this distinction between individualistic-market and communal-family imagery corresponds, respectively, to legitimations of authority that have been termed rational-legal and traditionalistic. Southern ideology was a blend drawing on both forms, but its accent clearly was on traditional justifications.

As in Japan, the myth that accompanied the spectacular growth of isolated mills was that these were families—in the South, "white families"—separated from the rest of the world. The mill owner was the model of "adulthood" and the millhands were his dependents for whom he assumed full responsibility.[99] The mill movement itself was legitimated by the claim that it was motivated by a concern for the poor, honest farmers and laborers of the state who desperately needed employment. In the words of one owner, "This was not a business, but a social enterprise. Any profit that might accrue to the originators of the mill was but incidental; the main thing was the salvation of the decaying community, and especially the poor whites, who were in danger of being submerged altogether. The record of these days is filled with a moral fervor that is astounding. People were urged to take stock in the mills for the town's sake, for the South's sake, literally for God's sake."[100]

Conflicts of interest between labor and management were obscured by appeals to regional and racial solidarity as the myth of the Lost Cause and the myth that the wealth of the aristocracy was depleted by Civil War and Reconstruction were advanced. According to the Mitchells, "The employers, certainly in the cotton manufacturing business, have tried to make their private interests appear as synonymous with the well-being of society, and have largely succeeded."[101] Such ideological efforts are not unique to the South, but the extent of their success and duration may be uniquely southern. Manufacturers had powerful allies in perpetuating these ideas in the southern clergy, as Liston Pope's account in *Millhands and Preachers* demonstrates. A similar flavor is echoed in the quasi-sociological interpretations of Glenn Gilman, a labor relations analyst who shared management's viewpoint on the textile industry and entitled one of his sections "The Folk Build the Mills." He claims that

> A relationship grew up between the communities and their mills that was and has remained unique in an industrial region. The communities built the mills, and the mills saved the communities. The mills "belong" to the communities. Either community initiative to begin with or community approval of an individual project brought them into being. It did not matter a great deal who owned the stock certificates that gave legal title to them—they remained "our mills" from the point of view of the community even after their initially widely distributed stockholdings had gravitated into the possession of a few people or a family who were interested in the mill as a primary source of income. The purpose for which the mills had been built and the return that the communities had expected to get from the mills had not altered. The purpose was to furnish payrolls.[102]

Even Woodward, who is not an apologist for the industry, says that profit alone "cannot account for the public zeal that . . . converted an economic development into a civic crusade inspired with a vision of social salvation."[103] The communal imagery of this ideology was especially southern. It contrasts with bourgeois England, for instance, where, according to E. P. Thompson, industrialization "was unrelieved by any sense of national participation in communal effort, such as is found in countries undergoing a national revolution. Its ideology was that of the masters alone."[104]

It is frequently assumed that paternalistic social values are inherently incompatible with the logic of industrialism.[105] Paul Gaston, for example, finds the values of the Old South incompatible with industrial development. "These three intertwining economic and social interests [in the Old South]—staple-crop agriculture, plantation aristocracy, and Negro slavery—produced a formidable defense mechanism that frustrated industrial and urban developments capable of undermining their foundations. The value system that grew naturally out of this order was inevitably hostile to the increasingly pragmatic and utilitarian cast of mind of nineteenth-century liberal development and suspicious of its notable shibboleths and achievements: economic individualism, urbanism, industrialism, and mass culture."[106] But paternalism and industrialism are not wholly incompatible, as the success of German and Japanese industrialization attests. One last way I can show a link between antebellum values and the New South creed is to recall the ideas of George Fitzhugh.[107]

In *Sociology for the South, or the Failure of Free Society*, published in 1854, Fitzhugh produced the South's most coherent ideological defense of slavery. This defense was, in Woodward's words, an "aggressive assault upon Adam Smith, laissez-faire, and all the political economists who advanced the proposition that social well-being was 'best prompted by each man's eagerly pursuing his own selfish welfare unfettered and unrestricted by legal regulations or governmental prohibitions.'"[108] Fitzhugh, who absorbed the ideas of conservatives such as Thomas Carlyle and Sir Robert Filmer, justified slaveholding in terms of the southern planter's "aristocratic and seigneurial prerogative and responsibility"—that is, his paternalism. Fitzhugh's image of slave society was that of the family, the same image that was later used by southerners to describe the mill village:

> For the Virginian [Fitzhugh] the family was everything, and
> society, government were but the family writ large—the au-
> thoritarian, patriarchal family. Aristotle had taught him "that
> the family, including husband, wife, children, and slaves, is
> the first and most natural development of that social nature."
> It was the model of all social institutions: "this family associa-
> tion, this patriarchal government . . . gradually merges into
> larger associations of men under a common government or
> ruler." It was the disproof of Locke, for "fathers do not derive
> their authority, as heads of families, from the consent of wife
> and children." It was the justification of domestic slavery
> for "besides wife and children, brothers and sisters, dogs,
> horses, birds, and flowers—slaves also belong to the family
> circle," and there they, like other weaker members, received
> the care, protection, and control they needed.[109]

Fitzhugh defended slaveholding by attacking the amoral individualism and libertarianism of northern capitalism. Speaking
to northern critics of slavery in *Cannibals All!* he said, "You, with
the command over labor which your capital gives you, are a
slave owner—a master, without the obligations of a master.
They who work for you, who create your income, are slaves,
without the rights of slaves. Slaves without a master!" The
"White Slave Trade" of the North, he said, was "far more cruel
than the Black Slave Trade, because it exacts more of its slaves,
and neither protects nor governs them."

Harvey Wish saw connections between Fitzhugh's paternalistic philosophy and industrial fascism. "However much his
own native kindliness would have compelled him to stop short
of the modern implications of his thought, there is little doubt
that his 'system' belongs within the ideological orbit of contemporary fascism. From Fitzhugh to Mussolini the step is star-
tlingly brief."[110] From the point of view of this chapter and its
focus on the South's conservative modernization, the important
point is that in his defense of slaveholding and paternalism,
Fitzhugh was not anti-industrial.

> Fitzhugh advocated a system of vigorous government par-
> ticipation in economic development, but he urged it upon
> Virginia and the Southern states as a solution to *their* prob-

lems. Both his economic and social aims and his means of attaining them were departures from the Jeffersonian tradition. He stressed the social values of manufacturing and commerce and the need for the growth of cities in the South to foster these arts. Government should be employed vigorously for planning and promoting schemes of internal improvements, developing financial and marketing facilities, and fostering transportation, particularly the building of railroads. "Our system of improvements, manufactures, the mechanic arts, the building up of our cities, commerce, and education should go hand in hand." Above all it was important to provide public education. "Poor [white] people can see things as well as rich people. We can't hide the facts from them. . . . The path of safety is the path of duty! Educate the people, no matter what it may cost!"[111]

Woodward finds this perspective inconsistent with southern thought. He explains it by saying paradoxically that Fitzhugh, the defender of slavery, was "decidedly *not* an agrarian." Fitzhugh, he says, "was not typical of anything. Fitzhugh was an individual—*sui generis.*"[112] Actually, Fitzhugh's viewpoint was quite southern, reflecting the values of an enlightened element of the landed upper class. Much as John Motley Morehead and others of North Carolina had done earlier in their report to the General Assembly in 1828, Fitzhugh advocated what would later be known as the Prussian route to modernity.[113] State encouragement of industry and state sponsorship of transportation and educational improvements were perhaps politically possible in 1854 when Fitzhugh wrote, but they were not possible three or four decades later when Daniel Tompkins and Henry Grady prescribed solutions for the South's chronic ills. During the period from 1854 to 1900, which spanned war and Reconstruction, the landed upper class lost control of the state twice—first to northern Republicans and their southern black allies and later, briefly, to the Populists. Not until 1900, when it restricted political participation to whites only, was the landed upper class of North Carolina securely enough in control to move in the directions to which Fitzhugh had pointed.

Conclusion

Earlier I discussed factors that impede industrialization in plantation societies. Landowners often oppose industry because they fear losing control over the rural labor force. Industrialization is also impeded by purely economic forces in plantation societies. Servile labor inhibits the home market for manufactured goods. After the Civil War, freedmen—economically enslaved by tenancy—provided no better a home market than had slaves during the antebellum period, yet the New South industrialized without their buying power. It did so by manufacturing a partially finished product, cloth, from local materials and selling the cloth outside the region. Wages had to be kept low because the South's principal competitive advantage in cotton manufacturing was its cheap labor. For these reasons, despite rapid industrialization, the South remained in a dependent relationship to New England. At least part of the ultimate value of the cotton crops still accrued to the North, where the final manufactured products, such as clothing, were produced and sold. Some of the usual multiplier effect of industrial growth was thus not achieved. Wages remained low, and some of the potential benefits of industrialization were lost to the community, though entrepreneurs benefited.[114] The growth of cotton manufacturing in North Carolina after the Civil War was change, dramatic in its rate, and yet it was no change, so continuous was it with the past. Fundamental social change is often resisted, but the textile mill crusade was popularly embraced. The slaveholders' hegemony, far from dying out, persisted as the paternalism of the plantation was translated into mill villages.

Barrington Moore has shown that industrialization is always a brutal process, especially for the lower classes, whose cheap labor pays for the costs of economic growth. In the South the costs were especially great because wages remained low. Taxes were minimized to attract other industry to the region; social needs were not met. Politically, the retention of nonwage black labor in the agricultural sector and cheap white labor in the industrial sector required strong authoritarian means. The traditional authority of the planter over the black man, extended to include white workers in the mill towns, helped to maintain the system. Paternalism was backed by the force of a repressive state. In the following chapters I shall suggest that state power was used in North Carolina to support the caste system and to curb potential labor unrest in the textile industry as well as to build an infrastructure of modern schools and highways in support of further economic development.

7. Populism, Progressivism, and Paternalism: The Politics of Development

Industrial labor relations and ideology in the South at the turn of the century, at least in the textile sector, reflected the moorings of southern industry in the agrarian social order. The social relations of millhands and owners were shaped not only by the dictates of machine production but by the ethos of plantation society that pervaded both factory and community life. As new technology permitted the employment of unskilled labor, much of it provided by women and children, an independent working class failed to emerge decisively despite occasional rumblings. Planters-turned-industrialists continued to rule.

The forces of conservative modernization shaped politics too, but here the pattern was more complex. The old slaveholders were defeated militarily when they fought to defend their world. During Reconstruction they were barred from public office. Their slaves were freed and given the vote. After Reconstruction many of the old slaveholders or their sons returned to power. They still owned the land, but, unlike modernizing agrarian regimes elsewhere with which they may be compared, their political options were limited. Thousands of black Republicans and later embittered white farmers contested their power to shape the region to fit their class interests. In North Carolina, especially, the planter-industrialists met new opponents and found new allies.

North Carolina is commonly viewed as politically distinct from other southern states. As I noted in chapter 1, V. O. Key spoke of a mood in North Carolina that was "at odds with much of the rest of the South." Key claimed that the state began a "modern era of liberalized Democratic government" about 1900, and he asserted that today "many see in North Carolina a closer approximation to national norms, or national expectations of performance, than they find elsewhere in the South." He highlighted the rule of an economic oligarchy in North Carolina by calling the state a "Progressive Plutocracy." He said that industrialization had "created a financial and business elite whose influence prevails in the state's political and economic life. An aggressive aristocracy of manufacturing and banking, centering around Greensboro, Winston-Salem, Charlotte, and Durham, has had a tremendous stake in state policy and has not been remiss in protecting and advancing what it visualizes as its interests." These interests include both "a sympathetic respect for the problems of corporate capital and of large employers" and "a sense of responsibility in community matters." In the viewpoint of Governor O. Max Gardner in 1946, this adds up to the "capitalist system liberally and fairly interpreted."[1]

If this imagery is accurate, it fits a very different political economy from the plantation society of the Deep South. It is sometimes pictured as the cultural triumph of the South's "common man." Quoting Frederick Jackson Turner's description of the spirit of the frontier, Glenn Gilman claimed that "political convictions born and nurtured in the Piedmont 'broke down the traditions of conservative rule, swept away the privacies and privileges of officialdom, and . . . opened the temple of the nation to the populace.'" Contesting W. J. Cash's interpretation of the mind of the South, Gilman argued that in North Carolina —"the most liberal politically of the Piedmont States"—"the society of the Piedmont owed little to the Tidewater and the Coastal Plain. . . . It was democratic rather than aristocratic. It was the South of Andrew Jackson and Tom and Nancy Lincoln, not of the Cavaliers. Its virtue and its vices were those of the frontier, not of the drawing rooms of Savannah and Charleston. It was not the region of the plantation owner, the Negro, and 'poor white trash;' it was the South of the Yeoman farmer, the white artisan, and the professions."[2]

Although superficially plausible, this popular image of state politics rests on the middle-class thesis of southern industrialization which I have suggested is incompatible with North Carolina's stratification history. The romantic ideal of a democratic spirit emanating from the "small farms and decentralized industry"[3] of the Piedmont region ignores the ideological and relational aspects of conservative modernization. It also ignores the economic and political dominance of Battles, Camerons, Moreheads, Pattersons, and the like that bridged the Old South and the New. Some of these landed families—the Camerons, Pattersons, Moreheads—were from the Piedmont, although this fact is overlooked in the regional stereotype.

I have not found the standard historical accounts very helpful for clarifying the politics of development in North Carolina. In Lefler and Newsome,[4] for instance, the reader encounters characterizations like "progressively conservative." Such concepts are not sufficiently abstracted from partisan labels to clarify the conflicts involved. Social processes such as class formation and conflict or social and political modernization are not treated systematically. The two most useful accounts of this period are Joseph Steelman's "The Progressive Era in North Carolina, 1884–1917," and Helen G. Edmonds's *The Negro and Fusion Politics in North Carolina, 1894–1901*, but neither provides fully the empirical foundations nor analytic treatment for an adequate sociology of politics.

Nor have I found the theoretical tools of political sociology directly applicable in this research. Too often theories of political modernization—for example, those of S. N. Eisenstadt[5] or S. P. Huntington[6]—reify social actions relevant to the process of development by treating these as the quasi-mechanical operations of an "organic" social system. Some of the variables they identify as important for understanding development are useful, nevertheless, "if one constantly translates the functional terminology, with its implicit adulation of authority and its references to abstract process of 'problem solving,' into the real actions of individuals."[7]

As I will show below, Lucien Pye's conception of "political development" as the tendency toward (1) increased government capacity, (2) differentiation, and (3) equality of participation helps to set North Carolina in a comparative context.[8] The most useful insight from the theoretical literature is the methodological suggestion that patterns of elite recruitment are both an important source of change and an indicator of change in the sociopolitical system.

> As a dependent variable [elite recruitment] expresses the value system of the society and its degree of consistency and contradiction, the degree and type of representativeness of the system, the basis of social stratification and its articulation with the political system, and the structure and change in political roles. As a factor which affects change, or as an independent variable, elite recruitment patterns determine avenues for political participation and status, influence the kind of policies that will be enacted, accelerate or retard changes, affect the distribution of status and prestige, and influence the stability of the system.[9]

The methodological strategy in the remaining chapters is to study the politics of development by looking at the people who were active in North Carolina politics near the turn of the century and to ask what interests they represented while the institutional arrangements were being created for industrialization. Such an approach is in line with questions many social scientists have seen as important for understanding development. As Salamon has said:

> Many of those who investigate modernization, in fact, consider the transformation of elite recruitment patterns the central feature of the whole modernization process. Cyril Black, for example, identifies "the transition from a political leadership wedded to the traditional system to one which favors thorough-going modernization" as "the central problem in political modernization." David Apter suggests that a "comparative study of modernization begins in the comparison of strategic career profiles in relation to stratification." And S. N. Eisenstadt argues that "modernization is born or pushed by 'charismatic' groups of personalities," so that "to understand

the process of modernization and especially the extent to which it creates the condition for sustained growth," it is necessary to "analyze exactly these relations between the innovating groups and the broader institutional setting."[10]

Who Made North Carolina "Modern"?[11]

Contrary to the stratification history suggested in the previous chapter, but according to the current view among southern historians, the men who came into power in the South after the failure of Reconstruction were "new men," who were primarily interested in business profits. They wished neither to restore the old order of the slaveholders that had collapsed nor to build an equitable and active, which is to say "modern," political system. If Lester Salamon's thesis, advanced in *The Social Origins of Mississippi Backwardness*, is correct that Reconstruction represented an attempt at political modernization, with the extension of suffrage to freedmen, their organization into political parties, and the willingness to use the state for social development, then the so-called Redeemers, the men who gained power after Reconstruction, were in this sense antimodern. Redeemers, or Bourbons as they were also called, were said to be interested simply in the unrestrained pursuit of profit at a time when great profits were to be made in commerce, cotton and tobacco manufacture, and railroad building. Speaking of these men in Alabama, Sheldon Hackney writes that

> the truth is that the Redeemers were not the modernizing elite that students of modernization see as a prerequisite of substantial change in social structure. They did not propose the creation of new institutions and they advocated no change of function for any existing institution. Retrenchment in governmental services and opposition to an expansion of the regulatory functions of government lay at the heart of their program. In fact, the Redeemers were so intent on exploitation that they were more analogous to colonialists than to a nationalistic leadership eager to adjust society to the needs of development.[12]

Lefler speaks of those who redeemed North Carolina from Reconstruction in the same way when he describes a leadership group that "favored the business interests, opposed social and educational progress, and neglected the common people."[13]

Among the most neglected and outraged of the common people were the state's many farmers. These farmers organized the People's party, which, after electoral failure in 1892, fused with Republican voters—former Unionist whites in the mountain counties and blacks in the coastal plain—to elect in 1896 one of the only Republican administrations in the South from the close of Reconstruction until the 1970s. According to propagandists and partisan historians, this administration was notable primarily for promoting "Negro Dominance." Four years later, a "Chastened Democracy" is said to have returned to power.[14]

Standard interpretations date political modernization in North Carolina from 1900. Under the leadership of Charles B. Aycock (1901–5), North Carolina's popular "Education Governor," the Democratic party is claimed to have launched a "political revolution": "Defeated by its stubborn resistance to reform, its adherence to conservatism and its championship of the special interests of the business classes and chastened by its experience of defeat, the Democratic Party returned to power with a more virile, youthful, progressive leadership; a program of public education and state development; a concern for the common man; and a greater responsiveness to the changing needs of a growing state."[15] In *Southern Politics*, V. O. Key concurred in the importance of this new progressive political elite. He believed that "North Carolina's spirit reveals itself in the purposeful direction of its social action commencing about 1900. Philosophers and historians find the origin, if not the explanation, of this spirit in the political struggles at the end of the past century, which propelled the state into its modern era of liberalized Democratic government."[16] Key thought that Aycock's victory began "a political and educational renaissance" —in other words, political modernization. This is what North Carolina schoolchildren are taught[17]—that "with Aycock came the dawn of a new day for North Carolina. An age of progress lay ahead." They learn that Aycock was "a new kind of Democratic leader." "He had a keen mind and a kind heart, and he was a friend of education, progress, and the Negro. . . . The Democratic party was again in control of the state. But the old party had been reformed. Its old leaders who had favored the business interests, opposed social and educational progress, and neglected the common people had been pushed aside."[18]

This view has recently been challenged by J. Morgan Kousser in *The Shaping of Southern Politics*. Kousser agrees with Key's assessment that the election of 1900 was the most critical in North Carolina's political development, but for a different reason. According to Kousser, the consequences of that election were grim, for he believes the "real" modernizers were the Populists who were ousted from office, not the progressives. In contrast to the typical picture of the Solid South, Kousser emphasizes that through the 1880s and 1890s there was great instability in southern politics, when a significant proportion of the southern population voted against the do-nothing Democrats. (From 1880 through 1896, the Democrats in North Carolina never won more than 54 percent of the gubernatorial vote, making its state politics the most competitive in the South.) When the fusionists, as the Populist-Republican coalition was called, came to power in North Carolina they represented a modernizing thrust, extending both the range of popular participation and state action. Kousser claims that "while they controlled the legislature," the fusionists "put through an impressive reform program, indicative of what opponents of the Democrats might have accomplished had they come to power elsewhere in the South."

> After restoring and liberalizing the alliance charter [the state charter of the Farmers' Alliance, out of which the People's party had developed] and seeking to lower bank interest rates, the legislature repealed the old county government law, thereby enabling localities to elect their own officials.
>
> Whereas the conservative Democratic regimes had starved public services, the Fusionists—in the midst of severe depression—substantially increased state appropriations for

public schools from the elementary to college level, set up teacher training institutes for local schools, and provided incentives for local school districts to raise their tax rates. The legislature also augmented expenditures for charitable and correctional institutions and intensified taxation of railroads and business. Governor Russell attacked the lease of the state-owned rail line to J. P. Morgan's Southern Railroad Company and called for public ownership of all railroads.[19]

The Democrats returned to power in North Carolina by waging a successful white supremacy campaign that resulted in constitutional disfranchisement of large numbers of blacks and illiterate whites. Unlike Key, who believed that the campaign brought to power a modernizing wing of the Democratic party, Kousser feels it signaled the decline of progress.

> With the suffrage restricted, both the Republican and Democratic parties shifted to the right, and turnout declined from 75% in the 1900 governor's race to less than 50% in 1904. No longer did either party have to concern itself with the illiterate or those too poor to pay the poll tax. Democratic legislatures kept taxes low, cut appropriations in some cases and failed to increase them in others, continued to pass partisan election laws and gerrymander voting districts, enacted few of the usual "Progressive" reforms, and none which protected workers or trade unions. The party convention almost endorsed the gold standard in 1902, elected the Southern Railroad's candidate to the United States Senate in 1903, a corporation lawyer to the governorship in 1904, and felt quite comfortable with the conservative Alton B. Parker as presidential candidate in that year.[20]

Thus it is unclear who modernized North Carolina. Was it the Aycock Progressives or the Populists before them? Also unclear is the relationship between the Aycock regime and the conservative Democrats who were ousted by the Populists. If the progressives were indeed new leaders, what was their social and economic basis? What was the relationship between their political victory and background trends in social stratification and economic development?

Figure 7.1 reports membership turnovers between legislative sessions in the North Carolina Senate from 1850 to 1921. Membership continuity was high during the antebellum years, when up to 60 percent of the senators returned from one session to another. Kousser's claim that the last quarter of the nineteenth century was a period of political instability is reflected in high senatorial turnover rates. The greatest discontinuity between sessions in the seventy years covered in Figure 7.1 (with the exception of Reconstruction) occurred in 1899, when forty-nine of fifty senators were replaced. Democrats regained control of the senate and wrote the constitutional amendment that disfranchised black voters and facilitated the Aycock victory in 1900. The data support the interpretations of both Key and Kousser that this and the general election that followed in 1900 (when 84 percent of the adult male population voted) were "critical elections"[21] in the state's political history. After this point there was much more continuity in the senate although never as high as antebellum levels.

Figure 7.2 reports the levels of state expenditures from 1890 to 1905. The data show that Kousser is wrong in claiming that the fusionists radically expanded state activity and the progressive Democrats cut appropriations. Instead the data support Key's claim that the Democrats extended the range of government services. This pattern is consistent with Sheldon Hackney's findings for Alabama in the same years. He found that tax policy revealed important differences between southern progressives and Populists. In his analysis of legislative behavior, Hackney found that Alabama Populists voted as a bloc against tax increases during the 1894–95 legislative session. He concluded that the "constant emphasis on low taxes and inexpensive government in Populist papers leaves little doubt that they were still wedded to the idea of minimum government, despite frequent infidelities of thought. Their fear of debt casts doubt on their grasp of the future needs and direction of society."[22] On the other hand, Hackney's analysis of roll call votes suggests that Alabama progressives—consistent with the North Carolina data in Figure 7.2—resembled a modernizing elite. "The signifi-

Figure 7.1. Turnover in North Carolina Senate

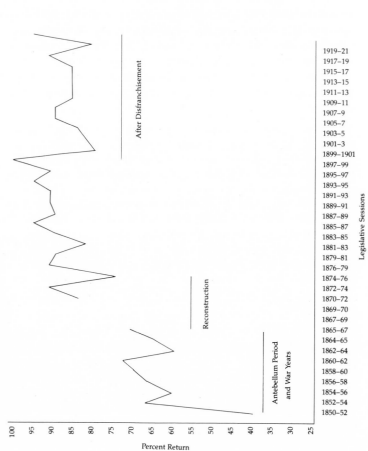

Source: *Journals of the North Carolina Senate,* 1850—1921.

cant thing about the Progressives' desire for social and economic development was that they wanted to use governmental action to stimulate such progress." The progressives, he concluded, "were earnestly interested in changing Southern society." They were "an innovating elite dedicated to rational growth."[23]

When political sociologists use the term "modernization," they mean not just the extension of the scope of state activity but also the expansion of popular political participation. As Kousser's research shows, however, the opposite occurred in North Carolina. The appearance of progressive legislation was simultaneous with the disfranchisement of thousands of voters, most of them black. Speaking of the changes in voter requirements throughout the whole South, Kousser writes:

> White turnout and opposition to the Democrats were almost always high or rising, or both high and rising, before disfranchisement, but the opposition collapsed and the participation rates of whites and blacks both plummeted immediately after the institution of new requirements. Extensive violence, intimidation, fraud, or a small but sufficient change in the election laws preceded passage of all major statutes and amendments. Although the relatively small declines in Negro voting previous to disfranchisement were enough to enable restrictive laws to pass, the laws did not simply mirror already established conditions. They had very large impacts on black and white turnout and voting for parties opposed to the Democrats.[24]

According to Kousser, North Carolina had the most competitive two-party system in the South prior to 1900. In the two previous decades its level of voter participation in governors' races never fell below 75 percent of the adult male population. Kousser compared the elections of 1896 and 1904 to estimate that disfranchisement reduced overall voter participation by 46 percent. Black participation was reduced by virtually 100 percent and white participation by an estimated 23 percent. George Rountree was an upper-class, Harvard-educated lawyer from the black belt who was a leader in the 1898 Wilmington riot that "overturned the legally elected government and killed 20 black

Figure 7.2. Total State Disbursements (in millions)

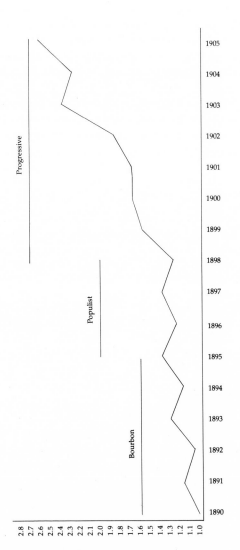

men." He was a member of the North Carolina House of Delegates and one of the men who drafted the disfranchisement laws in that chamber. Kousser refers to Rountree's papers to show that, along with blacks, lower-class whites were a direct target of the disfranchisement movement.[25] Opposition parties were hurt most by these measures. Fifty-three percent of the Republicans were disfranchised as compared with 46 percent overall.

How, then, are we to understand the ambiguous character of North Carolina's political development—its modern expansion of state activity and its regressive restrictions on participation? I will suggest one possible interpretation in the following chapters by looking closely at members of the political elite at the turn of the century and relating their actions to the background trends in social stratification and economic development.

8. Uneven Development and the Agrarian Revolt

North Carolina's orderly, routine politics during the twentieth century have been noteworthy among southern states. In part, the absence of demagoguery and race-baiting, characteristic of southern politics, contributes to the state's progressive reputation. Every political order consists of a structure of values, norms, precedents, rules, procedures, rituals, and beliefs that are differentially beneficial to actors in the community and serve as resources in determining who gets what. Political scientists refer to this phenomenon as a "mobilization of bias."[1] It is often difficult to see the "mobilization of bias" in a particular society because it tends to be taken for granted. The absence of overt challenges to order obscures certain aspects of political domination in modern North Carolina, where political domination has become routine and orderly. In V. O. Key's words, "The effectiveness of the oligarchy's control has been achieved through the elevation to office of persons fundamentally in harmony with its viewpoint. Its interests, which are often the interests of the state, *are served without prompting.*"[2]

One strategy for uncovering the structure of interests below the surface of "routine" politics is to study periods of crisis when the political order is challenged and tested. Crises are crises because conflict is irrepressible. The study of political crises may reveal social cleavages not otherwise apparent and enable the researcher to observe patterns of class structure and conflict that are thus indirectly revealed. The agrarian revolt of the late nineteenth century was a crisis that threatened the power and privilege of dominant groups in North Carolina.

In chapters 2 and 3, I noted that the self-sufficiency of the plantation, the principal social, economic, and political unit in

145

the South, limited community development. The South's economic infrastructure—its transportation, banking, educational, marketing, and urban institutions—were "all designed to reinforce the power of large, slave-based plantations."[3] This pattern was not restricted to the South before 1860. According to Phillip Muller,

> The war and reconstruction, destructive as they were, left intact Southern economic problems. Agricultural production continued to be dominated by staple, exportable crops. Manufacturing, by and large, still meant the preliminary, that is, low-profit margin, processing of agricultural commodities. The railroads had not solved their market-determined difficulties, nor had they discovered a rich, indigenous source of capital. Urban centers stood out as rare and anomalous phenomena in an agrarian setting.[4]

In both the Old South and the New, the large class of yeomen farmers were economically and politically deprived,[5] although perhaps not to the same extent as blacks.

The small farmers of North Carolina suffered great economic hardships during the 1880s and 1890s. In 1880, 75 percent of the state's labor force were employed in agriculture; cotton still was king. Prior to 1875, according to Muller, cotton prices fluctuated within a tolerable range from eighteen cents to twelve cents per pound. Prices began to fall, especially after 1883, and by 1894 they reached a low of five cents per pound. The farmer grossed no more than $10 per acre for his crop.[6]

The effect of declining cotton prices was worsened by the South's financial deficit. William E. Laird and James R. Rinehart argue that it was fundamentally this financial insufficiency, rather than agricultural prices alone, that inhibited southern economic development and accounted for the region's low per capita income.[7] The problem was particularly acute in North Carolina, where—as reported in chapter 4, Table 4.1—banking assets amounted to only eight cents per capita, the lowest level in the South. According to Herbert Mitchell, the specie assets of North Carolina's private banks totaled only $800,000.[8]

Laird and Rinehart argue that the South's financial disability resulted only in part from the invalidation of Confederate notes and the loss of over two billion dollars that had been invested in slaves. It was intensified by the national banking system which, they claim, operated with a "sectional bias" in the distribution of bank charters. Officially, the South was allocated $80 million worth of the authorized national bank circulation and New England only $45 million, but, according to Laird and Rinehart, "New England managed to obtain, in addition to her own note allotment, most of the South's as well."[9] They claim that Massachusetts alone garnered five times as much of the bank circulation as did the entire South. The region's participation in the national system was further limited by the system's high minimum capital requirements for establishments. Even those that were established, however, failed to serve farmers as a source of short-term credit because they were legally prohibited from lending on real estate. Seen in this context, the farmers' attacks on national finance policy and their demand for relief from inflation—often dismissed as "ideological primitivism"[10] or a "moral binge"[11]—appear quite rational.

The "solution" to the South's cash shortage was the notorious crop lien system, a form of debt peonage that bound tenants to landlords and enslaved small farmers to the rural merchants. Robert Allen describes the system as follows: "These merchants did not lend money but instead advanced goods that the farmer needed, in return for a lien upon his growing crop, usually cotton. High interest rates customarily were charged on these advances. Further, the crop that was mortgaged must be sold through the merchant who made the advance. The merchant class thereby increasingly gained financial control over the small farmers."[12] Essentially the same relationship held between tenants and planters, the latter serving the function of supply merchant. Laird and Rinehart report that southern farmers paid interest rates on their loans that ranged from 25 percent to 100 percent per annum.

Roger Ransom and Richard Sutch[13] argue that local merchants enjoyed virtual monopoly power in their small businesses and that they used this power "to prevent the production of agricultural commodities for home consumption and force the production of staple crops" in order to be assured a return on the credit they extended. They see this as the mechanism that caused an "overproduction" of cotton, commonly viewed as the single most important cause of the depressed state of southern agriculture. Recent econometric analysis, however, challenges the latter assumption.

In an extensive study of southern agriculture, Stephen DeCanio claims that the extent of cotton cultivation in the post-bellum South was economically rational.[14] He argues that by 1880 cotton led all alternative southern crops, such as corn, in value productivity. Its price, he contends, was not falling "relative to potential candidates for diversification."[15] He finds that the Deep South's comparative advantage in cotton over other crops was stronger, for example, that the Midwest's advantage in growing wheat. Examining the speeds of adjustment in the South to shifts in the price of cotton, he concludes that

> Southern cotton farmers were as flexible and as price-respon-sive as wheat farmers in the rest of the United States during the late nineteenth and early twentieth centuries. Neither relative cotton prices nor the agricultural terms of trade for the South declined steadily after 1880. These prices did fluc-tuate significantly, but adjustments to relative price shifts were fairly rapid in most southern states. No evidence of alleged traditionalism, or backwardness, or of merchants' insistence on cotton distorting Southern farmers' crop alloca-tion decisions, can be found in the estimates of cotton supply functions.[16]

DeCanio's analysis implies that credit insufficiency, rather than cotton overproduction, was the actual as well as the perceived nemesis of the southern farmer. The situation was somewhat different in North Carolina. According to DeCanio's estimates, North Carolina experienced the second greatest long-run and short-run price elasticities in cotton among the southern states. (Tennessee ranked first.) This means that in the short run, North Carolina farmers had comparatively more to lose from downward price shifts than did cotton farmers in the Deep South. In the long run, they enjoyed less of a comparative advantage in cotton cultivation than in other uses of the land. Also, the speed of adjustments in North Carolina to price shifts was relatively slow. These factors suggest that North Carolina cotton farmers were economically more vulnerable than their Deep South counterparts and may account in part for North Carolina's vigorous Populist movement.

There was not only an absolute decline in the economic position of small southern farmers. When they compared their prospects with other classes in the state, they felt relatively deprived as well. Sociologists have demonstrated that it is not simply absolute deprivation but perceived relative deprivation and disappointed expectations that are especially conducive to social protest.[17] The crop lien system hopelessly indebted farmers to the merchant class and tenants to their landlords. An antiquated tax structure placed an unequal burden on agrarians at a time when corporate taxes were minimized to encourage industrial development. Nationally, according to Simeon A. Delap,[18] farmers owned 24 percent of the country's wealth but were accountable for 62 percent of the taxed wealth in 1890. Even when their property was mortgaged, they were taxed as if they owned it free.[19] Tenants' needs were unarticulated. More prosperous farmers demanded increased social services such as education and agricultural assistance, but they were ignored while favors were given to railroads, which charged discriminatory rates, and to businesses. Further, the nation's tariff policy meant that farmers sold their crops in the world market but were forced to buy American manufactured goods at high protected prices. These factors—the tariff, the trusts, the railroads, and especially the money supply—were background conditions that fed into the dissent articulated by the People's party in the 1890s.

The Populist or People's party grew out of the Southern Farmers' Alliance, which had approximately 1.5 million members throughout the South and Midwest. A million or so more farmers were organized in the Colored Farmers' Alliance.[20] Although my interpretation differs from the literature at several points, recent scholarship, especially that of Lawrence Goodwyn, Robert C. McMath, Jr., and Michael Schwartz,[21] demonstrates the crucial significance of the Alliance experience to the course of the Populist revolt. According to Schwartz, historians have focused too much on the Populist party itself, which he calls a "leadership organization," and not enough on the Farmers' Alliance, a mass insurgent movement.[22]

The Alliance, according to Goodwyn, "was, first and most centrally, a cooperative movement that imparted a sense of self-worth to individual people and provided them with the instruments of self-education about the world they lived in."[23] Charles Macune of Texas, an intellectual architect of the movement, summarized its underlying philosophy when he stated, "I hold that cooperation, properly understood and properly applied, will place a limit to the encroachments of organized monopoly, and will be the means by which the mortgage-burdened farmers can assert their freedom from the tyranny of organized capital."[24] The most important form of cooperation was the Alliance Exchange. It has been called "the most ambitious counterinstitution ever undertaken by an American protest movement"[25] and "the world's first such working class institution."[26]

The central element of the Alliance program was the establishment of producers' and, to a lesser extent, consumers' cooperatives. Cooperative exchanges and state agencies were created to help farmers market their crops at optimum prices, to reduce the cost of farm supplies through wholesale buying, and to provide savings on food and consumer items. The Alliance Exchange system promised to bypass local merchants and landlords in the supply and marketing system. In North Carolina a statewide agency briefly conducted a $350,000 business in consumer goods. Alliancemen also established several tobacco warehouses and a factory, though with limited success.[27] Nonetheless, it is reported that in some counties, despite its brief history, the North Carolina Exchange "reduced prices as much as 60%, undermined the crop lien system, and had continued economic impact for 10 years after its demise."[28] In Texas, where the Exchange was born, Alliancemen realized that direct sales without credit failed to benefit the most needy farmers. As early as 1887 they moved to accept crop liens and to establish a cooperative credit system. This was met with great opposition from merchants, bankers, and, eventually, manufacturers who refused to sell to the Alliance. External pressures and particularly the lack of capital soon defeated the Exchange concept.[29] The collective experience, however, created the foundation for Populist support. According to McMath, "The cooperatives, particularly the state exchanges and agencies, gave the Alliance much of its internal cohesion." Such cohesion "would form the basis for such political solidarity as the Alliance subsequently achieved."[30]

Forty thousand local Alliance organizations spanned rural America[31] and created a basis for community in the South. In North Carolina by 1891, one hundred thousand farmers had joined the Alliance. Given the average family size in North Carolina at the time, this means that the Alliance touched the lives of roughly one-half million people or just under one-third of the state's total population.[32] McMath, especially, stresses the Alliance's community-building aspect, noting that, "particularly at the local level, [the Alliance] was a cohesive social institution as well as an agency for political and economic action."[33] Several observers have noted the "moralistic tone and revivalistic fervor" of sub-Alliance (local) meetings. Unlike town churches that "at least gave tacit approval to New South industrialism and to the hegemony of the Bourbon Democracy,"[34] and unlike the subsequent social gospel movement among national denominations that also served ultimately an integrative function, rural evangelical Protestantism within the Alliance context inspired demands for far-reaching social change.[35] But the community forged by the Alliance was not unstratified. McMath describes both "genteel" and "mudsill" elements in its membership, although he also claims that relatively "few wealthy planters" and few of the "most impoverished tenants" participated.[36] Schwartz, however, views the Alliance organization as much more stratified into a planter-dominated leadership and yeomen-tenant rank and file. "This marriage of planter groups with yeomen and tenant groups," he argues, "produced latent or overt conflicts and contradictions."[37]

Schwartz interprets the shift in strategy from economic struggle to political struggle following the Exchange failures as a retreat from the movement's radical premises, an outcome of its internal stratification. The Alliance leadership elite, he contends, had always favored politics. As large farmers, they were more interested in agricultural colleges and scientific services to modernize production than in solving the yeomen's credit problems. He suggests that this tension can be seen in North Carolina by comparing sub-Alliance concerns in planter-dominated units with those in less prosperous localities. "While the state leadership devoted the fall [of 1889] to organizing its entry into statewide politics [still within the Democratic party], the North Carolina rank and file raised $30,000 to help establish the Exchange." He contends that the entry into politics—an "attempted escalation" along lines compatible with elite interests in order to sustain movement momentum—"was bound to destroy the local and county organizations" favored by the rank and file.[38]

Schwartz does well to point out the internal stratification of the Alliance movement, somewhat minimized by McMath and especially by Goodwyn, but there is another way to view the transition from the Alliance to the People's party. McMath and Goodwyn both present evidence that the Alliance leadership was actually very hesitant to enter the political arena, especially as a third party.[39] Many conservative leaders such as Elias Carr, a rich North Carolina planter and president of the state Alliance, refused to break with the Democrats.[40] A straightforward interpretation of the third-party move assumes that the Alliance failure to raise enough capital to support cooperative counter-institutions such as the Exchanges forced farmers to struggle politically with national financial policy. According to McMath, "Viewed from a broader perspective, the exchange failed because it had attacked head-on the credit system that dominated southern agriculture. The exchange was unable to muster sufficient capital for such a task, but the experience convinced many Alliancemen, including Charles Macune, that agriculture would remain depressed until the nation's financial system underwent major changes."[41] Very similarly, Goodwyn argues that the political import of Alliance failures was radical: "The Alliance cooperative stood little chance of working unless fundamental changes were made in the American monetary system. This understanding was the germ of the Omaha Platform of the People's Party."[42]

The Farmers' Alliance made its greatest headway in North Carolina in the cotton-producing counties. In 1887 it spread from seven "heavily cottonized" counties to forty-six others, most of which produced cotton. Only then did it achieve success in noncotton localities.[43] In 1889, Colonel Leonidas L. Polk, North Carolina's first Secretary of Agriculture, was elected national president of the Alliance. His magazine, *The Progressive Farmer*, grew into the farmers' political voice. Members of the North Carolina Alliance briefly captured control of the state Democratic party in 1890, but few reforms actually were passed by the "Farmers' Legislature" in 1891 except for increased educational appropriations and, more important, the establishment of an agricultural college.[44] Agricultural conditions failed to improve, however, and many farmers grew more and more alienated from the Democratic party. These farmers, along with many others throughout the South and West, finally withdrew their support from the Democrats and organized the People's party.

Although it advocated a number of reforms, including government ownership or regulation of the railroads, the most familiar plank of the Populist or People's party was its demand for unlimited coinage of silver money.

> The federal government had stopped minting silver dollars in 1873, and instead paper money was issued by a number of private national banks acting in effect as sub-agents of the US Treasury. The farmers believed that this arrangement gave the private banks control over the monetary system and that

the banks exploited this control to keep the volume of money in circulation low, thereby keeping the cost of credit at a high level. Free coinage of silver, the farmers agreed, would increase the volume of money in circulation and compel the reduction of interest rates. Free silver thus became a rallying cry of the embattled white farmers.[45]

One of the most "radical" proposals of the Populists was the subtreasury plan. According to this scheme, the government would build warehouses for nonperishable agricultural goods where farmers could store their crops for a cash loan of up to 80 percent of market value, repayable at 1 percent interest when the farmer wished to sell his crop.[46] This plan would free the farmer from his situation of cashless debt peonage and allow him to weather times when commodity prices were low. The subtreasury plan "provided a handy political issue" for the new party.[47]

According to some authorities,[48] the subtreasury plan was devised in 1889 by Harry Skinner, a North Carolinian who was later elected to the United States Congress as a Populist. The bill was reluctantly introduced into the United States Senate by Z. B. Vance of North Carolina, who was pressured to do so by his constituency. North Carolinians figured prominently in the national leadership of the People's Party. They sent the largest state delegation to its founding convention in Cincinnati in 1891. But for his death, Leonidas Polk would probably have been the presidential candidate of the People's party. Harry Skinner was a candidate for vice-president but failed to win the party nomination. In 1896, Marion Butler, a United States senator from North Carolina, served as national party chairman. At the state level, by fusing with Republicans on issues and candidates, North Carolina Populists won their party's greatest electoral success in the South. They won control of the state legislature, and they helped to elect one of only two non-Democratic governors in the South from Reconstruction until the 1970s. Some historians view this North Carolina regime as "indicative of what opponents of the Democrats might have accomplished had they come to power elsewhere in the South."[49]

Who Were the North Carolina Populists?

Conflict continues among historians over how to interpret the southern Populist party. One historian has recently noted, "Few of the major studies of Populism are in even remote agreement on the question of what it meant to be a Populist."[50] The fact that Lyndon Johnson, Fred Harris, and Jimmy Carter as well as George Wallace, Lester Maddox, and Joe McCarthy have each been called a Populist shows how much confusion about Populism persists in our present use of the term. It is generally accepted, however, that the Populists were small farmers of humble social origins. In an important study of Alabama Populism, Sheldon Hackney found that, "Recruited heavily from among the downwardly mobile and geographically transient, they were vulnerable to feelings of powerlessness. They were largely superfluous farmers or ineffectively organized workers who were not linked to influential Alabamians by kinship or close association."[51]

There is considerably less agreement regarding the Populists' political orientation. Early treatments of Populism such as John D. Hicks's 1931 classic, *The Populist Revolt*, located the farmers as the source of twentieth-century liberalism, their demands being realized in Progressive and New Deal legislation. In his biography of Tom Watson and later in *Origins of the New South*, C. Vann Woodward advanced the liberal interpretation, arguing that the southern Populists rose above the white supremacy of their culture to champion the rights of the common man, black and white alike. As Lawrence Goodwyn has put it more recently, "The Populists were thus the last American reformers with authentic cultural credentials to solicit mass support for the idea of achieving the democratic organization of an industrialized society."[52]

A revisionist interpretation in the 1950s was Richard Hofstadter's *Age of Reform*, which viewed Populism as an irrational mass movement, an outcome of the structural strain experienced by American farmers and their subsequent status anxiety. Hofstadter's theory was influenced by sociological structural-functionalists. More recently, Sheldon Hackney applied Neil Smelser's strain model of social movements to Alabama Populism. He concluded that the Populists were neither radical nor conservative but rather, like Eric Hobsbawm's "primitive rebels," they were nonideological. According to Hackney, they wanted "neither revolution nor reform" but power. "Power, not a new system, was what the people required."[53] Radical historians responded to the status-strain theory by arguing that instead Populism was a radical class movement. In *The Populist Response to Industrial America*, Norman Pollack argued that "had Populism succeeded, it could have fundamentally altered American society in a socialist direction. Clearly, Populism was a progressive social force."[54] Subsequently, Christopher Lasch drew parallels between Populism and socialism[55] and Robert Allen interpreted Populist action as a militant response to monopoly capitalism.[56]

Historians also disagree over the relationship between Populism and modernization. Hicks, Hofstadter, and Woodward viewed the Populists as anti-industrial. In his analysis of Alabama legislative politics, Hackney concluded that the Populists were clearly "not modernizers," stressing their "constant emphasis on low taxes and inexpensive government."[57] More recently, however, Muller, writing specifically on North Carolina, has claimed that "industrial growth played a strong, positive role in the political program of both" the Alliance and the People's party.[58]

In order to interpret the North Carolina Populist movement and its role in the state's political and economic modernization, I analyzed county-level voting in the 1896 gubernatorial election to examine the social and economic bases for the movement's mass support.[59] The election was extremely complicated. From 1876 until 1894, North Carolina Democrats narrowly controlled the state legislature despite constant strong opposition from the Republican party with its two large blocks of mass support, blacks in the plantation counties of the East and subsistence farmers with former Unionist sympathies in the mountain counties to the West. Democrats used their legislative power to obstruct Republican voters and numerous other parties, such as the Greenbackers and the Prohibitionists, that were active in the 1880s. In 1894, however, Populists and Republicans allied in order to win control of the legislature.

Such cooperation must have been very difficult for southern Populists because the Republicans were extremely unpopular among the mass of nonmountain southern whites. According to Buck, "The practice of American politics in the years that followed the Civil War seemed based upon a theory that the two great parties were hostile armies in camps irreconcilably divided. Democrats were to Republicans, and Republicans were to Democrats, not opponents to be persuaded, but enemies to be remorselessly pursued and destroyed."[60] After all, a Republican administration and Congress had waged war against the South and imposed Reconstruction. Some members of the Farmers' Alliance were unwilling to break with the Democrats. Those that did abandon the party and, worse, in North Carolina, allied with the hated Republicans, paid a price. According to Hicks, "Only a Southerner can realize how keenly these converts to Populism must have felt their grievances. They became in the eyes of their Democratic neighbors political apostates and traitors to civilization itself, more to be reviled even than the Republicans."[61]

Nevertheless, the 1895 legislature reformed North Carolina's election laws and opened up the political process. In 1896 the "black counties" of North Carolina cast 33,900 votes as compared with only 18,543 votes in 1892.[62] This fact, plus the white Populist vote, which diminished traditional Democratic support and was necessary for electoral reform, undermined the Democrats for the first time since the end of Reconstruction. The Populists controlled the balance of power in state politics, even though their gubernatorial candidate, Gutherie, won less votes in 1896 than had the Populist candidate in 1892. The party won a majority in the 1897 legislature and five of eight seats in the United States House of Representatives.

As the election approached, many shifting alliances and counterstrategies were formed among the three parties. Nationally, both the Democratic and Populist parties nominated William Jennings Bryan as a "free silver" candidate for president. Fusion with the Democrats was made difficult, however, by their nomination of a conservative Maine banker for vice-president. In North Carolina, the leasing of the partially state-owned North Carolina Railroad to the Southern Railroad for ninety-nine years by Democratic Governor Carr outraged the Populists. Although "fusion" was not mentioned officially in state party platforms, Republicans and Populists endorsed similar issues and roughly the same slate of state officers, except for governor. The situation, however, was complicated. In some counties the Populists cooperated with the Democrats instead of with the Republicans.[63] A respectable number of black Republicans held an independent convention and repudiated the Republican nominee, Daniel Russell, an eastern North Carolina lawyer and planter whom they viewed as hostile to blacks.[64] Instead they endorsed Gutherie, the Populist candidate, an American Tobacco Company lawyer. Gutherie was a son-in-law of tobacco manufacturer Julian Carr, a liberal Democrat, and an associate of the Dukes. It is intriguing to speculate that this connection partially reflects the unique political economy of the tobacco industry. Carr operated a textile mill near Durham with black labor. A further connection is the fact that "it was the Republican 'angel,' millionaire Benjamin N. Duke of the Tobacco Trust, who kept the Populist state organ of Marion Butler solvent. During 1896," Carl N. Degler reports, "Duke secretly contributed $1,000 to the *Caucasian*, which was apparently unable to survive without this support."[65] Complicating matters further, however, and for inexplicable reasons, Gutherie repudiated fusion with the Republicans late in the race and urged Populist-Democratic fusion instead.

A linguistic analysis of Populist rhetoric reveals a great discrepancy between party platforms and campaign speeches made before North Carolina audiences in 1892 and especially in 1896. The Omaha Platform of the People's party endorsed wide-ranging reforms such as direct election of senators, initiative and referendum, income tax, and an eight-hour day. Robert Smith's content analysis of recorded speeches reveals that money and poor government were mentioned more times than all the other issues, including the subtreasury plan, railroad regulation, and the tariff. Reforms aimed at broadening popular participation, such as direct senatorial election or referendum, were never mentioned, probably because of the Populist fear of the black masses. The orators often denied that overproduction was the source of the farmers' troubles, a point supported by recent research into the region's agricultural economics. Although North Carolina Populist leaders such as Polk and Butler apparently viewed the free silver issue as "only a peg" to build support on,[66] by the election of 1896 it had become the central issue. According to Smith's analysis, "The main movement of thought was simply this: the monetary policy of the federal government caused the economic distress among the farmers."[67] This can be viewed as a watering down of Populist principles to appeal for broad support or as a rational, if very limited, response to the failure of the Alliance economic struggle.

Table 8.1 compares the eighteen North Carolina counties of greatest Populist strength in the gubernatorial vote of 1896 with the rest of the state. With one exception to be noted below, Populist support does not seem to have varied greatly with the socioeconomic composition of counties. Counties giving both high and low support to the People's party had almost identical proportions of planters, white yeomen, and white tenants. The table reports a higher proportion of blacks in Populist counties, but this reflects the sectional base of Populist support. If the twenty-five mountain counties of western North Carolina where the Populists gained little support are excluded, the Piedmont and coastal counties with low Populist votes had a higher proportion of blacks (40 percent). In fact, the relationship between Populist support and percent black was curvilinear. The Populist candidate did best in counties that were intermediate (25–45 percent) in the level of blacks as a proportion of total population.

Before making the analysis I had hypothesized that among the best predictors of Populist support would be the level of cotton cultivation and the level of white tenancy. Both variables reflect the pressure of commercialization, and I expected such

Table 8.1. North Carolina Populist Gubernatorial Vote, 1896, by Selected County Characteristics

Mean Characteristics for North Carolina Counties	High Populist Vote, 1896 (N = 18 Counties)	Low Populist Vote, 1896 (N = 79 Counties)
Political support		
Populist vote	23%	6%
Republican vote	34%	49%
Democratic vote	43%	45%
Socioeconomic variables		
Proportion planters (% farms above 500 acres)	3%	4%
Proportion white yeomen	55%	54%
Proportion white tenants	32%	33%
Proportion blacks	34%	30%
Economic variables		
Proportion acres devoted to cotton	17%	9%
Proportion acres devoted to tobacco	2%	2%
Agricultural value per capita	$46.53	$40.81
Average size farm	105 acres	103 acres
Percent white illiterates	14%	14%
Percent urban	4%	7%
Manufacturing value per capita	$12.94	$18.36

Source: *Twelfth Census of the United States, 1900*, Vol. 2, pp. 632–33; Vol. 5, pp. 108–9, 433, 565–66; Vol. 8, pp. 664–67.

counties to have been more receptive to the Populist demand for the maintenance of the price of agricultural commodities than, for example, mountain counties populated with subsistence agriculturalists.[68] The data show that cotton cultivation was indeed positively related to the Populist vote. The party did best in counties with high levels of cotton cultivation and also relatively high per capita agricultural values. As expected, they did less well in urban and manufacturing counties. If mountain counties are excluded, the per capita manufacturing value in high Populist counties averaged only $12.94 as compared with almost twice that, $22.38, elsewhere. (As noted earlier, industrialization functioned as a safety valve in depressed sections of the rural South and may have functioned as well to drain off dissent otherwise tapped by the Populists.) Populist strength was not, however, postively related to the proportion of white tenants. In fact, the reverse seems to have been true. I found a moderately strong negative partial correlation coefficient ($-.19$) between Populist voting and the proportion of white tenants in each county when I controlled statistically for the level of blacks and Republican strength. On the other hand, controlling for the same suppressor variables, I found a positive partial correlation coefficient of equal strength ($+.20$) between Populist voting and the proportion of white yeomen in each county.

The relative lack of support for the Populist candidate in counties with numerous white tenants and the party's greater success in areas of high yeomen concentration may reflect the legacy of the Farmers' Alliance in North Carolina. Schwartz reports that Alliance organizing activity met with its greatest success in the heavy cotton-producing counties,[69] as did the Populists, according to Table 8.1. Schwartz further claims that Alliance activities in North Carolina were often addressed to the interests of farmers who were still solvent, rather than to the needs of indebted tenants. Executives of the North Carolina Exchange, for example, observing the credit failure of the pioneering Texas Exchange, and especially the massive counterattack by merchants, had refused to sell supplies on credit. According to Schwartz, "The North Carolina leadership was unwilling to expose itself to such a personal risk, especially since the leaders themselves were prosperous farmers with little to gain from the Exchange. They therefore demanded a large fund to protect the transactions and refused to engage in any credit business."[70] Such policies, plus the campaign approach of the Populist speakers, may have failed fully to convince white tenants that their interests lay with the People's party.

Voting is not merely a reflection of social and economic patterns. It is also a response to perceived political conditions. The strongest single predictor of Populist support in a county was the level of Republican strength (with a negative zero-order correlation coefficient of $-.46$). From a stepwise multiple regression analysis of the statewide gubernatorial vote I discovered that 46 percent ($\bar{R}^2$) of the variance in voting among counties can be attributed to Republican strength. (The other variables in Table 8.1, excluding Democratic vote, explain an additional 12 percent ($\bar{R}^2 = .58$) of the variance.) Populists did best in counties where Republican strength was lower. This makes sense because both were opposition parties. In eastern counties Republicans drew support from black voters, while in the West Republican voting expressed opposition to the eastern plantation establishment.

I cannot completely determine from my analysis why certain counties expressed opposition to the Democrats by voting Republican while others did so by voting Populist, but there seems to have been a trade-off between these two parties. I found some support for this idea of substitutability in the regression analysis. An examination of the residual error vector shows that nine counties were highly deficient in Populist support. That is, judging from the general statewide relationship between the independent variables and Populist voting, as estimated by the regression equation, these counties had significantly lower support from the Populist candidate than predicted. Of these nine counties, five were represented by Republicans in the House of Delegates in 1895. The Republican gubernatorial candidate won in all but two. The idea of substitutability makes sense because Populists and Republicans did fuse in opposition to the Democrats.

A clearer picture of who the North Carolina Populists were and what their interests were can be obtained by looking at the social class composition of the party's leadership. But first a word of caution. Many biographical considerations besides social status determine a person's political behavior, including class consciousness, conscience, ambition, fear, and foolishness. One must not expect a perfect correlation between social position and behavior. Besides, the researcher often has only fragmentary historical evidence and must content himself with a qualitative sense of the class composition of political parties.[71] Another problem results from the fact that regardless of his personal social origins, once a political actor moves into an elite political position, his social contacts and, sometimes, his social loyalties change.[72]

The following quotation from Muller's "New South Populism" pointedly shows that party lines were far from pure within the social "elite" of North Carolina at the turn of the century.

> Although the elite tended toward the Democratic Party, it included spokesmen for virtually every position on North Carolina's limited political spectrum. State Alliance president and Democratic Congressman Sydenham B. Alexander, for example, was cousin to Alliance State Business Agent (and Populist) William Alexander Graham. Graham's brother, A. W. ("Gus") Graham, a Democratic candidate for Congress in 1894 on a frees [sic] silver platform, was law partner and brother-in-law of Robert Watson Winston, a self-proclaimed conservative Democrat. Winston's three brothers, Francis Donnell, Patrick Henry, Jr., and George Taylor Winston, all joined the Republican Party during the 1880's. R. W. Winston had married one of "Gus" Graham's sisters; a second sister married Judge Walter Clark. Clark, whom Winston called a "socialist" and a bitter opponent of the railroads, had been in the wedding party for Alexander Boyd Andrews, vice-president of the Southern Railway Company and political ally of Alliance Democrat Elias Carr, Democratic Senator Matt Whitaker Ransom, Republican Congressman Thomas Settle, and Republican Senator Jeter C. Pritchard. As a consequence of this chain of familial and personal relationships, Democratic and elite hegemony were functionally complementary without being mutually exclusive.[73]

The same caution regarding predictions can be made with examples from my own research.

Consider Politicians X and Y. Politician X served as a Democratic senator in the 1899 white supremacy session of the North Carolina General Assembly. He was a graduate of the University of North Carolina and a lieutenant in the Confederate army. A planter, lawyer, businessman, and statesman, he served as a representative in the United States Congress during 1883–87 and 1889–91. Politician Y also served as a representative in the United States Congress. He had a law degree from the University of Kentucky and was active in the state Democratic party. At one time he served on the governor's staff and was chairman of his county Democratic executive committee. From 1890 to 1896 he served as a member of the University of North Carolina Board of Trustees. After an unsuccessful bid for return to the Congress, having served in the Forty-fourth and Forty-fifth Congresses, he was appointed United States district attorney. He was subsequently elected president of the North Carolina Bar Association and vice-president of the American Bar Association. Surprisingly, although he is, to me, indistinguishable in class terms from Politician X, Politician Y was Harry Skinner, chairman of the Pitt County Populist executive committee and a two-term Populist representative in Congress. As I noted earlier in this chapter, he authored the party's subtreasury plan. Politician X—whose profile perfectly fits the ideal type of the planter-businessman who dominated the conservative Democratic party —was Thomas Gregory Skinner, Harry Skinner's older brother, a Democrat.

This example is sufficient to show the difficulty of predicting individuals' political behavior and to show that North Carolina Populist leaders do not fit the popular stereotype of Populists as "largely superfluous farmers." In his analysis of the Alabama legislature, Hackney observed that the Populist members were all "unknowns." None were "linked to influential Alabamians by kinship or class associations." None were college-educated.[74] North Carolina Populist leaders, in contrast, tended to be moderately well-to-do agrarians, sometimes with prominent family connections.[75]

The early leaders of the Farmers' Alliance in North Carolina were prominent members of the landed upper class. Colonel Leonidas Polk, the state's first commissioner of agriculture, had been a slaveholder before the Civil War, although his plantation was modest in size. As president of the Interstate Farmers' Convention that met in Atlanta in 1887, he had represented the "agricultural elite of the South." Polk's close friends, Elias Carr and Sydenham B. Alexander, both of whom served terms as Alliance presidents, were exceptionally large planters. Elias Carr was one of the richest men in North Carolina. These two men withdrew their support from the farmers' movement when it split with the Democratic party. At that time, Carr was governor of North Carolina.[76] Even without their support the fledgling party was not in the hands of small farmers. After the death of Polk, its three principal leaders were Marion Butler, Dr. Cyrus Thompson, and Harry Skinner, all three with prominent agricultural connections in eastern North Carolina.[77]

Marion Butler was the son of a moderately prosperous farmer and businessman in Sampson County. He graduated from the University of North Carolina in 1885 but deferred his law school plans because of his father's death to run the family farm. At the same time he served as superintendent of a local academy through which he gained access to county politics and the Alliance. He purchased a local newspaper, the Clinton *Caucasian*, which later grew into the statewide voice of the People's party. In 1891 he was elected president of the Alliance, was elected to the prestigious Board of Trustees of the University of North Carolina, and soon married into the "oldest and most influential family of Sampson County."

Dr. Cyrus Thompson was active in North Carolina politics from the early 1880s, when he served in the General Assembly. According to Muller, until the 1890s, when Alliance activity intensified, he devoted more time to his role as "gentleman farmer" than to politics or medicine. His family was identified as part of the "old Planter group" of Onslow County.

Harry Skinner also came from what Muller calls "high social status." His older brother was a successful planter, lawyer, and businessman as well as Democratic congressman. His uncle was

Thomas Jarvis, governor of North Carolina from 1878 to 1885. Muller fails to note that Jarvis, born in 1836, was not himself from a prosperous family. He got a degree from Randolph Macon College in Virginia, but his father was a "poor" Methodist minister. He taught school in Pasquotank County for a year, and he ran a store in Tyrrell County after the Civil War while studying law. He was elected to the North Carolina House of Delegates as a Conservative Democrat in 1868. Apparently, his real opportunity came when he entered law practice with Colonel David Carter in 1872. Carter was a very large planter with extensive land, banking, and insurance interests. Carter was descended from an old landed family that included a colonial deputy governor and a Revolutionary War general, and he was married to the daughter of a wealthy Beaufort County planter. In 1876, Jarvis was elected lieutenant governor, and he succeeded Governor Vance when the latter resigned to serve in the United States Senate.

Thus it appears that Populist leaders in North Carolina were moderately prosperous, well-connected gentlemen with roots in agriculture, though none were of the elite status of the small class of landed families consisting of Camerons, Battles, Moreheads, and the like described earlier. In some cases, personal ambition and the leadership opportunities a new party promised may have been motivating factors for their joining the People's party. H. Larry Ingle suggests this factor in his profile of William Hodge Kitchin, who was active in the People's party from 1894 to 1896.[78] Kitchin's father had married the daughter of a wealthy Edgecombe County planter and risen into the "lower order of the landed class." W. H. Kitchin graduated from Emory and Henry College in Virginia and was admitted to the bar in 1869. He won a large land case in California from which he earned $20,000. This provided the financial basis for his becoming, like his father, a gentleman farmer, although his principal interests were mortgages, timber, and real estate. He increased his landholdings by foreclosures on crop liens he acquired from local merchants.

Kitchin, by any standard, was a leading citizen of his small community, yet the instruments of power continued to elude him. As long as the Democratic Party did not recognize, much less fulfill, his aspirations, the growing third party offered him a chance to extend his influence and satisfy his hopes for political preferment. And, retaining his distrust of basic reforms, Kitchin could help move the Populists in a conservative direction.[79]

The instruments of power eluded not only William Hodge Kitchin but that whole class of moderately prominent land-holders whose principal power resource in the competition for privilege and prestige was land. The declining situation of agriculture in North Carolina—especially alongside the increasing prosperity of railroads, banks, and industry from which only the largest planters such as the Camerons could benefit—made them challenge the dominant political order. This suggests that the conflict between Populist and Democratic politicians was an intraclass struggle, at least for its leaders.

*The Politics of Participation
in the North Carolina Senate, 1895 and 1897*

To get a more complete picture of the class composition and interests of North Carolina's political parties during the process of the state's revolution from above, I have compared the membership and legislation of the 1895 and 1897 fusion senates with those of the 1899 white supremacy session. After the Populists failed to achieve electoral success in 1892, they fused with Republicans at the county level and, depending on local political conditions, they elected either Populist or Republican candidates. Most of the legislative accomplishments of fusion occurred in the 1895 session, which was composed of twenty-four Populists, eighteen Republicans, and only eight Democrats in the senate.[80]

Using the massive biographical index of the North Carolina Collection of historical materials in the Louis Round Wilson

Library, The University of North Carolina at Chapel Hill, I was able to obtain fragmentary biographical information on twenty-five of the fifty senators who served in the 1895 session. In his analysis of Alabama state legislators, Hackney identified thirty-six of sixty-five Democrats but only nine of thirty-five Populists in the House of Representatives.[81] He interpreted the lack of biographical information as an indicator of the Populists' obscurity and their lower social status. I was able to identify five of eight Democrats, ten of eighteen Republicans, and ten of twenty-four Populists.

Hackney found that although Populist leaders "were not from the lower class," they "started from considerably further down the social ladder than did comparable Democrats."[82] He found no college graduates among his sample of Populists. Although I cannot quantify my data, my sense is that the Democrats barely ranked first among the three parties in social status, these senators being mostly college-educated farmers and professionals (law, medicine, and journalism). Surprisingly, the Populists ranked not far below them as college-educated farmers and lower-status professionals (teachers and ministers). Ranking lowest were the Republicans, only one of whom attended college.[83] Most Republican senators were small-town businessmen and federal officeholders. Also surprisingly, the Populists were oldest, averaging forty-nine years; next were the Republicans, who averaged forty-seven. The Democrats were youngest, averaging only thirty-five years of age. For the most part, the Populists were political newcomers. According to the available information, only three of ten had prior statewide officeholding experiences. (One had served three terms in the house as an "Independent Democrat.") In sharp contrast, the Republicans were political old-timers. Six of the ten for whom I have information had served previously in the General Assembly, their occasional terms dating back as early as the late 1860s, 1870s, and 1880s. Three of the five Democrats served previously in the General Assembly although, because they were younger men, their terms were limited to the 1890s.

Seven of my sample of ten Populists were college-educated.

(It is possible that those for whom I could find biographical information were more prominent and of higher social status than were the others.) Five of the Populists attended the University of North Carolina, one Wake Forest, and one Trinity College. One of the Populists was a young lawyer with "agricultural pursuits." Two older men were college-eduated farmers. One was a farmer with a common school education who had served as a private in the Confederate army. One of the Populist senators was a Baptist minister and principal of a private academy; another was a college-educated farmer, minister, and doctor (apparently with no medical degree); one was a schoolteacher and justice of the peace. Another was a merchant who owned a "large" dry-goods, grocery, and hardware business in Greenville. He owned one-third interest in a small college and was president of the Tar River Transport Company and reportedly owned a "large farm in the country."

Of the ten Republicans for whom I have data, only one was college-educated. He was a graduate of the University of North Carolina and the Princeton University Law School and practiced law in heavily black Warren County. He was a former Democrat and, like several of the Republicans, a federal officeholder, serving as United States district attorney for the eastern district of North Carolina from 1889 to 1893. He moved to Oklahoma after the turn of the century. Another of the Republican senators was the son of a cotton mill superintendent from New England. Before becoming a merchant and postmaster in Goldsboro, he had served as a major in the Union army during the war. Another senator was a farmer, railroad foreman, contractor, and mayor of the small mountain town of Murphy. One Republican was a wagon and buggy manufacturer; another was a non-college-educated lawyer and federal solicitor; two were farmers. One was a "successful farmer" with a "small" mercantile business; another was a merchant.

Four of the five Democrats were college graduates. The fifth, for whom I had no educational information, was a lawyer. Two of the Democratic senators were lawyers. One senator was a Wake Forest–educated cotton farmer and merchant. Another was a physician and farmer from prosperous Edgecombe County. He attended Trinity College, the University of the City of New York, and the University of Virginia Medical College. Finally, one senator, a thirty-year-old graduate of Wake Forest, was owner, president, and general manager of the Charlotte *News.* He would later be known as the author of North Carolina's first Jim Crow law, which segregated public transportation. His father was a Confederate captain. One of his grandfathers was a Confederate colonel and the other was a general; both were planters.

A "sketch book" published commercially for the 1897 legislature included brief sketches of some members of the General Assembly.[84] Although I did not carry out biographical searches on these senators as I did the 1895 group, I compared my picture of the 1895 senators with the data from this source as a reliability check. As Tables 8.2, 8.3, and 8.4 show, there appear to have been fewer status differences between these Populists and Republicans than in my 1895 sample. It is not surprising to find, as shown in Table 8.2, proportionately more farmers (several of them college-educated) among the Populists than among the Republicans. Only three Democrats were described but, again, as in 1895, these stood out as higher-status persons. One was simply described as a lawyer. Another, a young University of North Carolina graduate practicing law in Greensboro, was a relative of a former Bourbon governor. The third, though very young, was described as a "typical North Carolinian of the old regime." Living on an "ancestral estate," he was interested in agriculture and banking. He also continued his grandfather's mercantile business which, at 101 years of age, was the "oldest business concern of unbroken succession in the State." His father, a businessman and planter, was a University of North Carolina graduate, who had served a total of twenty-one sessions in the General Assembly dating from 1844 to 1880. The young legislator also graduated from the University of North Carolina and had married into a distinguished Virginia family.

The preceding biographical analysis suggests that the Populist leadership in the North Carolina Senate represented not

Table 8.2. *Occupational Composition of the North Carolina Senate, 1897*

Occupation	Populists	Republicans
Farmer	8	1
Farmer-merchant	3	1
Lawyer	1	2
Physician	2	0
Minister	1	1
Businessman	2	2

Table 8.3. *Religious Composition of the North Carolina Senate, 1897*

Denomination	Populists	Republicans
Methodist	5	2
Baptist	3	2
Presbyterian	2	1
Episcopal	1	1
Other	2 Disciples	1 Catholic

Table 8.4. *Educational Composition of the North Carolina Senate, 1897*

Level of Education	Populists	Republicans
College	7	3
Noncollege	10	5

only the mass of small farmers in the state, but also large landowners. Surprisingly, in the two legislative sessions, fourteen out of twenty Populist senators (70 percent) for whom I was able to obtain educational data were college-educated. McMath and Schwartz both examined the socioeconomic status of state and national Farmers' Alliance leadership. McMath found that 18 percent of his sample were college graduates; Schwartz, using somewhat less conservative criteria, found that 38 percent of his leadership sample were "highly educated." Thus it appears that proportionately more of the Populist party leadership in North Carolina, at least in the state senate, came from elite social backgrounds than had a regional cross-section of Alliance leaders in the early 1890s.

The 1895 session of the General Assembly was important because it achieved the most significant legislation of the fusion period. I analyzed senate voting behavior to get an overall sense of the politics of participation and development during this period and to discern what issues divided the legislators. Published accounts do not indicate whether they were divided by class, sectional, or party loyalties.

There are many reasons why legislators vote as they do. They may vote against a bill with which they are sympathetic but which they feel is too weak, or they may vote for a bill they oppose as part of a compromise. Many votes reported in legislative journals are related to obscure amendments and often to motions regarding the passage of a bill. A vote to "table" a bill, for instance, may either be an attempt to kill a bill or to delay a final vote in order to drum up more support for it. Thus, rather than interpreting individual votes, it is safer to observe average or typical voting patterns among legislators over a large number of issues. To do this, I calculated voting similarity scores for each pair of senators on 120 roll call votes reported in the senate *Journal* in which there was disagreement. (Two hundred votes were unanimous.) I then used a multidimensional scaling program (KYST) to plot a spatial representation of the senators' proximity to one another in terms of their "average" voting patterns. This is shown in Figure 8.1.[85]

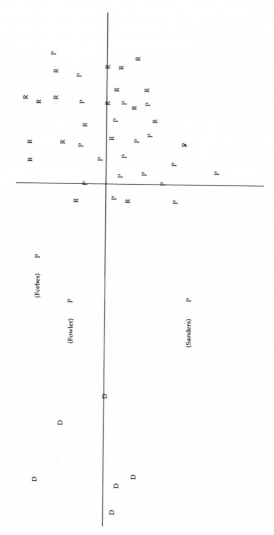

Figure 8.1. Two-Dimensional Representation of the Fusion Senate, 1895

In his landmark study, Hackney interpreted the Alabama Populist movement as a nonideological "power oriented protest movement" because his analysis of roll call votes showed that its leaders were "inconsistent and divided." He could discern no pattern of class-conscious voting.[86] I was therefore surprised to find a tight cluster of Populists and Republicans united in opposition to a smaller cluster of Democrats. Judging from the overall structure of voting in the 1895 session, North Carolina Populists were not "inconsistent and divided." Their proximity to Republicans is remarkable, given the traditional southern antipathy toward Republicanism since Reconstruction—their cooperation is an indication of the lengths to which Populists would go in opposition to the Bourbon Democrats.[87]

As Figure 8.1 shows, only three of the Populists voted against the Populist-Republican coalition with any frequency, siding as often with the Democrats. One of these, O. M. Sanders, was a senator from the Piedmont about whom I have no information. The other two were from black-belt counties. J. E. Fowler was the lawyer educated at Wake Forest and the University of North Carolina with "agricultural pursuits." A. A. Forbes, the least typical of the Populists for whom I have information, was the Greenville farmer-businessman who was president of the Tar River Transport Company. The information on the content of roll call votes reported in the senate *Journal* is too skimpy to permit thorough analysis of individual voting patterns, but I was able to discern a few votes that may shed some light on these three senators' party defection.[88]

Conservatives believed that the extension of government services meant higher taxes and, hence, an attack on the privileges of wealth. Sanders voted against a road improvement bill and against a bill to raise revenues. Forbes and Fowler did not vote on the latter. Like Forbes and Fowler, he voted with the Democrats that counties, not the state, should pay for the expenses of convicts used on road projects. Forbes and Fowler voted with the Democrats against abolishing the state board of education and against reducing appropriations to the national guard. (Black-belt politicians were eager to keep decisions affecting their counties at the state level, where they could not be influenced by the majority blacks. The national guard may have been viewed in the black belt as an important social control device.) Fowler and Forbes voted with the Democrats against altering Raleigh's city charter (presumably affecting representation), and they voted against one version of a bill for popular election of justices of the peace. (This bill was supported primarily by Republicans, presumably confident of continued Negro support. Although they courted black voters, the Populists did not really want to alter traditional white political dominance.) Finally, Forbes, the black-belt businessman, voted against the local self-government act, the Populists' principal legislative accomplishment.

In an excellent chapter entitled "Triumph of Fusion, 1894–1895," Helen Edmonds summarizes the accomplishments of the 1895 legislature.[89] It responded to the farmers' indebtedness to the merchant-banker class by limiting the legal rate of interest to 6 percent per year. It responded to the farmers' demand for school improvements with a 20¢ per $100 property tax and a 60¢ poll tax to supplement the public school fund. They also allocated $25,000, refunded to the state by the Congress, for the public school fund. But the most important accomplishments of fusion were the attacks on the prevailing "mobilization of bias" in state politics that prevented popular participation.

The senate passed an election law that simplified registration procedures and, more important, decentralized the control of election machinery that, in the past, had been an instrument of Democratic force and fraud. Their "crowning achievement" was the restoration of self-government at the county level. After Reconstruction, the Democrats had provided in the state's new constitution that county officials be appointed by the General Assembly. Thus, in order to minimize the influence of blacks in counties where they were a majority, the Piedmont and mountain counties were denied local self-government in the name of eastern white supremacy. By restoring local self-government, the fusion senate undermined one of the principal political props of the caste system. They also provided for the popular election of county school officials.

As noted in Table 7.2, the Populists' increase in spending (an indicator of attitudes toward government activity) was not dramatic. Certainly it was lower than expenditures of subsequent Democratic sessions. The fusion appropriations were, however, something of a departure from the do-nothing, spend-nothing policies of the Bourbon Democrats who preceded them.[90] Although they were significant, they were not a great departure from the legislation of 1891 that established an agricultural college. Altogether the legislature spent $72,161.74 in 1895 as compared with $66,520.78 in 1893.[91] As Steelman has concluded, "The legislature did not live up to the expectations of reformers. It failed to take forthright action against trusts, and to appeal the homestead law. The slate of reform proposals given widespread publicity in the press fared badly in the legislature."[92]

The important question is why the Populists went no further with social reforms. Their party platforms had attacked monopoly capitalism and called for "trust-busting" and public ownership of the railroads. They had demanded real reforms in agricultural economics. Forces operating on at least two levels account for the ultimate political failure of North Carolina Populism. On one level are the politics of fusion that collapsed in 1897. On another level are the internal contradictions of the movement itself.

On the first level, in order to understand the breakdown of fusion politics in North Carolina, I examined the 1897 session of the state senate, a session marred by discord within Populist ranks. The legislature that year "did little to distinguish itself."[93] It passed three very minor reform acts in regard to railroad regulation, but mainly it tinkered with legislation from the previous session, correcting some minor flaws. Edmonds reports that legislators amended county government structures slightly and altered city charters to allow greater local control,[94] although, more cynically, McNeill contends that "the majority of the laws that were passed attempted to enable the Republicans to keep in power."[95]

The failure of the legislature cannot be blamed on the Republican administration. Governor Russell is said to have "proved himself to be more in sympathy with Populist than with Republican aims, and a man capable of keeping himself in step with the most progressive thought of his time."[96] In his inaugural address Russell attempted to reduce white fears of "Negro domination" with the acknowledgment that "there should be no attempt to avoid the necessity of protecting the tax-payers of these municipalities against the danger of misrule by propertyless and ignorant elements." In addition, however, he called for a surprising number of reforms. He demanded increases in school taxes, a system of apprenticeships and re-formatories, court reform, and, most significant, railroad reform, noting that the needs of outside capital did not necessarily correspond to the public good in the state. He promised to oppose the Democrats' eleventh-hour lease of the North Carolina Railroad to the Southern system. Sounding more like a Populist than a Republican, he claimed that the time was approaching when North Carolinians could look foward to the conversion of private railroads into "public highways owned and controlled by the nation."[97] For a variety of reasons, however, the governor's message produced few legislative results.

One of the very first issues facing the legislature in 1897 was the election of a United States senator. The Republicans nominated the conservative incumbent Jeter C. Pritchard. The Populists nominated Cyrus Thompson and the Democrats nominated Rufus Doughton. Nationally much was at stake in the election. Republicans held forty-two of eighty-eight seats in the United States Senate. With a Republican vice-president to break ties, the party needed only two more seats to gain a majority. This made North Carolina a "pivotal seat in the whole free coinage controversy." Surprisingly, with so much at stake, several Populist senators cast their votes for Pritchard, who was re-elected. Populist leaders were stunned. According to Marion

Butler, "The election of Mr. Pritchard, the candidate of Hanna, Sherman, and Wall Street, to represent the silver sentiment of North Carolina in the U.S. Senate discovers a startling crisis in the history of the People's Party."[98]

Reasons for the split among Populists have not been fully understood. The "bolters," as Populists who broke rank were known, are said to have been led backstage by Congressman Harry Skinner, "either to uphold the pledge of fusion or for patronage." Personal ambitions cannot be ruled out. Harry Skinner, slow to break with the Democratic party for fear of jeopardizing white supremacy, was an unlikely defender of fusion commitments on moral grounds. He may have eyed Butler's seat in the United States Senate, for which cooperation with Pritchard forces and party disloyalty would have been perhaps small prices. Whatever its origins, "the rift in Populist ranks . . . contributed manifestly to the downfall of the party and the collapse of the Fusion government."[99] From this time on, the bolters are assumed to have voted with the Republicans, and the majority Populists, led by Marion Butler's brother, voted with the Democrats.[100]

Figure 8.2, a two-dimensional representation of 1897 roll call voting proximity,[101] shows that the situation was not as simple as traditional accounts suggest. The two-cluster voting structure of 1895 (Figure 8.1), in which Populists and Republicans were firmly unified against the Democrats, disappeared. Instead, the 1897 configuration shows three separate party clusters in which Populist and Republican groups were bridged by nine "bolting" Populists. Table 8.5 compares socioeconomic indicators of the counties represented by these two groups of Populist senators. On the average, the bolters represented counties with larger farms, proportionately more white yeomen and fewer white tenants, slightly higher agricultural values, much less manufacturing activity, and proportionately fewer urban residents than did the group of loyal Populists. Economically, such counties should have favored Populist programs. My guess is that political rather than economic factors influenced the aberrant voting pattern.

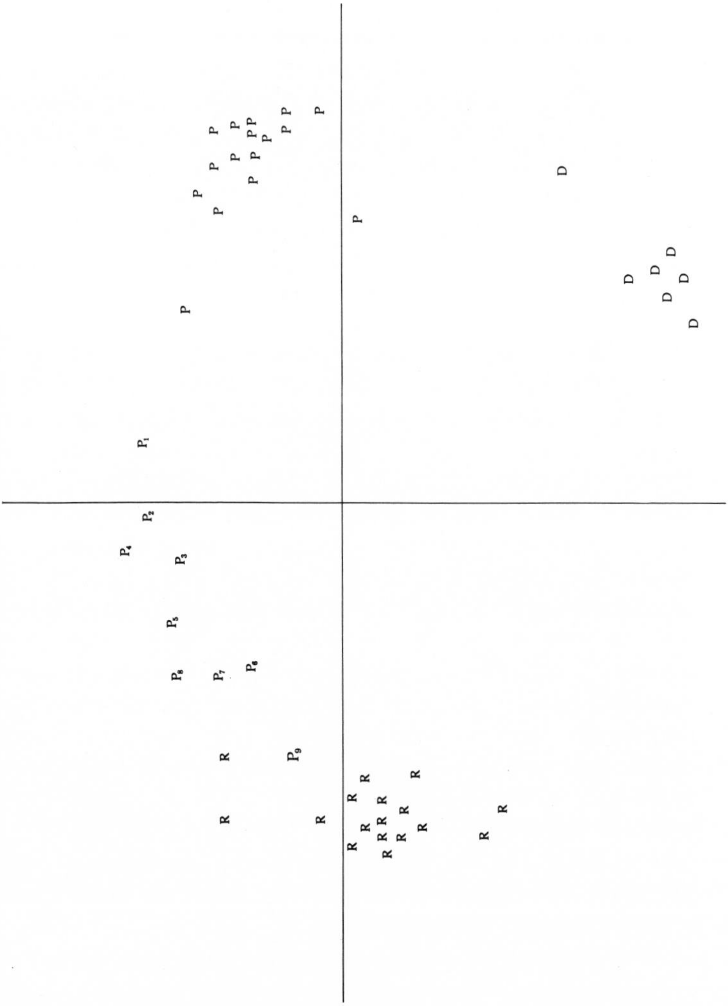

Figure 8.2. Two-Dimensional Representation of the Fusion Senate, 1897

Several of the bolters came from counties where black Republicans controlled local politics and had elected a black leader to represent them in the United States Congress. Few of the bolters were from Harry Skinner's First Congressional District. As shown in Table 8.5, they represented counties that, on the average, had given the Populist gubernatorial candidate less support (11 percent) than had the counties represented by the loyal Populists (15 percent). In counties represented by the latter, the Democratic candidate won a majority of the votes (44 percent), whereas the Republican winner, Russell, carried the counties represented by the bolters (47 percent).

An interesting pattern emerges when political conditions of the individual counties represented by bolters are matched with the latter's voting records. County votes for Governor Russell in the bolters' home counties were as follows: $P_1 = 64$ percent, $P_2 = 52$ percent, $P_3 = 54$ percent, $P_4 = 45$ percent, $P_5 = 51$ percent, $P_6 = 43$ percent, $P_7 = 40$ percent, $P_8 = 42$ percent, and $P_9 = 33$ percent. This is just the reverse of what one might expect. Those nearest in voting to the loyal Populist caucus represented counties with relatively greater Republican strength, whereas those nearest the Republican cluster represented counties with weaker Republican support. Those nearest the majority Populists, however, P_1 through P_5, each represented eastern counties with large black populations. The others represented western counties with a stronger tradition of white Republicanism. For example, P_9 was an Anson County merchant, endorsed by the Republican party on a fusion ticket, representing a senatorial district that had also elected a Republican senator who appears nearest P_9 in the figure. Apparently, a greater amount of Republican pressure was needed at home to pull black-belt Populists partially into the Republican camp, whereas less political pressure was required to pull western Populists further toward cooperation with the Republicans.

An alternative explanation for deviant voting might hypothesize that bolting senators were new recruits to Populist thinking, with less firm ideological commitments and perhaps representing counties that had less experience with Alliance principles. On the other hand, if bolting members of the Populist

Table 8.5. *Comparison of 1897 Senate Voting Clusters by Average County Background of Populist Senators*

County Variables	"Bolting" Populists	Loyal Populist Majority
Political support		
Populist gubernatorial vote (1896)	11%	15%
Republican gubernatorial vote (1896)	47%	41%
Democratic gubernatorial vote (1896)	42%	44%
Socioeconomic variables		
Proportion planters (% farms above 500 acres)	3%	4%
Proportion white yeomen	57%	50%
Proportion white tenants	28%	36%
Proportion blacks	41%	42%
Economic variables		
Proportion acres devoted to cotton	13%	15%
Proportion acres devoted to tobacco	1%	4%
Agricultural value per capita	$45.68	$43.04
Average size farm	118 acres	108 acres
Percent urban	1%	9%
Manufacturing value per capita	$13.08	$28.48

Source: *Twelfth Census of the United States, 1900*, Vol. 2, pp. 632–33; Vol. 5, pp. 108–9, 433, 565–66; Vol. 8, pp. 664–67.

caucus voted as they did in response to constituency pressure to honor the fusion pledge, then perhaps they were not necessarily hostile to their party's economic reform program. A closer look at their voting behavior suggests that the latter was at least partially the case. In a majority of instances (eleven times) bolters voted with the majority of their party on Populist reform bills such as railroad regulations. Four other times they were evenly split. Only on legislation such as that affecting city charters, presumably having to do with local control and party representation, did they consistently vote against the Populist majority (which voted in such instances with the Democrats against Republican bills).

Several of the bolters were in fact strong advocates of reform. Dr. David Reid Parker (P_2) was a prosperous planter, who had been associated with Leonidas Polk from the mid-1880s in speaking for farm interests. He was among the earliest organizers of the Farmers' Alliance in the state. Surviving evidence indicates that[102] he was the only Populist speaker during the campaign of 1896 to have continued the demand for public ownership of the railroads and for the subtreasury plan. Another bolter, Senator E. T. Clark (P_1) from Halifax County, valiantly proposed two significant railroad reform bills prohibiting the use of free passes and establishing reasonable fares and rates, but they were defeated. Further evidence of motivation is provided by the case of Senator G. H. Cannon (P_8), who usually supported reform legislation. Cannon was elected on a fusion ticket representing heavily black Brunswick and New Hanover (Wilmington) counties, the home district of Governor Russell. At one point during the session when he refused to support a Republican move he disapproved, he stated, "I want this caucus to understand that I voted for Senator Pritchard at Governor Russell's solicitation and I stand by Russell all the time and I bid you goodbye."[103] Since Russell had promised to support reforms favored by the Populists, it is possible that the bolters, long condemned for their disloyalty, may have voted out of a mixture of both idealism and necessity because of the political realities of their home counties.

Thus it appears that the bolters' real disloyalty was in matters of party politics, such as the advantages to be had by manipulating electoral rules, rather than in economic reform. This raises the question of what were the fundamental priorities of the loyal Populist delegation in the General Assembly. What was the point of Populist officeholding?

My analysis suggests that the Populists sought power rather than revolutionary social change. This conclusion is similar to Sheldon Hackney's interpretation of Populist goals. I think Hackney is wrong, however, in seeing the Populists as nonideological and not conscious of class interests. Fundamentally, their leaders were socially conservative landowners. They wanted power to improve the lot of commercial farm interests, but when it came to taking action, Populist leaders were unwilling to alter the traditional agrarian order. Nor was it altogether in their interests to do so.

There is ample evidence to support an interpretation often made by radical scholars such as Roberta Ash[104] that the free silver impulse was simply a corruption of the Populist movement. Surely the move partially represented a brokerage party approach to politics. Marion Butler said in 1895: "I am in favor of making the next fight chiefly on the financial question as the overshadowing issue, that we may bring with us all who oppose the financial position of both old parties."[105] No doubt some Populist principles were compromised in the bid for national office, though others, such as the demand for a ten-hour work week, may have been added for their strategic value. On the other hand, however, I see the financial issue at the base of the movement from the beginning. I do not agree that the movement's failure resulted simply from the decision to enter the national political arena. Rather, its decline, as I will show, was ultimately caused by internal contradictions that were present from the beginning. If the Populist movement is viewed as essentially a capitalist reform movement, then its real goal appears to have been power at the national level to influence fiscal policy. This was a logical development from the failure of Alliance Exchanges, not a departure. Although the Populists necessarily made weak overtures to groups like the Knights of Labor in an effort to win national power, I cannot accept Goodwyn's romantic argument that they truly attempted to forge a "national coalition of the 'producing classes.'"[106] The Knights, as McMath notes, had absolutely no interest in such concepts as the subtreasury plan.[107] Goodwyn claims that the "populists were not capitalist reformers,"[108] yet this is precisely what they seem to have been.

Although perhaps drawing too heavily on the Alabama experience, Carl Degler's treatment seems to be among the most on target of recent interpretations of Populism.[109] In *The Other South*, Degler stresses the conservative roots of southern Populism. He does so recognizing that a threat to the dominance of the Democrats "cut like a knife into the going politico-social order of the South." To support his contention that the Populists were not radicals, he accepts on face value the words of Marion Butler in 1894: "The People's Party is composed of the most conservative elements of the old parties. It is composed of men who want the present wrongs righted by the due process of legislation and execution of law. The old party machines are today playing the part of anarchists by refusing to observe and execute laws, and playing the part of traitors and tyrannists by passing laws in the interest of the few against the many."[110] In a good overall assessment of Populism, Degler concludes,

> The Populists did not object to the system; they merely wanted a fair chance to prosper under it. They had been led to believe—for they were fervent followers of Jefferson and other early patriots—that America was the home of opportunity. A chance to realize that promise was what they felt being denied them and which could be theirs if the principles of Populism were put into practice. They were not revolutionaries; they were just people who asked that the rules of the system be obeyed. And if the rules were honored, the Populists believed, all would be well.[111]

Degler views the Populists' cooperation with blacks and Republicans as pragmatic. "The Populists," he says, "were not philosophical egalitarians; they were simply Southern farmers who wanted to defeat the Bourbons, and they needed black votes to do it." He writes further, "Undoubtedly, it was the recognition that black farmers were indeed in the same economic boat as white farmers, regardless of the sincerity of Populist interest in Negroes, that moved many blacks to support Populist candidates."[112] But as my biographical analysis shows, Populist leaders were not simply "white farmers," but representatives of a lower level of the landed upper class. Although all were affected by declining agricultural prices, planters, yeomen, and black and white tenants were not in the same economic boat.

Table 8.6 summarizes the complex class structure of rural, nineteenth-century North Carolina. It uses Max Weber's multidimensional model of stratification with particular emphasis on a neglected aspect of the model[113] that conceives class position as determined by location in three different market structures: labor, credit, and commodity markets. The schema reveals an often overlooked but fundamental class antagonism within the Populist movement. Tenants and landowners share common interests in commodity and credit markets. Both are dependent (directly or indirectly) on external buyers and lenders (although to the extent that planters assume the latter role landowners and tenants are opposed to one another over interest rates). The Populists tried to unify agrarian classes in opposition to merchants and especially to financiers, including the government. Tenants and landlords stand clearly opposed to one another, however, in the labor market, where they conflict over crop shares. In his outstanding work *Agrarian Revolution,* Jeffery Paige has shown that the conflict between farmers and businessmen usually results in reform in the commodity market—lowered interest rates, price supports, and the like—the aims, in other words, of Populist politics.[114] In contrast, however, the antagonism between landowners and sharecroppers often results in revolution, as attested by communist regimes in China and Vietnam. This tendency for revolution occurs because the economic weakness of the landed upper class makes them less able than businessmen to compromise and thus more likely to use

Table 8.6. *Class Structure in Rural North Carolina*

Rural groups	Class Position				Status	Party Tendency
	Commodity Market	Credit Market	Labor Market			
Planter/ industrialists	Sellers of agric./indus. products	Lenders (via banking interests)	Employer (farm and industrial labor)		White	Democrat
Smaller planters	Seller	Borrower	Employer (farm labor)		White	Populist
Independent farmers	Seller	Borrower	Self-employed		White	Populist
Merchants	Buyers of agricultural products	Lenders	Employers		White	Democrat/ Republican
Tenants and sharecroppers	Sellers	Borrowers	Employees		White/ Black	Populist/ Republican
Subsistence farmers (mountains)	Limited sellers	Borrowers (limited)	Self-employed		White	Republican

force in a zero-sum conflict with their labor force over land and production shares.

Generalization from the Alabama Populists, if they were indeed uniformly poor, has perhaps obscured this fundamental class conflict within the Populist movement. Robert Allen, writing from the black perspective on social reform movements in America, is one of the few writers, along with Schwartz, to have recognized this conflict. Allen notes that in 1891, the Colored Farmers' Alliance proposed a strike of black cotton pickers, who were demanding a wage increase. Colonel Polk, president of the white Alliance, defeated this move, advising white farmers to let their crops rot before paying more for agricultural labor. Polk attempted to conceal the class conflict within the movement by charging that blacks were attempting "to better their condition at the expense of their white brethren. Reforms should not be in the interest of one portion of our farmers," he said, "at the expense of another." Allen concludes:

> Underlying this dispute was a difference in class interest between the two groups. Many of the white farmers, especially the leaders of the agrarian revolt, were farm owners and their ideology tended to be that of a landowning class. Between white and black farmers, who were overwhelmingly sharecroppers differing only in degree from landless farm workers, there was a smoldering class conflict not altogether unlike the contemporary conflict between farm owners and farm workers. This class conflict theme was never articulated.[115]

It was this internal contradiction, this political Achilles' heel, that ultimately made the Populists vulnerable to assault by the opposing Democratic party.

9. The Conservative Triumph

Although fusion political reforms removed one of the props of the caste system, there is little doubt that North Carolina's three parties agreed that the Negroes' role in state politics should be minimal. Populists flirted with black support, but the name of their organ, Butler's *Caucasian*, reflected their attitude toward white supremacy. Sensing the political climate in the state in 1899, Republican Governor Russell defended his Republican administration against charges of "Negro dominance" in his biennial message to the legislature:

> By the constitution and laws of the State, the power of appointment to office is vested in the Governor as to many constitutional and statutory offices. It has been charged in the public press in other States, and the impression seems to prevail among many people in various sections of the United States and perhaps, in foreign countries, that North Carolina has been under negro government, and that the Governor of the State has appointed large numbers of colored persons to office. It appears from an account made of the commissions issued from the executive office to persons appointed by the Governor, that I have appointed in the two years [1896–98] to civil office eight hundred and eighteen (818) persons, of whom not more than eight (8) were colored.[1]

No doubt the Democrats understood this taken-for-granted condition of state politics, but charging "nigger rule" was their best political strategy. Speaking of the 1896 election, Edmonds reports that "when discouraging Negroes from supporting Russell, [the Democrats] referred to his calling the Negroes 'savages.' When discouraging the Populists from supporting him, they called him a 'nigger lover.'"[2] In response to the potential threat to the class system and to traditional privileges the Democrats had previously enjoyed, the Democrats launched a massive and effective white supremacy campaign in 1898. It was a brilliant maneuver in "symbolic politics" that preyed upon the poor whites' traditional antipathy toward blacks.[3]

Freud conceived of the unconscious as a collection of once-conscious thoughts that have been repressed. While no doubt the process of selective forgetting occurs for psychological reasons, a sociological interpretation of the unconscious is that it consists of impulses and experiences for which there is no vocabulary. Experiences that cannot be put into words cannot be articulated—they are "unconscious." By extension, we can speak of a "public unconscious" and refer to aspects of social life for which we lack a vocabulary and hence consciousness. The public vocabulary, an important aspect of the "mobilization of bias" in a political system, may either repress genuine communication—as do terms in our current public vocabulary such as "peace with honor," "national security," "national interest," "energy crisis"—or facilitate it.[4]

Just as the image of the mill town as a "white family" functioned to repress working-class consciousness, public denunciations of "nigger rule" by upper-class Democrats functioned to blind white farmers and tenants to their class interests. Georgia Populist Tom Watson told tenants this in an effort to unite poor white and black farmers, but "this is the closest, incidentally, that Watson or any other Populist came to saying that racial prejudice and hostility were deliberately created to gain advantage for the dominant economic interests." He said, "Now the People's Party says to these two men [black and white], 'You are kept apart that you may be separately fleeced of your earnings. You are made to hate each other because upon that hatred is rested the keystone of the arch of financial despotism which enslaves you both. You are deceived and blinded that you may not see how this race antagonism perpetuates a monetary system which beggars both.'"[5]

The target of Watson's rhetoric was the eastern financial system, not the southern stratification system. North Carolina Populist leaders did not use this vocabulary. They failed to warn their constituents of the uses of racist rhetoric in the political order. Consequently, they were defeated by the distinguished, upper-class white supremacy orators who traveled throughout the state fanning the fires of racial hatred. Edmonds writes, "The November election of 1898 restored North Carolina to Democratic control."[6] Forty Democrats, seven Republicans, and only three Populists were elected to the state senate.

The Populists' failure was not, as Lasch suggests, simply a failure of theory.[7] When forced to choose between their desire for power and the defense of their class position, Populist leaders, like Colonel Polk in his response to the proposed strike of black cotton pickers, chose against an honest treatment of southern stratification. I suggest that this was a key factor in their political demise. Potential class antagonisms between planters and tenants within the Populist movement seem to have prevented education in matters of social structure and class interests that might otherwise have inhibited the appeal of Democratic rhetoric. Genuine class consciousness in the rural South, however, was an awesome possibility in the 1890s—one that potentially threatened not only the hegemony of planter-industrialists but that of Populist leadership as well. Dissident agrarian leaders entered the political arena to challenge the nation's fiscal policy. They were willing to enlist what support they could find, whether black tenants or Knights of Labor. But to teach the truth of southern stratification was more of a departure from mainstream political culture than they were willing to make.

White Supremacy and the Senate of 1899

Although the Democrats who regained control of state politics in 1899 are referred to by historians as "progressives," their principal accomplishments were negative; they overturned prior fusionist legislation. Foremost was the reversal of political reforms. County-level offices were again made appointive by the legislature. Among their principal achievements was the formulation of a constitutional amendment, which they successfully put before the people, restricting suffrage to literate voters. A short-lived "grandfather clause" was added to "protect" illiterate white voters, though there is evidence that they, too, were targets of the restriction.[8] One contemporary political observer's analysis of the national election of 1896 held true as well for North Carolina Democrats: "It was not free silver that frightened these plutocratic leaders. What they feared then, what they fear now, is free men."[9]

The Democrats who entered the house and senate of the General Assembly in 1899 were an outstanding group of men. White supremacy orators of the vicious campaign against the fusionists played an important part in the house leadership. According to Edmonds, "On the county and municipal government committee were George Rountree, H. W. Stubbs, Francis D. Winston, 'white supremacy' orators; on the election law committee were H. W. Stubbs, Francis D. Winston, Frank Ray, and Locke Craig, 'white supremacy' campaigners; and on the constitutional amendment committee were George Rountree, Francis D. Winston, and Lee Overman, 'white supremacy' advocates."[10] These were able spokesmen for upper-class interests. Kousser describes Francis D. Winston: "Born in 1857 of F.F.V. lineage, Winston attended Cornell and graduated from the University of North Carolina. A member of the proper gentry church (Episcopal), Winston followed his father's path into law and the state legislature, and he surpassed his parent by attaining the lieutenant-governorship in 1904." Of George Rountree he says: "Though Rountree's ancestors settled in Virginia too late to be among the first families, they did predate the Revolution, and his father was a rich North Carolina businessman. Graduating from Harvard in 1877, George Rountree became a lawyer, politician, and pillar of the Episcopal church. A leader in the 1898 Wilmington uprising which overturned the legally elected government and killed twenty black men, Rountree displayed small concern for either Negroes or lower-class whites."[11]

To evaluate the relationship between such politicians and the Democrats and fusionists who preceded them, I studied the men elected to serve in the 1899 senate.[12] I found biographical information for thirty-seven of the forty Democrats. Of these thirty-seven, twenty-four were college graduates, seven attended common schools, and two studied law but had no college degrees. No educational information was available for four of the men. Most were graduates of the University of North Carolina, although several attended Wake Forest and Trinity. Other colleges attended include the University of Virginia (three), Davidson (two), Medical College of the University of Maryland, Harvard, and Princeton (one each). The senators averaged forty-six years of age, ranging from seventy-four to twenty-nine.

In sharp contrast with the Populists and Republicans in the fusion senates, the Democrats' occupational composition is consistent with my interpretation of North Carolina's development as a revolution from above. Many Democratic senators occupied positions of high social status and combined economic interests in agriculture, business, and industry. I estimate that at least seven, and probably more, of the senators were planters. Several others had significant agricultural interests, although I was unable to determine the extent. Very incomplete data on family origins suggest that at least seven senators were sons of planters. Unlike the Populists, whose occupations were more exclusively agrarian, these members of the landed upper class had investments in agriculture, manufacturing, banking, railroads, and businesses.

Table 9.1 summarizes the occupational composition of the Democrats in the senate. Since several of the senators pursued multiple careers, more than thirty-seven occupations are listed. The most typical occupation was law, and this represents a real change from the two previous sessions. Twenty-three senators were lawyers. Several were corporate lawyers, at least six representing railroad companies in their private practices. Several of the lawyers were also associated with banks, cotton mills, and a power company. This is why Key pictured these men as representing the urban and industrial interests of the state.[13] However, I reject his thesis that their political victory represented the rise of industry over agriculture in North Carolina. I discovered

Table 9.1. Occupational Composition of Democrats in the 1899 Senate[1]

Occupation	Number
Lawyers	23
Farmers[2]	16
Businessmen	6
Merchants	5
Ministers	1
Physicians	1

1. The total number of occupations is greater than the total number of Democratic senators because many of these legislators pursued multiple occupations.
2. Category includes both "farmers" and "planters."

that at least eight of the lawyers had personal agricultural interests. The following brief biographical sketches illustrate the Democrats' combination of economic interests and suggest their continuing position in the agrarian social structure. This pattern is strikingly similar to that described in chapter 5, where I examined the economic elite.

Democratic Senators, 1899

Julius C. Black. Lawyer. Trinity College. Son of a physician.

Joseph A. Brown. Farmer, hotel manager, sawmill owner, railroad contractor, owner of a mercantile business, and manufacturer. The son of a physician and planter, his education was limited. Attended commercial school one year.

James A. Bryan. Farmer with a Princeton law degree. Owner of several sawmills. President of the Atlantic and North Carolina Railroad. President of the National Bank of New Bern. His father was a "big landholder," attorney, and member of the legislature and of the Constitutional Convention of 1835. Senator described as a "descendant of one of the state's oldest families."

Thomas Cheek. Tailor. Common school education.

Thomas J. Clinton. Farmer. Sheriff. Common school education.

William J. Cooke. Lawyer with a Harvard law degree. Mayor of Asheville. Owned a large farm in Buncombe County and reputedly kept the largest herd of a certain hog species in the United States. Son of a prominent lawyer and businessman.

R. A. Cooley. Lawyer. Graduated from Wake Forest.

George Cowper. Lawyer with a degree from the University of North Carolina. Son of Richard Green Cowper, a Hertford County planter who served in the house and senate of the General Assembly.

Frank A. Daniels. Lawyer with a University of North Carolina degree. Law partner with Governor Aycock, city attorney of Goldsboro. Brother of editor Josephus Daniels.

William C. Fields. Lawyer, University of North Carolina degree, with interests in a mercantile business, manufacturing, and farming. Superintendent of county schools and solicitor of inferior court.

Robert B. Glenn. Lawyer for Southern Railroad and Western Union Company. Graduated from Davidson College and the University of Virginia. Had served as U.S. attorney for western North Carolina. Succeeded Aycock as governor of North Carolina, 1905–9.

Frank C. Hairston. Farmer. Educated at the University of Virginia.

Archibald A. Hicks. Lawyer. Attended Yadkin College. Mayor of Oxford. One of the organizers of the First National Bank of Oxford.

Isham Hill. Merchant.

John Q. Jackson. Lawyer, farmer, educated at Trinity College.

Fernando James. Lawyer, graduate from the University of North Carolina, mayor of Greenville, 1882–92. Son of a Pitt County physician.

Thomas J. Jerome. Lawyer, educated in common schools. General counsel for the Asheboro and Aberdeen Railroad, Seaboard Air Line Railroad, and "numerous other corporations."

F. P. Jones. Lawyer. Town counsel for Dunn, North Carolina. Attended Floral College.

J. A. T. Jones. Primitive Baptist minister.

Michael Hoke Justice. Lawyer, farmer, judge. Son of a Baptist minister. Attended Golden Grove Seminary.

Wiley L. Lambert. Lawyer. Owned business and residential properties, "extensive" land. Father died when he was young. Attended public schools and read law. Grandparents on both sides were planters.

David Lowe. Large cotton farmer. Mercantile business. Tannery business. Never attended college. Served as colonel in the state militia, 1847–54.

Stephen McIntyre. Lawyer, handled interests of numerous railroads and cotton mills. "Financially interested in cotton mills and banks." Owned valuable farm land. Vice-president of National Bank of Lumberton; director of Mansfield and Jennings Cotton Mills. Grandfather built mills in western North Carolina. Father was an extensive agriculturalist.

Oscar Mason. Gaston County lawyer. Mother's family name is associated with planters and cotton mill builders in Gaston County.

Thomas J. Murray. Madison County sheriff and tax collector. Common school education.

Francis Osborne. Attorney for Southern Power Company and several railroads. Mayor of Charlotte by age twenty-five. Attended Davidson College and University of Virginia. Son of Judge James W. Osborne, a graduate of the University of North Carolina, who held state and federal offices. Mother said to have been from an "old and distinguished family." Francis served as attorney general of North Carolina from 1892 to 1896 until ousted by Populists.

J. W. S. Robinson. Postmaster, farmer, merchant. Common school education.

Thomas Gregory Skinner. Described as "lawyer, statesman, planter, businessman." Graduate of the University of North Carolina. Member of U.S. Congress, 1883–87, 1889–91. Nephew of former governor. Brother of Populist congressman, Harry Skinner.

Robert Lee Smith. Lawyer. Attended Trinity College and the University of North Carolina.

Dr. R. H. Speight. Physician with a "lucrative and successful practice." Planter (cotton and tobacco). Director, Central Hospital, Raleigh (mental hospital). Director, state prison. Graduate of the University of North Carolina and Medical University of Maryland. Son of a judge.

Charles Stanback. Farmer. Educated at Trinity College.

Edwin L. Travis. Lawyer.

Hallett S. Ward. Lawyer. Attended the University of North Carolina. Mayor of Plymouth in Beaufort County.

F. A. Whitaker. Wake County farmer ("one of the best in the state"). Attended Wake Academy.

William L. Williams. Cotton planter, born on "Williams Plantation." Member of a "prominent and historic" family involved in state politics and planting back to the colonial period. "Good educational advantages."

John N. Wilson. County attorney of Guilford. Special counsel to Southern railways. Graduated from the University of North Carolina.

These are the men who, according to Key, ushered in the "modern era of liberalized Democratic government" in North Carolina and brought about a "political and educational renaissance."[14] Were they in fact what Lefler calls "a more virile, youthful, progressive leadership" than the Bourbons who had controlled the state from the end of Reconstruction until 1894?[15] I think the answer is *no*. Unlike the Populists who were political newcomers, the Democrats who entered the senate in 1899 were not new men.

Senator Black served in the senate in 1883; Brown in 1893. Cheek served in the house in 1889 and in the senate in 1893. Fields served in the house in 1874 and 1875 and in the senate in 1887 and 1893. He was also a solicitor of the inferior court for a number of years. Glenn was in the house in 1880 and 1881. He also served as district solicitor in 1885 and 1886 and as a presidential elector for several elections. James served in the senate in 1893 and was mayor of Greenville for a decade before that. Justice served in the senate in 1877 and the house in 1895 and 1897. He was a presidential elector in 1884 and served as a judge for seventeen years. Robinson was a member of the house in 1885. Skinner had already served eight years in the U.S. Congress beginning in 1883. Smith served previously in the house; Speight served in the 1891 senate. Stanback served in the 1889 senate. Thomas served in the house in 1893. Williams served in the 1889 senate.

These were not new men to state politics. They shared twenty years of collective legislative experience in the General Assembly. In addition, six other senators had extensive prior political experience as Democratic mayors, judges, and county officials. Still others had acquired political seasoning as city and county lawyers. The oldest senator, David Lowe, age seventy-four, had been a justice of the peace in Lincoln County for forty years. Hardly a newcomer to public affairs, he had served as a colonel in the antebellum state militia from 1847 to 1854.

My research contradicts the state's popular self-image as articulated by most state historians. It supports the interpretation advanced by Steelman who, although he did not look closely at senatorial membership, nevertheless saw little discontinuity between the Bourbons and the progressives.

> The Campaign of 1898 witnessed the resurgence of a conservative faction in the Democratic Party. It is patently misleading to imply that the party in giving lip service to some of the demands of the Populists underwent a fundamental change of ideology. Furthermore most of the "new leaders" in the party had gotten their start in public life under the tutelage of Matt W. Ransom, acknowledged leader of conservative Democrats. The trend toward conservatism was discerned before and after the election, and the powerful hold of railroad interests upon the party was especially deplored. Promises . . . did not indicate the Democrats had made a radical break with the past. Bourbons had made and broken virtually all these promises beforehand.[16]

Steelman, overreacting perhaps against the Key-Lefler interpretation, minimized the policy changes set in motion by the Democrats beginning in 1899. But as Figure 7.2 showed, the level of government spending—one indication of modernization—doubled between 1898 and 1905. If not because of the entry of new men into state politics, why did this particular form of modernization occur when it did? To answer this question, we must look more closely at the administration of Governor Charles B. Aycock.

Progressivism and Paternalism: The Aycock Regime

Passage of the fusion election laws in 1895, which removed electoral machinery from Democratic control, produced many more votes in black-belt counties than had been cast in 1892. Repeal of this law in 1899, which meant the return of force and fraud to the voting booth, restricted black participation and aided both the election of Aycock to governor and the subsequent passage of the disfranchisement amendment. The effects of both restriction and intimidation are evident in the voting statistics. In 1896, 5,438 voters in New Hanover County (Wilmington) cast 41 percent of their votes for the Democrats. In 1900, 2,966 voters cast 99.9 percent of their votes for the Democrats. Only 1,340 people voted in 1904. Similarly, in Edgecombe County, 4,953 voters cast 55 percent of their votes for Russell in 1896, while in 1900, 4,143 people voted 90 percent for Aycock. Only 1,767 people voted in 1904.[17] Under the leadership of Aycock, the Democrats simultaneously expanded state activity and restricted popular political participation.

Governor Aycock has a hallowed image among southern politicians. Key credited him with leading an "educational and political renaissance." Schoolchildren are taught that he was a "new kind of Democratic leader." John S. Ezell included him among a few "progressive governors" whose "contributions were among the greatest in southern history."[18] Rupert Vance eulogized him, saying: "In fact, North Carolina has long ceased to think of him as her 'white-supremacy governor'; to all the state, white and black, he is the 'educational governor.' This man, a politician, a man of the common people, fighting an issue based on prejudice, emerged by rising as far above prejudice as it has proved possible for any native-born Southerner to go."[19]

Aycock was an upwardly mobile member of North Carolina's small middle class. His biographers, R. D. W. Connor and Clarence Poe, describe his ancestors as "plain and simple farmers."[20] His father, Benjamin Aycock, a small slaveholder, was a staunch Confederate who served in the state senate during the Civil War. He also served eight years as clerk of the superior court of Wayne County. The governor-to-be grew up during Reconstruction, and this is said to have left an imprint on his political outlook. In his own words, he viewed Reconstruction as "the intolerable burden of negro government." Aycock entered the University of North Carolina in 1877; among his classmates were many lifetime associates. Charles McIver, Edwin Alderman, and James Joyner—future educational leaders, the last two, county school board members with Aycock in Goldsboro—were there, as were Rufus Doughton, Locke Craig, and Francis D. Winston—future political leaders. Aycock practiced law in eastern North Carolina, where he was active in county politics as a member and superintendent of the school board.

When Aycock became the Democratic candidate for governor, Furnifold M. Simmons was the party chairman and campaign manager who had just engineered the 1898 legislative victory. Simmons was elected to the U.S. Senate in 1900 at the same time Aycock was elected governor. He ran the Democratic party until 1930. V. O. Key claimed that, beginning around 1900, the interests of the "aggressive aristocracy of manufacturing and banking, centering in the Piedmont" were "served without prompting" by the "Simmons machine." The "Simmons machine" drew its support from Piedmont and mountain Democrats. Internal party conflict came from the black-belt counties. "In North Carolina opposition to the political machine, to the economic oligarchy of manufacturing and financial interests, comes from the counties with the most Negroes." Thus, for Key, the election of Aycock and Simmons spelled the political victory of the industrial Piedmont over the plantation system of eastern North Carolina. This "political revolution," as Lefler refers to it, is supposed to have reflected in the political arena changes already wrought in the stratification system, that is, the rise of the middle class. Key says, "In Alabama, black-belt whites are often among the political big shots who set the style of state policy and politics. The lesser role of plantation princes in North Carolina's executive and legislative affairs contributes not only to a de-emphasis of harsh, racial attitudes but also to less effective assertion of the extremely conservative viewpoints of all kinds that are usually associated with a plantation economy."[21]

I believe that this is a very misleading picture of North Carolina's political economy. Opposition to machine candidates in the eastern counties, as Key partly acknowledges, reflected the high level of white tenancy as well as the legacy of Populist sentiment in the black belt. Insurgents from eastern counties occasionally won electoral victories. One was W. W. Kitchin, son of the Populist leader W. H. Kitchin, who was elected governor in 1908. Such candidates typically claimed that the Democratic machine was "subservient to the special interests—tobacco and power companies, cotton mills, railroads, and the business and urban classes—and neglectful of the interest of the mass of farmers, industrial laborers, and the common people generally."[22] As the Populists before them, however, most of these liberal Democrats, including Kitchin, failed to sponsor reforms when elected.[23] None of this implies a "lesser role of plantation princes" in North Carolina affairs.

Key fails to mention that Furniford Simmons was not a new face as chairman of the state Democratic party in 1900; he had been party chairman when the Bourbon Democrats were ousted by the fusionists. Nor does Key note that Simmons was a wealthy eastern North Carolina cotton planter. Branson's 1869 *Directory* reported that his father owned a 2,200-acre plantation. One of his biographers reports that Simmons "was born into abundance" and that while he was in the U.S. Senate he owned "farms" in Jones County and near New Bern where he practiced law. Simmons was the political protégé of Senator Matt Ransom. Ransom was born in 1826 into an influential Warren County family. He graduated from the University of North Carolina in 1847 and became state attorney general in 1852. Ransom served as a major general in the Confederate army and surrendered with Lee. After the war he planted cotton and practiced law. He served in the U.S. Senate from 1872 until 1895. One of his biographers described him as "one of the largest landed proprietors and most successful planters in the State." Simmons, who had served in the U.S. Congress in the 1880s and had become state party chairman in 1892, inherited control of the party when Ransom died.

This information and my profile of state senators suggest an alternative view of North Carolina's political development—that in 1899 the old Bourbon coalition of big agriculture and industry returned to power in the legislature. The elimination of the fusion election machinery ensured the Democratic party's control of the general election of 1900. In this election the influence of big business, and especially the railroads, was widely felt. In self-congratulatory language, the *Charlotte Observer*, a newspaper owned by cotton mill industrialist Daniel Tompkins, declared that "the businessmen of the State are largely responsible for the victory. Not before in years have the bankmen, the mill men, and the business men in general—the backbone of the property interest of the State—taken such sincere interest. They worked from start to finish, and furthermore, they spent large bits of money in behalf of the cause. . . . Indeed North Carolina is fast changing from an agricultural to a manufacturing State."[24]

During the campaign, Simmons sought financial support from business interests. Through former Governor Thomas J. Jarvis he promised the "large corporations" that "in the event of Democratic victory their taxes would not be increased."[25] Once in office, the Democrats defeated a measure to levy a graduated income tax on railroads. They created a corporation commission that "voted against reduction of freight and passenger rates and dropped all charges pending against railroads."[26] The state's railroads had been assessed for tax purposes at $42 million although their real worth was estimated to have been nearer $150 million. Governor Aycock agreed not to have them reassessed until 1903. Although he is classed as a progressive, Aycock did not support the legalized primary, antitrust measures, child labor reforms, and other typical progressive reforms. His published speeches indicate the strong degree to which he supported the traditional caste system. In a campaign speech, for example, Aycock is reported to have said: "I do not believe the Fusionists intended to give us bad government; they simply could not help it. I assert that such a condition with them is inevitable because the party has not behind it virtue and intelligence, but it has the evil influence of 120,000 negro votes. No government can be better than the average of the virtue and intelligence of the party that governs."[27] Aycock's paternalistic attitude is revealed in his gubernatorial acceptance speech:

> May this era of good feeling among us be the outcome of this content. Then we shall learn, if we do not already know, that while universal suffrage is a failure, universal justice is the perpetual decree of Almighty God, and that we are entrusted with power not for our good alone, but for the negro as well. We hold our title to power by the tenure of service to God, and if we fail to administer equal and exact justice to the negro whom we deprive of suffrage, we shall in the fullness of time lose power ourselves, for we must know that the God who is love trusts no people with authority for the purpose of enabling them to do injustice to the weak.[28]

In an overall assessment of the accomplishments of Aycock and the North Carolina progressives, Steelman concluded that his "search for an explanation of why North Carolina acquired the reputation, early in the 20th century, of being a 'preeminent' state of the 'new South,' progressive in outlook, enlightened in political, social, and economic matters has probably raised more issues than it has resolved."[29]

I think it can be argued that along with public health leadership and its good roads movement, championed by Bennehan Cameron, North Carolina's progressive image rests chiefly on its leadership among southern states in building a modern system of public education. Charles Aycock led not only North Carolina but the South in the public crusade. Whenever they speak of Aycock, North Carolinians are fond of telling that he died of a heart attack near the end of a speech extolling the value of universal education before the Alabama Educational Association. The concluding words of that speech were to have been: "Equal! That is the word. On that word I plant myself and my party—the equal right of every child born on earth to have the opportunity to burgeon out all that there is within him."[30]

According to Steelman, "There is considerable evidence to support the thesis that the crusade for public education, of which Charles B. Aycock was the acknowledged leader, was launched in earnest only after strong criticism had been leveled against the literacy clause of the suffrage amendment."[31] A grandfather clause protected illiterate white voters only until

1908. To answer challenges to this proviso, as the white supremacy campaign went on, Democrats began to say that if the state had an adequate school system literacy would be no problem, and they pledged to build one. This proved to be a brilliant campaign strategy. I suggest that it undermined Populist resistance by championing educational reform, one of the farmers' demands, and it assured the support of middle-class progressive elements throughout the state.

Education, Modernization, and the Middle Class

According to Barrington Moore's concept of a revolution from above, conservative modernization is typically sponsored by a landed upper class in cooperation with a weak and dependent middle class. North Carolina was still largely a rural state at the end of the nineteenth century. The weak position of its small middle class can be illustrated with a brief look at the careers of the state's most celebrated journalists, Walter Hines Page and Josephus Daniels, both of whom wanted change but lacked power to bring it about.[32]

Walter Hines Page was born in 1855 at the site of what is now Cary, North Carolina. His grandfather, Anderson Page, was a planter who owned twenty slaves and one thousand acres of land in Wake County. Anderson Page sent several of his sons to college, but not Frank Page, Walter's father. Although he identified his occupation as "farmer," Frank Page owned only four slaves at the beginning of the Civil War, and his agricultural holdings were small.[33] He was a hardworking businessman who founded two communities in North Carolina, Cary and Aberdeen. Unlike the Camerons, who were strong enough to survive war and Reconstruction, Frank Page was ruined by the Civil War. His lumbering business was destroyed, and his land had been trampled by both armies. He had no livestock and no money. His family's one resource was a peach orchard that survived the war and yielded a good crop in 1865. Walter was ten years old when the war ended, and he is said to have sold peaches to occupying troops in Raleigh. In time, however, Frank Page recouped his losses. He built hotels in Raleigh and opened up the Pinehurst region of the state. He built the Aberdeen and Asheboro Railroad, grew rich, and bought land.

Walter Page, like a number of whites who boycotted the University of North Carolina during Reconstruction while it admitted blacks, went to college out of state. He attended Randolph Macon College in Virginia and did graduate work in Greek at Johns Hopkins. He failed to find work as a journalist in his poor home state and worked instead as a reporter in Missouri and Washington. He returned to North Carolina in the 1880s to edit the Raleigh *State Chronicle*, which was partially owned by Julian S. Carr (himself an upwardly mobile member of the middle class who had recently become a Durham tobacco manufacturer) and was partially backed by Frank Page. Walter Page was critical of the Bourbon order, advocating industrial progress and public education. His editorials often described small towns in the postbellum South as vigorous middle-class islands in an otherwise stagnant and "mummified" plantation society. His views were not fashionable, and he failed to make a success of the paper. According to Joseph L. Morrison,

> Page had turned his *State Chronicle* into a daily in hopeless competition with two others for the meager advertising in the state capital (population 9265 in 1880). Editor Page had been delighted with a clear news beat fashioned for him by Josephus Daniels who sent him in a detailed story about a disastrous fire at Wilson. Out of Page's delight with Daniels' enterprise came an invitation to edit, in Page's absence, the *State Chronicle* for the two weeks around Christmas in 1884. In reality Page was using the vacation to shop around for an out-of-state job and, not being able to win appointment as State Printer from the succeeding legislature, Page had to strike his colors.[34]

Page found another job over Christmas and left North Carolina. Tired of the criticism his editorials generated and eager for recognition, he complained of "an intolerance in North Carolina that is oppressive. Men do not have the chance to rise in life that they have elsewhere."[35] Josephus Daniels, then only twenty-two, took over as editor of the *State Chronicle*.

Daniels was one of twelve children of a store clerk and part-time shipbuilder. His father died when he was young, and he was raised by his mother. The family had no money, but Josephus, like his older brother Frank, who later practiced law with Charles Aycock, managed to get an education. He succeeded where Page had failed with the *State Chronicle*. Nevertheless, life was hard for him. For financial reasons he, too, was forced to leave the state. Daniels took a job as chief of the Appointment Division of the Department of the Interior in Washington, a patronage position in return for his editorial support of Senator Matt Ransom, the conservative Confederate. According to his biographer, "Daniels was genuinely reluctant to become a Washington bureaucrat, but North Carolina could not in those hard times afford him a living."[36] Later Julian Carr bought the Raleigh *News and Observer* and turned it over to Daniels to operate as the organ of the North Carolina Democrats. He supplemented his income as state printer, a reward for his party loyalty, until he was replaced by the Populists.

These two careers illustrate the precariousness of middle-class careers in nineteenth-century North Carolina. Both Page and Daniels were progressives who favored industrial and educational development. Because his views were unpopular at the time, Page left the state for a successful journalistic career. By the age of forty he was editor of the *Atlantic Monthly* and soon organized Doubleday, Page and Company. Daniels managed to build a successful journalistic career in the state by allying himself with such powerful Democrats as Matt Ransom. He wrote vicious editorials against blacks and Populists in the *News and Observer*. Although he was considered to be in the liberal wing of the party, he was allied with the conservatives and his editorials played an important part in the white supremacy campaign. Daniels traveled throughout the South studying the measures used in other states to disfranchise blacks, and he brought back to North Carolina the plan adopted by the 1899 legislature to restrict suffrage. His career typifies the alliance between the weak middle class and the dominant landed upper class that characterizes conservative modernization.

An important vehicle for middle-class expression in North Carolina during the 1880s was the Watauga Club, an informal group of middle-class reformers that developed "into the core of a statewide network of 'involved' individuals."[37] At its center was young Walter Hines Page, whose *State Chronicle* became its semiofficial voice. Prominent members (of an "official" total of eighteen) included Josephus Daniels; Charles Dabney, a University of North Carolina chemistry professor, later president of the University of Cincinnati; Richard H. Lewis, M.D., later president of the American Public Health Association; Joseph Hill Brown, later president of Citizens' National Bank in Raleigh (in which he began his career as a teller); and Charles D. McIver, later president of North Carolina Women's College and president of the Southern Educational Association. Most of the Wataugans were indeed "middle class," although a few of its members were well connected. Frank Moving, for example, was born into a family of "prominent planters" at Movingburg, North Carolina. He established the Caraleigh Cotton Mills and became a director of the Raleigh Banking and Trust Company. Other middle-class members included Arthur Winslow, an M.I.T.-trained mining engineer and later president of the United States and British Columbia Mining Company; John W. Thompson, a businessman; Edward Moses, superintendent of Raleigh schools; and William Peele, a humorist and lecturer.[38]

The Wataugans espoused typical progressive positions, including professionalism, efficiency, the elimination of political corruption, and the expansion of government services and regulation.[39] Demands for the expansion of public services, especially education, are commonly believed to have united the state's farmers and its small middle class—two groups bypassed by North Carolina's economic development in the 1880s—in opposition to the Bourbon regime. Lefler writes: "The demands for trained men in industry, voiced by Walter Hines Page and the Watauga Club of Raleigh and the crusade for agricultural education carried on by Colonel L. L. Polk, editor of the *Progres-*

sive Farmer, finally led to the chartering of the State Agricultural and Mechanical College in 1887."[40] Muller echoes this, saying that "two class movements, the one middle class, the other agrarian, and their institutional representatives, the Watauga Club of Raleigh and the Farmers' State Alliance, joined to promote the 'New South.'"[41]

This is a misleading interpretation, for the middle class allied itself not with the Populists, who wanted power, but with the Democrats, who had power. Muller contradicts his own interpretation when he reports that the Wataugans "intended to omit any mention of agriculture in their proposal for a technical college, until Page commented that the 'd—n farmer legislature' would pass nothing 'unless there was some agriculture in it somewhere.'"[42] The Wataugans identified with business interests, not with the farmers. For example, some years later, Page wrote Daniel Tompkins that it "was the businessman who had [sic] to lead our old commonwealths out of the rut that the politician got them into."[43]

When these middle-class progressives diagnosed the social ills of their state, they might have looked above at the landed upper class and called for land reform, or they might have challenged the political power of the railroads and the economic exploitation in the mill towns. Instead, they located the sources of North Carolina's backwardness below them.[44] Partly, the problem was the blacks. Social control of black voters, the necessity of which the middle class took for granted, produced force and fraud in politics. Disfranchisement, they thought, would eliminate political corruption, and, in Aycock's words, "usher in a period of social and economic stability."[45] Some of North Carolina's problems resulted from the condition of lower-class whites. Walter Hines Page described the illiterate white farmer as "the real curse of the land. He is the fellow for whom Southern civilization sacrifices itself. . . . Better white men cannot rise for him. He is at once the worst and most persistent product of slavery. The sorry Southern white man; his like exists in other parts of the country, but he does not set the pace elsewhere."[46] Page's famous commencement address to North

Carolina State University, delivered in 1897 after he had become *Atlantic Monthly* editor and entitled "The Forgotten Man," is a classic statement of middle-class ideology. In that speech he addressed the region's fundamental problem: it was the mass of common people. The forgotten man had "become not only a dead weight but a definite opponent of social *progress.*" The solution for the South was education, which, of course, the middle class could provide. "The battle is practically won when the whole State stands secure on this platform. *That a public school system generously supported by public sentiment and generously maintained by both State and local taxation, is the only effective means to develop the forgotten man.*"[47]

Southern historians have failed to grasp the profoundly conservative quality of educational reform. Far from challenging the dominant order, the southern educational movement served the needs of the South's developing industrial system, just as progressivism generally contributed to the development of the American corporate economy.[48] Writing of the Progressive Era in American life, Lasch argues that such reformers as Jane Addams and John Dewey "sought not so much to democratize the industrial system as to make it run more efficiently. These reformers wished to substitute 'education' for older and cruder methods of social control, techniques that appeared to them not only offensive in themselves, since they rested on coercion, but inexcusably inefficient." Lasch quotes John Dewey: "We are likely to take the influence of superior force for control, forgetting that while we may lead a horse to water we cannot make him drink; and that while we can shut a man up in a penitentiary we cannot make him penitent." Lasch concludes that "even when they originated in humanitarian impulses, progressive ideals led not to a philosophy of liberation but to a blueprint for control."[49]

Schooling fulfills several important functions in an industrial society. Schools teach not only academic skills but also discipline and conformity to authority, thus producing a literate and disciplined work force.[50] They identify some students as "talented" and contribute to their mobility while legitimating others' lack of mobility as a matter of "personal deficiency."[51] Finally, by training citizens, schools contribute to the prevailing bias in the political system.

Middle-class reformers in North Carolina were not blind to the social control functions of education as the following quotations from Aycock's addresses show:

The Social Control Function / In his famed "Universal Education" speech, Aycock compared education to breaking a mule.

> But this is your unbroken mule. We call it "breaking" them. What is "breaking" a mule except training him, educating him, bringing out of him what there is in him? Why, when you buy a mule fresh from a drove it takes two white men and one 15th amendment to hitch him to a plow. And when you get him hitched up he plows up more cotton than he does grass; but after you have broken him, trained him, developed him, educated, why the old mule goes right along.[52]

Improvement of the Work Force / Speaking before the Manufacturers' Club of Charlotte, Aycock said:

> I am anxious to see every agency which tends to increase the wealth of the State prosper and receive that encouragement which comes from a friendly view on the part of those who possess governmental powers. . . .
>
> I urge you (therefore) with all your might and power to put yourselves in the front of this great movement for universal education. With education will come renewed activity, increased and better work, higher skill, and consequently higher wages. Every one must recognize that the wealth of the State is dependent upon the wages which are paid to the earners, and these wages in turn are dependent upon the capacity of the wage earner, and this capacity is dependent upon the quickness and skill which comes with an acquaintance with books.[53]

The Selection Function of Education / Aycock said:

> We have in the South today our Hills, our Lamars, our Becks, our Vests, our Vances, and our Hamptons (all of them products of the period before the War); but no man can go through the country and lay his hand on the head of a single child and say that here is a Lamar, here a Vance, or a Vest, or a Hill, or a Hampton, or a Beck. It is the business of the schools to find for us these splendid children and develop them into these great leaders.
>
> We want the schools to find all the strongest and best in competition one with the other until the fullest power of each shall be developed. In doing this we shall get the largest contribution to society.[54]

Social Control for Blacks / When Aycock spoke of universal education he had in mind education for blacks as well as whites. He believed that emancipation had undermined the paternalism of the plantation system. When the tenancy system replaced plantation supervision, a decrease in social control resulted. The paternalism of the schoolhouse could restore this control:

> I find in the State men who think that the negro has gone backward rather than forward and that education is injurious to him. Have these men forgotten that the negro was well educated before the War? Do they not recall that he was trained in those things essential for his life work? He has been less educated since the War than before. It is true that he has been sent to school, but his contact with the old planter and with the accomplished and elegant wife of that planter has been broken. This contact was in itself a better education than he can receive from the public schools, but shall we, for this reason, say that he is incapable of training? Ought we not, on the contrary, to study the conditions and realize that the training which he needs has not been given to him since the War in like manner that it was before?[55]

Speaking of the weak middle class in Germany, Barrington Moore, paraphrasing Marx and Engels, referred to "a commercial and industrial class which is too weak and dependent to take power and rule in its own right and which therefore throws itself into the arms of the landed aristocracy and the royal bureaucracy, exchanging the right to rule for the right to make money."[56] It is not too much of an exaggeration to suggest that in North Carolina, the small professional middle class that included a number of important southern reformers allied itself with the landed upper class that sponsored industrialization and, after 1900, expanded the range of state activity, thereby exchanging the right to rule for the right to teach school.[57]

The class position of middle-class professionals, especially educators, was improved by disfranchisement because they benefited from increased public expenditures. With blacks out of the political process for the first time since Reconstruction, the landed upper class could begin to use state government as an instrument for modernization. Education, like public health improvement and road building, was complementary to North Carolina's changing political economy. Other political goals of the middle class, however, such as corporate regulation, were not realized. During the first decade of the twentieth century, a number of progressive measures were advocated by reform candidates such as the "Fifth District Combine" centered around Greensboro. The reform slate included the son of a former Populist leader, William Kitchin, a Roxboro lawyer, for governor, and two Greensboro lawyers, Aubrey Brooks and Edwin Justice, who were candidates, respectively, for Congress and House Speaker of the General Assembly. These men failed to alter North Carolina's profoundly conservative course.

Many progressive reforms were effectively blocked in North Carolina by the economic elite. A number of the state's business leaders, calling themselves "Independent Democrats," met in Greensboro in 1902 to oppose the "liberal" directions they feared the Democratic party was taking.[58] Included among several mill owners were two Holts and a Battle. John Fries of the Wachovia manufacturing and banking establishment was there, as was J. M. Odell, mill owner and banker. Many of these men belonged to the group of antebellum industrial families discussed in chapter 5. Newer mill men such as Caesar Cone were also present. Other prominent participants included Henry Page, brother of Walter Hines Page and president of the Aberdeen and Asheboro Railroad; W. W. Clark, son of Walter Clark, chief justice of the state Supreme Court; P. J. Sinclair, a newspaper owner and large cotton planter who had served as a colonel in the Confederacy; and J. P. Caldwell, editor of Daniel Tompkins's *Charlotte Observer*. The group endorsed Lindsay Patterson, who was, by then, a Republican, for governor. Patterson, a cotton manufacturer, was the son of Samuel F. Patterson, the brother of Rufus Patterson (who was serving as Democratic commissioner of agriculture), and the brother-in-law of John Fries. They also endorsed John Motley Morehead, who defeated Aubrey Brooks in the congressional contest. This group reads like a *Who's Who* of chapter 5. As politically active representatives of the landed upper class and its business partners, I suggest that these men had the power to set limits and directions for North Carolina's political and economic development.

Conclusion

In chapter 6, I argued that Germany and the American South occupied comparable niches in the world market system in the nineteenth century. Both societies exploited servile labor to produce agricultural commodities, wheat and cotton, for export. Labor-repressive agricultural relations required authoritarian measures for social control, and the landowning classes of both societies developed antibourgeois sentiments and aristocratic pretensions despite their involvement in the capitalist world system. This involved risks, however, and it created social tensions. Efforts to manage these tensions—in Germany and Japan, the popularization of the principles of conservative modernization in fascist mass movements, and in America, the expansion of slaveholding into the Southwest to retain political parity in the federal system—pitted these societies against political and economic developments in the "core" regions of the capitalist system. The landed classes of both societies responded similarly to external pressures—in Germany to foreign threats and in the South to northern restraints on geographical expansion of the slave system—with nationalism, militarism, and industrialization. Because the South lost its nationalist struggle, its subsequent modernization could not be like Germany's. Most important, with military occupation and the enfranchisement of freed slaves, the landed upper class temporarily lost control of the state. Consequently, they could not use government, as was done in Germany, as an instrument of modernization and repression.

Conservative Democrats regained control of North Carolina politics after Reconstruction, but that control was never secure until 1900. From 1880 through 1896, the Democrats in North Carolina never won more than 54 percent of the gubernatorial vote. Blacks and their white Republican allies in the mountains remained a threat. The Populist revolt also threatened the control of the landed upper class but, as we have seen, Populist leaders were unwilling to alter the agrarian social structure. When the Democrats regained control of the legislature in 1899, they began simultaneously to expand government activity and to reduce popular political participation. My research strongly suggests that, contrary to popular opinion, these were not new men in state politics. Only with the elimination of blacks from the political process (achieved by legal suffrage restriction) could they begin to use the government again, as planters had done in the early 1860s when they prepared for war, to bring about an industrial revolution from above.

I noted at the beginning of chapter 7 that Cyril Black identified "the transition from a political leadership wedded to the traditional system to one which favors thorough-going modernization" as "the central problem in political modernization."[59] Despite North Carolina's reputation as the most progressive of the southern states, its political elite did not favor thorough-going modernization. Much of North Carolina's industry was integrated into the traditional rural social structure. The wealth and power of the planter-industrialists depended upon maintenance of the system of nonwage agricultural labor and cheap industrial labor. After 1899 they used government to uphold the caste system. Strong labor laws and the occasional use of force kept industrial workers under control. But the state needed some reforms. Road building, public health, and educational development—programs on which the state's progressive reputation is based—not only undermined the Populists' political opposition and coopted the state's small middle class, but benefited the state's expanding industrial system as well. Since they were again securely in control of the state apparatus, the Democrats could be sure that these programs supported their class interests.[60]

10. "Softly, Do You Not Hear . . . ?"

In the 1970s, as economic decline threatens northern industrial cities like Detroit and New York and a southerner has been elected president, the nation seems fascinated by the apparent economic prosperity and cultural vitality of today's South. Re-dubbed the "Sunbelt" to include California and the Southwest, and viewed in more favorable light than the segregationist South of the 1950s with its "massive resistance," the southern periphery has become, in the eyes of some, "an industrial and financial colossus." Kirkpatrick Sale has observed that the "southern rim" presently has a "gross national product bigger than any foreign country in the world except the Soviet Union." Were it a separate nation, by most standards the South would be "a world power on the scale of the present superpowers."[1]

In the concluding paragraph of *The South since 1865*, John Samuel Ezell wrote in 1963: "Slightly less than one century after the Civil War, the question 'What is the South?' should instead be phrased, 'What was the South?' Even for those who argue that this is not accurate—that the South continues to be a distinct and separate region—there, nevertheless, can be only one valid definition for that uniqueness, a 'state of mind.'" Whatever was distinctly southern, it is frequently thought, has retreated to the penumbra of southern consciousness.[2] A corollary to the notion that the South since 1865 has been a new South is the belief that its growth was made possible by the sudden and complete fall, because of the war, of its planter aristocracy. Eugene Genovese, who understands that class as well as anyone, says: "For the Old South, without a complicated state machine, traditional officer corps, and bureaucracy, there were no institutional mechanisms for shaping the new region in the mold of the old. When the planters went down, their way of life went down also. For the adherents of the old regime

Appomattox literally marked 'when the world ended.' "[3] Consequently, historians typically have treated the birth of the New South as an immaculate conception. In a 1948 presidential address to the Southern Historical Association, for example, Robert Cotterill claimed that to southerners of the 1880s, the cotton mill movement appeared as something revolutionary, "unrelated to the past, barren of ancestry, destitute of inheritance."[4]

It has also been common wisdom that no southern state showed more vitality after the Civil War than poor, humble North Carolina. Key wrote: "After the War the odd child bestirred itself sooner and more productively than its prouder neighbors. It seemed less shackled than they by the ghosts of lost grandeur; it had less grandeur to lose." Politically as well as economically, North Carolina is thought to have broken with southern tradition. "The spirit of the state has not tolerated strident demogoguery." It "has no place for a Huey Long. . . . The spirit that is unchained to a social and economic hierarchy of great tradition and authority has no place for a Byrd machine."[5]

I have presented an interpretation of North Carolina's political economy in the nineteenth century that challenges this picture of its radical discontinuity with the past and from its neighbors. From a close look at the actions of the supposedly "new men" of politics and industry in late nineteenth-century North Carolina, I have tried to infer patterns of class stratification and social change. The state's political economy in that period, it seems to me, suggests more continuity than change. I have shown its similarity to other societies where the landed upper classes were the principal agents of industrial development. I have drawn inferences from this comparison that I believe help to clarify the nature of economic development, industrial relations, ideology, and political modernization in North Carolina and the Upper South.

At the end of this research, as I review historical and sociological interpretations of southern life, none seem so penetrating as W. J. Cash's *Mind of the South*. Cash's work has been praised and faulted by many. It is full of hyperbole and contradictions. Genovese has justly criticized Cash for muddying the fact of antebellum planter hegemony with his claim that parvenu planters usually failed to live up to the ideal of the Virginia cavalier. All ruling classes, Genovese rebukes, are "acquisitive." Their origins usually are "violent and ugly."[6] Woodward criticizes Cash, despite the title of his book, for viewing the South as "mindless" and for minimizing the region's intellectual journey from Jefferson's liberalism to Fitzhugh's paternalism.[7] I reject Cash's tendency to psychologize, to reduce the facts of southern history to characterological dimensions such as the "savage ideal." Nonetheless, in his central thesis of the continuity of southern institutions, I find W. J. Cash right on target.

Cash contended that despite modifications wrought by industrialization and commercialization, "the extent of the change and break between the Old South that was and the South of our time has been vastly exaggerated." This is wholly consistent with the theme of conservative modernization developed in this book. I have depicted a revolution from above in North Carolina resting on agriculture and aimed at sustaining the position of a traditional landed upper class. Similarly, Cash read the "greatest uneasiness" in the minds of the South's "master class" as they viewed their grave postbellum economic troubles as well as the political threats from below that culminated in the Populist revolt. According to Cash, the result of the planters' assessment was "the feeling that somehow another line must be found; that without ever abandoning cotton-growing of course, *the arm of the land must somehow be extended.*" According both to Cash and the interpretation advanced here, the South's version of progress extended the social relations of plantation production to New South mills and schools and realized the aim of the planters. "So far from representing a deliberate break with the past, the turn to Progress clearly flowed straight out of that past and constituted in a real sense an emanation from the mill to maintain the South in its essential integrity."[8] Cash goes beyond merely claiming that the cotton mills were built by planters. He depicts southern industrialization as if it were a military campaign.

> So under the drive of this conviction in themselves and their fellows, there began to grow up in the minds of some of the best of these masters (the old Confederate captains in large part) an idea—a dream. Let us, in this quandary, take a page from the book Yankeedom. Let us meet the old enemy on his own ground. Let us, in short, turn to Progress.
>
> Let us introduce the factory in force. Let us, in particular, build cotton mills, here in the midst of the cotton fields. Let us build a thousand mills—and more than a thousand mills, and erect the South into a great industrial and commercial empire.[9]

When one recalls the conviction of North Carolina's greatest planter, Paul Carrington Cameron, that the forges and furnaces that had brought war might also foster manufacturing and economic independence for the South, one must agree with Cash's assertion that "in the feeling of the South, Progress stood quite accurately for a sort of new charge at Gettysburg."[10] Yet Cash's stress on southern continuity has met stiff opposition. One of Cash's most ardent critics has been C. Vann Woodward, whose *Origins of the New South* is the best-stated exposition of the thesis of the discontinuity of the New South from the Old South.

In response to Cash's rhetorical question about skyscrapers in the southern Piedmont—"Softly, do you not hear behind that the gallop of Jeb Stuart's Cavalrymen?"—C. Vann Woodward recently retorted, "The answer is 'No!' Not one ghostly echo of a gallop. And neither did Jack Cash. He only thought he did when he was bemused." Woodward believes that "slavery and secession, independence and defeat, emancipation and military occupation, reconstruction and redemption," rather than a unique class structure, made the South a distinct region. More than events, they are profound changes in social structure that have caused southerners to feel "the solid ground of continuity give way under their feet." According to Woodward, the Civil War "proved to be the death struggle of a society, which went down to ruins. . . . An old order of slave society solidly supported by constitution, state, church and the authority of law and learning and cherished by a majority of the people collapsed, perished and disappeared."[11]

It is hard to understand why historians have been so hostile to Cash's thesis and why, on the other hand, as Sheldon Hackney notes, "there has been no major challenge to *Origins of the New South*."[12] Perhaps there is something to Michael O'Brien's observation that "if Southern history is a remorseless unity, unbroken in its social conservatism and unchallenged by a significant radicalism, the task of the Southern liberal is futile."[13] In arguing, as Hackney summarizes, that "the Civil War deflected the course of southern history and altered the nature of southern society,"[14] Woodward makes a case for the impermanence of southern institutions. This forces him, however, to deal with the paradox of *apparent* continuity in the South. He attempts to do so by accepting as "Cash's main contribution" the "genuine insight into class relationships in the South" and the facticity of what Cash termed "Proto-Dorian Consensus." Woodward argues, "The lower-class white's obsessive anxiety for racial hegemony trapped him into submission to upper-class hegemony. More than it did anywhere else in the country, this class hegemony prevailed in the South, and it survived in various guises the real breaks in historical continuity."[15] This is a peculiar argument in which Woodward gives much ground. He explains the appearance of continuity in southern history in terms of the persistence of upper-class ideological hegemony, itself seen as a consequence of false consciousness of the mass of white southerners. However, since as Antonio Gramsci has shown, ideological hegemony is cultural control, one must wonder how this control was possible unless the landed upper class remained in political and economic control as well. This, of course, is equivalent to what Cash was trying to say.

When *Origins of the New South* is searched for empirical support for the claim that the middle class built the New South, the evidence is not there.[16] Woodward lacked support for his fundamental contention that New South leaders "were of middle-class, industrial, capitalist outlook, with little but a nominal connection with the old planter regime."[17] The only evidence he cited for who built the mills was Broadus Mitchell's impressionistic account of 1921, which Mitchell contradicted in a subsequent publication.[18] Disconfirming evidence was dismissed. For example, the numerous Confederate officers who headed southern businesses[19] were treated as token, showpiece employees of Yankee-owned enterprises. Woodward's stress is on an absentee-owned "colonial" economy that does not accord with my evidence.

As more studies are made of the class structures and industrial elites of New South states, I believe evidence will mount against the middle-class thesis. In addition to the evidence from North Carolina, other state studies begin to suggest this. Recent studies of Mississippi and Alabama by Salamon and Jonathan M. Wiener[20] demonstrate that the planters retained economic control in the Deep South. There is evidence against discontinuity in the Upper South as well. In his review essay, Hackney noted one "substantial contradiction" to Woodward's thesis in William Cooper's *The Conservative Regime: South Carolina, 1877–1890*. He writes, "According to William J. Cooper, Jr., the South Carolina Bourbons were not former Whigs nor were they the agents of northern capital. Far from being new men, they were the offspring of planters."[21] Hackney warns that South Carolina may simply be a "special case." Although Cooper's study somewhat lacks analytical depth, his empirical findings are compatible with my interpretation of North Carolina's development. Cooper found that South Carolina Bourbons "retained close ties with the land and with agriculture" and at the same time "welcomed industry to South Carolina and worked to create a favorable atmosphere for its growth." Similar to the pattern of North Carolina's conservative modernization, Cooper interprets South Carolina's conservatives as having "attempted to recreate what they considered the foundations of ante-bellum South Carolina."[22]

Further, indirect support for the continuity argument comes from studies of Virginia and Georgia. Raymond Pulley's study of Virginia Progressivism closely accords with my interpretation of North Carolina's reform movement during the Aycock administration. He concludes that the social reforms of the Progressive era thus went hand-in-hand with political consolidation in giving new life to Old Virginia. The educational and social reforms undertaken in Virginia between 1900 and 1910 were closely related to the political changes in the same period. School expansion, penal reform, and social work, like the franchise contraction and the primary system, were designed to promote the state's traditionalist order. Through preventive social work old family Virginians such as the Valentines and Munfords hoped to forestall racial and class conflict and encourage social peace.[23]

Finally, in a forthcoming restudy of the "power structure" of Atlanta, Georgia, Floyd Hunter has traced the origins of Atlanta's present economic elite back to the Civil War and beyond. He found, for example, that the family of R. W. Woodruff, currently president of Coca-Cola and at the apex of Atlanta's power structure, dates back in Georgia to the late 1820s, when the family owned a grist mill and "numerous other enterprises" before they entered textile manufacturing. Hunter concludes, "After having reviewed the material I had gathered on the history of Atlanta's leadership sector, the prevailing notion that the Civil War had caused widespread and chronic distress among the landowners and capitalists of the day seemed to me less credible."[24]

These studies suggest the value of a new approach to southern development. Studies by sociologists and historians have been constrained in the past by unilinear models of economic modernization, drawn from the English experience, that have tended to equate development with the rise of the middle class. In developing ideal type descriptions of three alternative routes to modernity—bourgeois, fascist, and communist revolutions—that nation-states have taken, Barrington Moore has greatly advanced sociological theory.[25] His work invites a fresh look at development histories.

Interesting patterns, as yet unexamined in the development literature, emerge when Moore's historical typology is combined with Immanuel Wallerstein's structural model of the capitalist world system. These patterns help to reconstruct the contexts in which the development of particular societies such as the American South has taken place. This theoretical synthesis reveals that history's first wave of industrialization—which has been mistaken by many scholars as the only way development is achieved—occurred slowly during the late eighteenth and early nineteenth centuries in the commercial "core" of the capitalist world, most notably in England under the auspices of the middle class. In making room for their revolutionary economic practices in a traditional world, this class extended the range of individual liberty and strengthened parliamentary democracy. A different kind of industrial development occurred in "semi-peripheral" regions of the world market late in the nineteenth century. Almost simultaneously southern planters and Prussian Junkers allied with nascent industry in their societies to impose change from above. Finally, a third phase of industrialization, even more rapid and authoritarian, has developed during the twentieth century following peasant revolutions in "peripheral" and "semi-peripheral" regions such as Russia and China.

Moore relates modes of surplus extraction and the relative strengths of social classes to the routes chosen by particular societies in the course of their development. His typology is not a predictive theory, although its explanatory power is enhanced when its starting point in surplus extraction is linked with world system analysis. His methodology reveals why Germany, for example, was more likely to have followed a fascist rather than a bourgeois path, but he does not deal directly with the question of why some societies, such as Spain or Portugal, hardly industrialize at all.[26]

Many historical conditions—demographic factors, structural locations in trade markets, capital availability, international conflict, political resources of leadership classes and the power of lower classes to resist, manufacturing base, and others all interact to influence whether or not agrarian societies modernize.[27] As we find that planters remained economically and politically dominant throughout all the southern states in the late nineteenth century, these are the historical variables that must be examined in each state to determine whether or not its planters were attracted to manufacturing.

North Carolina had a limited but significant antebellum industrial base. Demographically, it was the reverse of the Deep South with its small core of plantation counties and larger yeomen rim. The vast yeomen numbers represented a political threat to upper-class privilege, especially when they moved to unite with the black underclass, as they did during the Populist episode. Ultimately, the economics of agriculture and especially cotton production shaped the balance of these forces. When profitable cotton growing was endangered by price declines, especially in the Upper South, cotton manufacturing became more attractive. Planters-turned-industrialists sustained a local market for cotton and profited from its heightened value as a manufactured product, while all the hoopla about industrialization promised a way out for some of the bankrupt farmers and avoided rural revolution.

Indirect support for this argument is presented in Table 10.1, based in part on econometric data from Stephen DeCanio,[28] which reveals a positive correlation between (estimated) long-run (1883–1914) price elasticities for cotton growing and the per capita value added by manufacturing in ten southern states. It shows that the more vulnerable a state to drops in the price of cotton (as compared with other products), the greater its manufacturing activity. North Carolina ranked as the second most vulnerable state to drops in cotton prices. In contrast, Mississippi, with the second lowest price elasticity, could better weather price declines. DeCanio reports that the Deep South's comparative advantage in cotton growing relative to other crops was so great that it was economically irrational for planters there to do other than plant cotton. This factor, plus the labor needs of cotton production and the relatively small proportion of yeomen, no doubt disinclined Mississippi planters from promoting industry, unlike their peers in the Upper South.

The hallmark of conservative modernization is the preservation of the traditional agrarian social structure—the primary

Table 10.1. *Comparison of Estimated Long-Run Price Elasticities for Cotton Growing (1883–1914)*[1] *and Total Value Added by Manufacturing Per Capita (1890 and 1900),*[2] *for Ten Southern States*

	Estimated Price Elasticity	1880 Mfg. Value Added Per Capita (dollars)[3]	1900 Mfg. Value Added Per Capita (dollars)[4]
Tennessee	1.269	24.04	53.52
North Carolina	.778	14.36	50.12
Louisiana	.414	25.75	87.71
Arkansas	.364	8.42	34.46
Georgia	.326	23.63	48.12
South Carolina	.297	16.81	43.83
Florida	.278	20.58	69.64
Alabama	.247	10.74	44.15
Mississippi	.212	6.64	26.06
Texas	.183	13.02	39.17

1. Source: Stephen DeCanio, *Agriculture in the Postbellum South*, p. 260.
2. Source: *Twelfth Census of the United States, 1900*, Vol. 8, pp. 982–89.
3. Correlation coefficient between price elasticity and 1880 manufacturing value = .39.
4. Correlation coefficient between price elasticity and 1900 manufacturing value = .20.

source of the upper class's wealth and power—simultaneously with the sponsoring of industrial growth. This may, however, create insoluble long-run problems. If industrialization is thoroughgoing, the landlords may set in motion forces that undo agrarian dominance. On the other hand, if industrialization is not thoroughgoing, many of the benefits of industry are never experienced. This has perhaps been the situation in North Carolina, where the upper class successfully integrated textile manufacturing into the agrarian social structure, but the state industrialized without developing the buying power of its population by selling a partially finished product, cloth, to another region. As I suggested in the contrast with the situation in the tobacco industry, the state's only competitive advantage in textile manufacturing was cheap labor. This, and the preservation of nonwage agricultural labor, helped keep North Carolina in a dependent relationship with the rest of the American economy.

In a discussion of Japan entitled "The Fate of Paternalism in Modern Bourgeois Society," Genovese has examined the paradoxical nature of conservative modernization. He concludes that paternalistic relationships ultimately are incompatible with the logic of industrialism. Without accepting this contention altogether, I agree that "the relevant question centers on whether the older paternalism—the actual personal relationship of patron and client—can be sustained within a new economic system that is essentially bourgeois in its social relations."[29] The effects of conservative modernization, the legacy of paternalism, are still visible in North Carolina today, approximately one hundred years after the state's industrial take-off. Industrial paternalism has been sustained, but rural North Carolina has changed dramatically.

Agricultural modernization in the South has several sources. Evidence supports the planters' claim that industrialization would benefit North Carolina's depressed rural economy. Anthony Tang's study of economic development in the southern Piedmont demonstrates that industrial-urban development has helped to absorb underemployed farm labor. The effect has been substantial increases in farm income per worker without reductions in output.[30] Salutary effects of industrial growth have been compounded by state and federal agriculture reform programs.

North Carolina led the South in land reclamation with passage of a land drainage act in 1909. According to Tindall, this was "rationalized as a safety valve for the dispossessed" tenancy. The legislature also considered, but failed to pass, a program to encourage tenant land purchases. During the Depression, southern congressmen are said to have "hastened" to support federal crop limitations and price supports.[31] Federal programs prevented the collapse of southern agriculture during the Depression by subsidizing farmers and providing meager welfare relief for impoverished tenants. Although welfare payments allowed Deep South planters to keep a reserve labor supply on the land with minimal costs,[32] the long-run effects of reform encouraged modernization.

Urban-industrial labor demands, subsidized acreage reductions and price supports, shifts to less labor-intensive crops, and the attraction of northern cities to outmigrants from the rural South all have contributed to reductions in the rural work force and encouraged both mechanization and a shift from farm tenancy to wage labor.[33] In the first decade after World War II, the proportion of North Carolina's work force employed in agriculture declined from 42 percent to 29 percent.[34] In the decade from 1964 to 1974, tenant-operated farms declined from 27 percent of total farms to 12 percent. The proportion of total black farms operated by tenants declined even more sharply from 55 percent to 18 percent.[35]

Farm sizes in North Carolina have also been affected by these changes. The average farm in 1974 was 123 acres. A steady downward trend in farm sizes—from an average of 369 acres in 1850 to 101 acres in 1900 and to a low of 65 acres by 1930—was reversed after World War II.[36] The current pattern of land ownership in North Carolina has not been examined, but a trend toward more extensive corporate farming is evident. Four exceptionally large farms have been established in eastern North Carolina since 1970. The largest is the colossal First Colony Farms, which covers 375,000 acres and is expected to employ a thousand workers. This $200 million business is principally owned by North Carolina–born Malcolm McLean of New York. McLean, who built a large trucking firm in Winston-Salem, is a director of R. J. Reynolds Industries and of the Diamondhead Corporation, which owns the Pinehurst, North Carolina, resort.[37] This example suggests a continuing relationship between land ownership and industrial ownership in North Carolina that should be examined more closely.

Changes in agricultural organization are striking, but the continuities in North Carolina industry, where the effects of conservative modernization are still painfully obvious, are equally apparent. Luther Hodges's description in *Businessman in the Statehouse* of his years as governor reflects the legacy of the state's revolution from above. His career provides a benchmark for what has changed and what remains the same.

Hodges was born in Virginia in 1898, the year of North Carolina's white supremacy campaign. He was one of nine children of a tenant farmer who was forced off the land by declining tobacco prices and into a textile mill owned by the Moreheads, eight miles away in Spray, North Carolina. Hodges began working as an office boy in the mill at the age of twelve. After college he returned as personnel manager of the Leaksville-Spray area mills, by this time owned by Marshall Field and Company of Chicago. Eventually he left North Carolina, having become general manager of all the Marshall Field mills and vice-president of the company in 1943. In 1950, Hodges retired from the textile business. In 1952 he ran for lieutenant governor of North Carolina.

Hodges's career in the textile industry reveals changes in the industry structure—opportunities for upward mobility and absentee ownership. His actions as governor, described in two chapters of his autobiography,[38] reveal much about North Carolina's current political economy. In one chapter, appropriately entitled "Labor and Management, Law and Order," Hodges defended his use of state police and national guardsmen to end a textile strike at Henderson, North Carolina—an action he admits nearly cost him Senate confirmation as United States secretary of commerce in the Kennedy cabinet.

In the following chapter, he described the creation during his administration of the Research Triangle, a research and development complex centered near North Carolina, North Carolina State, and Duke universities. What could he do as governor, he asked rhetorically in his book, to raise per capita incomes—then forty-fourth out of forty-eight states—in North Carolina? To attract industry to the state, he lowered corporate taxes and advertised this fact in the *Wall Street Journal*. Although he did not say it, he could not attract high-wage industries to North Carolina because this might have meant unionization that would have threatened the delicate balance in the textile industry during a period of labor conflict. (It has been documented several times that textile mills use their power to keep high-wage industries out of their communities.[39]) Instead, he built the Research Triangle, a government-backed, privately financed project directed by business and university leaders, including several textile manufacturers. Called "the marriage of North Carolina's ideals for higher education and its hopes for material progress,"[40] the Triangle capitalized on previous educational investments—the political solution, as I have suggested, to an earlier period of unrest. High-wage industrial workers remained in the North, but management came South, a reversal of an earlier pattern of development.[41] By encouraging the research and development divisions of large corporations to locate at the Research Triangle Park, North Carolina finally began to acquire a politically safe, high-income middle class, which, via a revolution from above, the state had managed to industrialize without.[42]

The two policies described by Luther Hodges, labor control and state-sponsored economic development, are consistent with earlier observations that during the course of conservative modernization, the state is both an instrument of repression and of modernization. (This dual quality is what made the Aycock administration at the turn of the century difficult to comprehend.) In addition to its right-to-work laws and its tradition of "union-busting," the repressive aspect of government activity in North Carolina is also reflected in the state's judicial system. Despite the state's liberal image, this is the reason Angela Davis, speaking in Paris, called North Carolina "America's South Africa." A recent report shows that "although North Carolina has only an average crime rate, it locks more of its people behind state prison bars, proportionately, than any other state."[43] Despite the fact that North Carolina ranks thirty-fourth in the number of serious crimes committed, it has the highest ratio of prisoners to citizens (1:410) in the nation. California, by comparison, ranks first in the number of serious crimes committed but eleventh for its prisoner/citizen ratio (1:887). (Other southern states also have high prisoner/citizen ratios. Georgia ranks second, Florida ranks fifth, South Carolina ranks seventh, and Alabama ranks ninth nationally.) According to the report, North Carolina has the reputation of being one of the most conservative states in the United States in granting pardons and among the most severe in its penalties. One-third of all the prisoners on death row in the United States are in Raleigh's Central Prison.

Both the success and the failure of North Carolina's industrial revolution are reflected in current labor statistics. Although it ranks second among the fifty states for its percentage of nonagricultural work force in industry, North Carolina ranks last in its level of industrial earnings and its level of unionization. In a recent analysis of the gap between average earnings for gainful employment in the United States and the average in North Carolina, Emil Malizia points out that "many believe that this earnings gap can be explained by the assertions that: [1] North Carolina is a state that has a concentration of low wage industries [and 2] North Carolina workers are less productive than U.S. workers in general." Analyzing the effects of such factors as productivity differences, industrial composition, cost of living differences, and levels of unionization, Malizia finds, instead, that "North Carolina workers produce more output in return for a dollar's wage than do United States workers in the same industry" and that "North Carolina industries generally show rates of profit higher than comparable United States industries regardless of whether they are high profit or low profit industries nationwide." Malizia concludes that

> (1) The size of the earnings gaps in southern states represents a problem of major importance for people interested in economic justice. Practically all industries located in North Carolina tend to pay their workers less than in comparable industries outside the South. (2) The corporate sector is rewarded for paying lower wages in North Carolina by reaping higher profits. (3) The analysis of productivity does not justify paying North Carolina workers lower wages because of their productivity. (4) The degree of unionization positively influences the level of earnings.[44]

In an article entitled "Something Could Be Finer Than to Be in Carolina," Barbara Koeppel stresses the continuing efforts of state government to keep wages low and profits high in North

Carolina. Responding to an advertisement in *Forbes* boasting that "North Carolina has a commitment to provide the most favorable climate to industry that is possible," Koeppel claims, "When the industrial establishment feels particularly threatened, strong medicine is applied and the strike-breaking apparatus is marshaled for the attack." Recalling an unsuccessful strike in 1972, she reports:

> When bargaining proved fruitless, the [Communications Workers of America] called a strike which lasted almost seven months and ended in failure when intimidation and arrests took their eventual toll. Morale collapsed as the sheriff, local police, and state troopers moved into action. "They park their cars nearby, hover over the picket line, sport guns, and swing billy clubs. Arrests are made for the slightest infraction, or on trumped up charges, like 'excessive noise,'" [Wilbur Hobby, president of the North Carolina AFL-CIO] recalls. Thus, the strikers along with those already too frightened to join the picket line, are subdued; the next time, if there is one, they will be less likely to risk their jobs for nothing.[45]

North Carolina's persistent underdevelopment was illustrated recently in an interview in *The South*[46] with Kaguo Chiba, Japan's consul-general in Atlanta, who said that his country plans to concentrate much of its international investment in the South. Much of this will be in North Carolina, which produces one-fourth of the total U.S. textiles and currently is home for forty-four foreign textile manufacturers. Though we frequently hear that American industry cannot compete against cheap Japanese labor, in textiles, at least, the reverse seems to be true:

> We fought the southern textile industry for years, but couldn't get through the import quotas and tariffs. So now we are going to make our textiles here, using southern labor, southern materials, and Japanese machines.
>
> There are good reasons for us to come here. The South has the only resource of good labor left in the US. Southern labor is in fact cheaper to us than Japanese labor. The South

also has vast reserves of land and energy. This Japan does not have, and so we have had to limit our internal industrial growth. We are now permitting only "sophisticated" non-polluting industries like electronics to be built.

Older industries, like textiles, are being phased out in Japan and exported to other countries.

In chapter 3, I showed that there are important parallels between North Carolina and Japan in industrial relations and ideology, reflecting their common legacy of conservative modernization. Chiba hints at this when he says: "We find ourselves more welcome in the South than anywhere outside California. . . . Your way of life here is much closer to ours than in other parts of the US. Southerners conduct their business with courtesy, as do we."

Thus we see, at the core of southern history, patterns of political and economic domination that have persisted despite vast social change. No one would deny the varied faces of North Carolina and the South in 1900: there were planter-industrialists cultivating cotton with black and white tenant labor and building textile factories; there were impoverished yeomen farmers trying to keep their land, first with cooperatives and then with politics, while many among them slipped into tenancy or into the new mill villages; also there were tobacco manufacturers arising from local craft industries to the apex of national capitalist achievement and, alongside them, a new landless black proletariat in the bustling tobacco cities like Durham which they created; finally, there were the small-town businessmen and the middle-class reformers, among the latter especially educators and journalists, eager for progress that to them implied, among other things, greater opportunity and prestige for professionals. All these social worlds were lived in the South at the turn of the century according to their own internal principles, and yet they were located within a highly complex and interdependent class structure. Despite the new forces their social relations implied, all were shaped by the background dynamics of plantation agriculture. The old premises of the agrarian order and the old paternalist grammar were translated into new forms in the post-bellum South without destroying old institutional foundations. Profound as some of these changes were, when compared with the continuities of class and politics in the region, the New South of 1900 seems to us now, if not to its contemporaries, as hardly new at all.

Notes

Chapter 1

1. Hugh Lefler and Albert Newsome, *North Carolina* (1973), p. 520.
2. See Table 4.1.
3. *Compendium of the Tenth Census of 1880*, p. 396.
4. *Abstract of the Twelfth Census of 1900*, p. 350, and *Compendium of the Tenth Census*, p. 719.
5. V. O. Key, *Southern Politics*, p. 205.
6. Ibid., p. 206.
7. *The University Gazette* of the University of North Carolina, 4, no. 13 (6 August 1976): 3.
8. Joseph F. Steelman, "The Progressive Era in North Carolina, 1884–1917," p. ii.
9. J. Morgan Kousser, *The Shaping of Southern Politics*, p. 291.
10. Indicative of such theoretical developments that establish broad sociological approaches on the insights of stratification research by scholars such as Lenski and Moore are Randall Collins's *Conflict Sociology* and Anthony Giddens's *The Class Structure of the Advanced Societies*.
11. An exemplary introduction to and application of political-economic analysis is Daniel Chirot's *Social Change in a Peripheral Society*, an analysis of Wallachia, a Balkan colony, from 1250 to 1917.
12. Ibid., p. 2.
13. Taken together, Eugene Genovese's *The World the Slaveholders Made* and *Roll, Jordan, Roll* are perhaps the finest attempt to demonstrate the dialectical interplay among these factors in a concrete instance, that of the slave South.
14. C. Wright Mills, *The Sociological Imagination*.
15. The scope of this present analysis is unfortunately one-sided in that, for the most part, it focuses on highly visible, upper-status individuals to the exclusion of the mass of yeomen, tenants, and millhands whose role in North Carolina's development was equally important if ultimately less influential. The choice is a methodological one which I hope to remedy with subsequent research more attuned to this extremely neglected aspect of the social history of the South.

Chapter 2

1. Gunnar Myrdal, "The Drift Towards Regional Economic Inequalities in a Country"; Andre Gunder Frank, "The Development of

Underdevelopment"; Immanuel Wallerstein, "Dependence in an Interdependent World." The work of these scholars is representative of a perspective on underdevelopment known as "dependency theory," an alternative to cultural explanations of economic development that has become popular among students of Latin America. In *Latin America*, p. 2, Ronald Chilcote and Joel Edelstein compare these two models: "One suggests that the development of areas like Latin America will come about through outside influence and assistance; this explanation is embraced by the *diffusion model*. The second explanation, incorporated in the *dependency* model, views foreign penetration as the cause of underdevelopment in Latin America and implies that underdeveloped countries can develop only if both their internal structures and their relations with other nations undergo a complete change." Important formulations of the dependency model include Theotonio dos Santos, "The Structure of Dependence"; Susanne Bodenheimer, "Dependency and Imperialism"; Dale L. Johnson, "Dependence and the International System," pp. 71–111; and Osvald Sunkel, "Big Business and 'Dependencia.'"

2. Frank, "Underdevelopment," pp. 3–4.

3. For a brief overview see Immanual Wallerstein, "Three Paths of National Development in the Sixteenth Century," and for fuller treatment see his *The Modern World-System*.

4. Wallerstein, *Modern World-System*, pp. 349, 351. Also see Wallerstein, "Class-Formation in the Capitalist World-Economy."

5. Wallerstein, *Modern World-System*, p. 350.

6. See L. J. Zimmerman, *Poor Lands, Rich Lands*.

7. Wallerstein, *Modern World-System*, p. 302. In "Three Paths of National Development," pp. 91–92, Wallerstein has defined the structural positions in the world system as follows: "The core areas [in the sixteenth century] were the location of a complex variety of economic activities—mass market, industries such as there were (mainly textiles and shipbuilding), international and local commerce in the hands of an *indigenous* bourgeoisie, relatively advanced and complex forms of agriculture (both pastoralism and high-productivity tillage with a high component of medium-sized, yeoman-owned land). The peripheral areas, by contrast, were monocultural, with the cash crops being produced on large estates by coerced labor. The semiperipheral areas were in the process of deindustrializing." Wallerstein illustrates the operation of the world system by showing the interdependent roles of Poland (periphery), Venice (semiperiphery), and England (core) during the sixteenth century.

8. The exportation of the grosser forms of exploitation to foreign lands and peoples is one reason why western Europe modernized

democratically. This option did not exist during the nineteenth century when the South launched its industrial revolution, nor does it exist today for Third World nations whose own populations must bear the costs of rapid modernization. See Barrington Moore's *Social Origins of Dictatorship and Democracy* for a discussion of the relationship between exploitation and alternative routes to modernity.

9. Eugene Genovese, *The World the Slaveholders Made*, p. 23.

10. See Jerome Blum, "The Rise of Serfdom in Eastern Europe," and Daniel Chirot, "The Growth of the Market and Servile Labor Systems in Agriculture."

11. See also Wallerstein's account of this process as it occurred in Poland in "Three Paths of National Development," pp. 96–97.

12. Chirot, "Servile Labor Systems," p. 67.

13. George Beckford, *Persistent Poverty*.

14. This is the central thesis of dependency theory. Plantation economies are not the only societies in the Third World whose growth is limited and directed by external forces. Recent articles, especially those by Bodenheimer and Sunkel, focus on "dependent industrialization," which in Latin America is increasingly dominated by multinational corporations and geared to the needs of external, developed economies.

15. See Andre Gunder Frank, "Economic Dependence, Class Structure, and Underdevelopment Policy."

16. Genovese, *World Slaveholders Made*, p. 11.

17. Beckford, *Persistent Poverty*, pp. 33–34. Italics added.

18. See Beckford, *Persistent Poverty*, and Edgar Thompson, *Plantation Societies, Race Relations and the South*.

19. Beckford, *Persistent Poverty*, pp. 183–86.

20. Douglass North, "Agriculture in Regional Economic Growth," p. 951.

21. Santos, "The Structure of Dependence," p. 231.

22. Myrdal, "Regional Economic Inequalities," p. 389.

23. Immanuel Wallerstein, "The Rise and Future Demise of the World Capitalist System," pp. 387–417.

24. It seems, however, that there are limits on their growth potential. See Wallerstein, "Dependence in an Interdependent World," pp. 1–26.

25. This pattern of growth is outlined in North, "Agriculture," pp. 949–50.

26. As North, ibid., p. 941, notes, "To the extent that a region's income directly flows out in the purchase of goods and services rather than having a regional multiplier-acceleration effect, then it is inducing growth elsewhere, but reaping few of the benefits of increased income from the export sector itself."

27. Paul Baran, "On the Political Economy of Backwardness," p. 293.

28. See Andre Gunder Frank's discussion of "bourgeois nationalism" in Latin America in his "Economic Dependence," pp. 39–45. Also see Bodenheimer, "Dependency and Imperialism."

29. For information on Japanese modernization see Moore, *Social Origins*, pp. 228–313, and Thomas C. Smith, *The Agrarian Origins of Modern Japan*.

30. The use of state power in the world periphery to counter market forces parallels mercantilist policies in the core states. See Dudley Seers, "The Stages of Growth of a Primary Producer in the Middle of the Twentieth Century." For an empirical demonstration that withdrawal is sometimes a viable development strategy even in very small, backward societies, see Lawrence Busch, "Patterns of Dependence," who compares the more equitable economic growth of Guinea, which broke out of its dependency on France, with the Ivory Coast, which has not despite political independence. Growth in the Ivory Coast, although contributing to a higher GNP than in Guinea, nonetheless continues to benefit largely the metropolitan enclave and especially its French population. Richard Rubinson, "The World-Economy and the Distribution of Income within States," pp. 638–59, explains intersocietal differences in inequality as a consequence of the relation of states to the world economy. His cross-sectional regression analysis shows the effects of indicators of state strength, direct foreign financial control, and dependence on external markets on the degrees of inequality.

31. Baran, "Backwardness," p. 297. In the following chapters I will test this assertion by asking what role if any the "keepers of the past" had in North Carolina's dramatic industrial revolution that occurred after the devastation of the Civil War.

32. See especially Charles Wagley, "Plantation America."

33. Thompson, *Plantation Societies*, p. 221.

34. Beckford, *Persistent Poverty*, pp. 54–55.

35. See R. T. Smith, "Social Stratification, Cultural Pluralism, and Integration in West Indian Societies."

36. Beckford, *Persistent Poverty*, p. 204.

37. Thompson, *Plantation Societies*, p. 116.

38. The following paragraphs are principally an exposition of Genovese's interpretation. His works include *The Political Economy of Slavery*, *The World the Slaveholders Made*, and *Roll, Jordan, Roll*.

39. Genovese, *Political Economy*, p. 23.

40. Ibid., pp. 181, 21. The last phrase is borrowed from Paul Baran.

41. Ibid., p. 165.

42. Quoted in ibid., p. 173.

43. Ibid., p. 20.

44. See especially Baran, "Backwardness," p. 289.

45. Robert Fogel and Stanley Engerman, *Time on the Cross*, pp. 70, 196. The investment return from New England textiles, for comparison, was 10.1 percent between 1848 and 1853.

46. Fogel and Engerman's method of estimating profitability and relative efficiency of southern agriculture has been challenged by other econometricians who believe they present a falsely sanguine view of the cotton economy. See especially Paul David and Peter Temin, "Slavery," and Gavin Wright, "Prosperity, Progress, and American Slavery."

47. Fogel and Engerman, *Time on the Cross*, pp. 253–54.

48. Ibid., pp. 71, 255.

49. David and Temin, "Slavery," pp. 42–43.

50. Genovese, *Political Economy*, p. 187. Genovese adds that "for individual planters, however, investments in industry usually formed a minor interest, rarely large enough to influence significantly their social outlook." It is interesting in this connection to note that proslavery advocates such as George Fitzhugh were *not* anti-industry. (See my discussion of Fitzhugh in chapter 6.)

51. Diffee Standard and Richard Griffin, "The Cotton Textile Industry in Antebellum North Carolina," pp. 24–25.

52. Wallerstein, "Rise and Future Demise," pp. 399–400.

53. Gavin Wright, "Prosperity, Progress, and American Slavery," pp. 308, 304.

Chapter 3

1. C. Vann Woodward, *Origins of the New South, 1877–1913*, especially pp. 291–321.

2. As does C. Vann Woodward, Genovese, in *The Political Economy of Slavery*, p. 37, claims that the "colonial" status of the South did not end with the Civil War and emancipation. Its "colonial dependence on the British and Northern markets did not end when slavery ended. Sharecropping and tenancy produced similar results. After the Civil War, the colonial bondage of the economy was preserved but the South's political independence was lost."

3. Douglass C. North, "Agriculture in Regional Economic Growth," p. 948.

4. Thomas C. Cochran and William Miller, *The Age of Enterprise*, p. 34.

5. Quoted in Hugh Lefler, ed., *North Carolina History Told by Contemporaries*, pp. 251–55.

6. North, "Agriculture," p. 949.

7. These themes of concern are reported in Clarence Danhof, "Thoughts on the South's Economic Problems."

8. Robert Fogel and Stanley Engerman, *Time on the Cross*, p. 251.

9. Gavin Wright, "Prosperity, Progress, and American Slavery," p. 329.

10. See H. H. Winsborough, "The Changing Regional Character of the South."

11. According to Fogel and Engerman, *Time on the Cross*, p. 247, per capita income in the South was also 69 percent of the national average in 1840.

12. George B. Tindall, "The South Pits Itself against History as It Rises Once Again."

13. See 1970 United States Department of Labor report, *State Economic and Social Indicators*, especially pp. 16, 30, and 40.

14. See J. L. Spengler, "Southern Economic Trends and Prospects."

15. Fogel and Engerman, *Time on the Cross*, p. 249.

16. Woodward, *Origins*, p. 294.

17. Danhof, "Thoughts on the South's Economic Problems," especially pp. 44–51.

18. Howard Odum, *Southern Regions of the United States*, pp. 219 and 461.

19. Rupert Vance, *Human Geography of the South*, pp. 467–81.

20. Pablo Gonzales Casonova, "Internal Colonialism and National Development," pp. 27–37.

21. William Appleman Williams, "The Vicious Circle of American Imperialism." The sociological literature on metropolitan dominance also shares this view. See Rupert Vance and Sara Sutker, "Metropolitan Dominance and Integration."

22. Geoffrey Faux, "Colonial New England," p. 17; Lee Webb, "Colonialism and Underdevelopment in Vermont," pp. 29–33. My thanks to David Walls—whose paper "Central Appalachia" is an excellent discussion of the literature on internal colonialism—for showing me these applications of the colonial model.

23. Michael Hechter, "Regional Inequality and National Integration," p. 99. See also Hechter's *Internal Colonialism*.

24. Hechter, *Internal Colonialism*, p. 161. Hechter's analysis grew from Wallerstein's suggestion that "core states [of the world economy] because of their complex internal division of labor begin to reflect the pattern of the system as a whole." Wallerstein showed that as early as the sixteenth century, England was well on its way to becoming Britain, "which would have regional homogeneity within a relative heterogeneity for the nation as a whole." See Immanuel Wallerstein, *The Modern World-System*, p. 354.

25. Hechter, *Internal Colonialism*, p. 33.

26. Pierre van den Berghe, "Education, Class and Ethnicity in Southern Peru." Only the native American population in the United States meets these criteria for an internal colony. Blacks and women have also been described as "colonized" groups, but here the term has been so weakened that it means no more than exploitation.

27. On this matter, Barrington Moore, in *Social Origins of Dictatorship and Democracy*, pp. 152–53, writes, "Labor-repressive agricultural systems, and plantation slavery in particular, are political obstacles to a *particular kind* of capitalism . . . competitive democratic capitalism. . . . Slavery was a threat and an obstacle to a society that was indeed the heir of the Puritan, American, and French Revolutions. Southern society was based firmly on hereditary status as the basis of human worth. With the West, the North, though in the process of change, was still committed to notions of equal opportunity. In both, the ideals were reflections of economic arrangements that gave them much of their appeal and force. Within the same political unit it was, I think, inherently impossible to establish political and social institutions that would satisfy both." Speculating about the consequences if the South had won the Civil War, Moore adds that "then the United States would have been in a position of some modernizing countries today, with a latifundia economy, a dominant antidemocratic aristocracy, and a weak and dependent commercial and industrial class, unable and unwilling to push forward toward political democracy."

28. William Nicholls, *Southern Tradition and Regional Progress*, pp. ix, 15.

29. Moore, *Social Origins*, p. 486.

30. Lester Salamon, *Social Origins of Mississippi Backwardness*. No page citations are available at this time for Salamon's text, but I was very fortunate to have access to the author's manuscript. An earlier version of this work is available as a Harvard University dissertation.

31. Salamon has in mind the *politically* closed society as described by James Silver, in *Mississippi*, not the sort of economic closure described in chap. 2.

32. Moore, *Social Origins*, p. 418.

33. Ibid., especially pp. 433–52.

34. Paul Baran, "On the Political Economy of Backwardness," p. 300.

35. Sheldon Hackney, *"Origins of the New South* in Retrospect," p. 191.

36. Woodward, *Origins*, pp. 29, 140.

37. Glenn Gilman, *Human Relations in the Industrial Southeast*, pp. 69–70.

38. Liston Pope, *Millhands and Preachers*, p. 15.

39. Melton McLaurin, *Paternalism and Protest*, pp. 42–43.

40. Hackney, *"Origins,"* p. 191.

41. Genovese, *Political Economy,* p. 159.

42. Leonard Reissman, "Social Development and the American South," pp. 105–6. Italics added.

43. See Glaucio Soares, "Economic Development and Class Structure," pp. 198–99.

44. Reissman, "Social Development," p. 107.

Chapter 4

1. Neal R. Peirce, *The Border South States,* p. 117.

2. Robert Winston, "North Carolina," p. 731.

3. Robert Wilson, *Southern Exposure,* p. 180.

4. Guion Johnson, "Social Characteristics of Ante-Bellum North Carolina," p. 156.

5. Hugh Lefler and Albert Newsome, *North Carolina* (1973), p. 314.

6. See Roland B. Eutsler, "The Cape Fear and Yadkin Valley Railroad," pp. 427–41, for a picture of early transportation limits.

7. Lefler and Newsome, *North Carolina* (1973), p. 319.

8. Ibid., p. 324.

9. North Carolina voted not to secede, but the likelihood of becoming a battleground after Virginia's and South Carolina's secession forced the opposite action. Sadly, North Carolina's poor, nonslaveholding yeomen made good cannon fodder. North Carolina lost more dead in the Civil War than any other southern state.

10. Comparisons with Virginia are misleading because of the 1860 census's inclusion of the area that soon became West Virginia, a region of small farms.

11. For a good discussion of North Carolina's subregions see Samuel H. Hobbs, Jr., *North Carolina,* pp. 67–88.

12. See especially V. O. Key, *Southern Politics,* pp. 215–18.

13. Johnson, *Ante-Bellum North Carolina,* p. 58.

14. In Alabama, in 1860, there were 696 farms over 1,000 acres each out of a total of 55,128 farms, whereas there were only 311 such farms in North Carolina out of a total of 75,205 farms (*Eighth Census,* Vol. 2, p. 210).

15. Using the official census classification of planters as farmers owning at least twenty slaves, a little less than 6 percent of the Old South's white population were planters.

16. Lefler and Newsome, *North Carolina* (1973), p. 323.

17. Gail O'Brien, "A Study of Power and Influence in Mecklenburg County, 1844–1854."

18. Gail O'Brien, "War and Social Change."

19. Harriet Herring, "Early Industrial Development in the South," p. 2.

20. Lance Davis et al., *American Economic Growth,* p. 441.

21. Liston Pope, *Millhands and Preachers*, p. 4.
22. Holland Thompson, *The New South*; Broadus Mitchell, *The Rise of Cotton Mills in the South*.
23. Broadus Mitchell, "Growth of Manufactures in the South," pp. 22, 23.
24. Holland Thompson, "The Civil War and Social and Economic Changes," pp. 17, 20.
25. Mitchell, "Growth of Manufactures," p. 24.
26. Herbert Collins, "The Idea of a Cotton Textile Industry in the South, 1870–1890," p. 358.
27. These instances are reported in Richard Griffin, "Reconstruction of the North Carolina Textile Industry, 1865–1885," pp. 44–47.
28. C. Vann Woodward, *Origins of the New South, 1877–1913*, p. 133.
29. Mitchell, "Growth of Manufactures," pp. 24–25.
30. Herring, "Early Industrial Development," pp. 1–4.
31. Ibid., p. 4.
32. Ibid., p. 7.
33. Ibid., p. 5.
34. Diffee Standard and Richard Griffin, "The Cotton Textile Industry in Antebellum North Carolina," pp. 21, 33.
35. Ibid., p. 22.
36. Herring, "Early Industrial Development," p. 2.
37. Standard and Griffin, "Cotton Textile Industry," pp. 23–26.
38. Herring, "Early Industrial Development," pp. 9, 8. Italics added.
39. Ibid., p. 8.
40. Griffin, "Reconstruction," p. 34.
41. Herring, "Early Industrial Development," p. 1.
42. J. Carlyle Sitterson, "Business Leaders in Post–Civil War North Carolina, 1865–1900," p. 113.
43. Dan Lacy, "The Beginnings of Industrialism in North Carolina, 1865–1900," p. 74.
44. Harry Boyte, "The Textile Industry," p. 11.
45. Sitterson, "Business Leaders," pp. 114–15.
46. Griffin, "Reconstruction," p. 34.
47. Standard and Griffin, "Cotton Textile Industry," p. 160.
48. Griffin, "Reconstruction," pp. 51–53.
49. Harry M. Douty, "The North Carolina Industrial Worker, 1880–1930," pp. 8–9.
50. I am most grateful to William Powell for introducing me to Branson's directories as a convenient information source.
51. Griffin, "Reconstruction," pp. 48–49.
52. Lester Salamon, *Social Origins of Mississippi Backwardness*.
53. Biographical profiles have been drawn from information in Jerome Dowd, *Sketches of Prominent Living North Carolinians*, and from Volume 6 of *North Carolina Biography* (no author given).

54. Ben Lemert, *The Cotton Textile Industry of the Southern Appalachian Piedmont*, pp. 31–45.

55. Lefler and Newsome, *North Carolina* (1973), p. 524.

56. Douty, "North Carolina Worker," p. 12.

Chapter 5

1. Paul Gaston, "The 'New South,'" p. 322.

2. Henry Grady, "Cotton and Its Kingdom," pp. 719, 721.

3. Quoted in Paul Gaston, *The New South Creed*, p. 66.

4. Quoted in Paul H. Buck, *The Road to Reunion, 1865–1900*, p. 145.

5. Another point to which New South advocates added their share of confusion is the extent of northern investments in southern business. Gaston notes that in 1883, Grady "announced that 'northern capital has been coming into the South very rapidly for several years,' but the next year he lamented that 'capital has been kept out of the South by prejudice.'" See Gaston, *New South Creed*, p. 71.

6. Buck, *Road to Reunion*, p. 145.

7. Grady, "Cotton," p. 724.

8. Hugh Lefler and Albert Newsome, *North Carolina* (1973), pp. 576–77, 522.

9. Michael Schwartz, *Radical Protest and Social Structure*, pp. 80–88.

10. *Twelfth Census*, Vol. 5, pp. 310–11.

11. Unless otherwise indicated, biographical information is from Samuel A. Ashe, ed., *Biographical History of North Carolina*.

12. Frank Parkin, *Class Inequality and Political Order*, p. 13.

13. Burton Alva Konkle, *John Motley Morehead and the Development of North Carolina, 1796–1866*, pp. 127 and 195. Konkle traces the Moreheads in America back to the "son of a distinguished London and Edinburgh merchant and colonizer" who came to Virginia in 1630 (p. 2). The distinguished Scottish family is said to have been celebrated in the balladry of Sir Walter Scott.

14. Kemp P. Battle, "James Smith Battle," p. 14.

15. Ibid., p. 16.

16. Charles Richard Sanders, *The Cameron Plantation of Central North Carolina*, p. 1.

17. Samuel Ashe, "Duncan Cameron," p. 45.

18. Sanders, *Cameron Plantation*, p. 6.

19. Cameron may even have been the single largest slaveholder in the South. Herbert Gutman uses Cameron's plantation records in his analysis of *The Black Family in Slavery and Freedom, 1750–1925*, pp. 169–80.

20. Sanders, *Cameron Plantation*, p. 6.

21. Ibid., p. 7.

22. Samuel A. Ashe, "Paul Carrington Cameron," p. 49.

23. See the Cameron Family Papers, no. 133, housed in the Southern Historical Collection of The University of North Carolina at Chapel Hill.

24. Sanders, *Cameron Plantation*, p. 8.

25. Ibid., p. 11.

26. Buck, *Road to Reunion*.

27. Ibid., p. 300.

28. *Twelfth Census of Manufactures*, 1900, Part III, "Special Report on Selected Industries," p. 25.

29. Buck, *Road to Reunion*, pp. 155, 156.

30. George Edwards, "Development of American Security Capitalism," p. 124.

31. Thomas Cochran and William Miller, *The Age of Enterprise*, p. 191. Also see Edwards, "American Security Capitalism," pp. 124–25.

32. Buck, *Road to Reunion*, p. 156.

33. Lefler and Newsome, *North Carolina* (1973), p. 517.

34. Glimpses of North Carolina's railroad history can be found in Peter S. McGuire, "The Seaboard Air Line," and in Roland B. Eutsler, "The Cape Fear and Yadkin Valley Railroad." C. K. Brown, "The Southern Railway Security Company," describes an abortive attempt by the Pennsylvania Railroad to secure control of southern railroads that failed in the Panic of 1873 but presaged the growth of the Southern and Atlantic Coast Lines. John F. Stover's *The Railroads of the South, 1865–1900*, is a general discussion of the role of northern finance in southern railroads.

35. C. Vann Woodward, *Origins of the New South, 1877–1913*, pp. 291–92.

36. Ibid., p. 311.

Chapter 6

1. Barrington Moore, *Social Origins of Dictatorship and Democracy*, pp. 438, 433–52.

2. Thomas C. Smith, *The Agrarian Origins of Modern Japan*, pp. 201–13.

3. Moore, *Social Origins*, p. 434.

4. Robert Cole, *Japanese Blue Collar*, pp. 271–72.

5. Moore, *Social Origins*, p. 436.

6. Alan Palmer, *Bismarck*, p. 1.

7. Theodore S. Hamerow, *Restoration, Revolution, Reaction*, p. 51.

8. Erich Eyck, *Bismarck and the German Empire*, p. 259.

9. Although Bismarck had both industrial and agricultural investments, the bulk of his personal wealth came from vast timber holdings in Prussia that were greatly enhanced because the tariff included lumber imports. See Palmer, *Bismarck*, p. 204.

10. Moore, *Social Origins*, pp. 440, 442.

11. See Reinhard Bendix, *Nation Building and Citizenship*, pp. 66–126.

12. Immanuel Wallerstein, *The Modern World-System*, p. 351.

13. The South's ambivalence toward industry, which Eugene Genovese analyzed, was overcome as the region prepared for war. I suspect that the workings of the South's revolution from above can be seen clearly in the workings of the Confederacy and the wartime activities of the state. On this see Genovese's discussion of the role of the southern industrialists in the war, pp. 201–6, in *The Political Economy of Slavery*.

14. Reinhard Bendix, "Tradition and Modernity Reconsidered," pp. 292–346.

15. Without knowing of my interest in comparing North Carolina's labor relations with those of Germany and Japan, Donald Roy, an expert in southern labor research, suggested that I read Robert Cole's *Japanese Blue Collar* to get an understanding of southern labor relations. The parallels between Japanese and southern industrial relations are striking. Such patterns are a legacy of the conservative modernization both societies experienced.

16. C. Vann Woodward, *Origins of the New South, 1877–1913*, p. 150.

17. Harriet Herring, "Early Industrial Development in the South," p. 8.

18. Eugene Genovese, *The Political Economy of Slavery*, pp. 13, 30–31.

19. Broadus Mitchell and George Mitchell, *The Industrial Revolution in the South*, p. 205.

20. W. J. Cash, *The Mind of the South*, p. 205.

21. Mitchell and Mitchell, *Industrial Revolution*, pp. 122–23.

22. Herring, "Early Industrial Development," pp. 8–9.

23. Mitchell and Mitchell, *Industrial Revolution*, p. 11. Also see Harriet Herring's *Welfare Work in Mill Villages* for general background.

24. Melton McLaurin, *Paternalism and Protest*, pp. 38–39.

25. Thomas Cochran and William Miller, *The Age of Enterprise*, p. 72.

26. Cole, *Japanese Blue Collar*, p. 175.

27. See Arthur M. Whitehill and Shin'ichi Takezawa, *Cultural Values in Management-Worker Relations*, pp. 101–10. An interesting parallel in survey research is Robert Blauner's finding that in comparison with other American workers, southern textile workers were much *less* "alienated" than one would theoretically expect from the nature of their job tasks. Blauner interpreted this surprising finding as an effect of the social cohesion in southern mill villages. See Robert Blauner, *Alienation and Freedom*, pp. 58–88.

28. Cole, *Japanese Blue Collar*, p. 7.
29. Ibid., p. 271.
30. Ibid., 174, 173.
31. Mitchell and Mitchell, *Industrial Revolution*, p. 247.
32. Ibid., p. 100.
33. Maxcy L. John, "Mark Morgan," p. 287.
34. Glenn Gilman, *Human Relations in the Industrial Southeast*, p. 144.
35. Gilman rejects Cash's argument that the plantation provided the model for these social relationships. Instead, he claims that they reflect the personalistic orientation of the folk society of the Carolina yeomanry, the democratic ethos of the frontier. Howard Odum made the same arguments in his *Way of the South*, pp. 19–21.
36. Cash, *Mind of the South*, p. 217.
37. Cole, *Japanese Blue Collar*, p. 175.
38. Harry Boyte, "The Textile Industry," p. 23.
39. See especially ibid., and McLaurin, *Paternalism and Protest*, p. 67. The latter argues that "extreme individualism, lack of education, and deep racial prejudices, all heritages of the Old South, seriously hampered the development of a traditional economic class consciousness among southern mill workers." Labor militancy in otherwise culturally similar southern coalfields shows that these are not sufficient conditions for explaining the absence of occupational consciousness among textile workers.
40. The social history of Appalachian coal towns has been as much, or even more, neglected as has the history of Piedmont mill villages. An excellent introduction to their history is Ron Eller's "Coal, Culture, and Community." An interest in the similarities and differences between mining and mill villages in the South was a principal motivating factor for my doing this study and represents the next stage of my research.
41. For an introduction to this subject, see Theodore Dreiser, ed., *Harlan Miners Speak*.
42. Rupert Vance, *Human Geography of the South*, pp. 291–98.
43. A University of Pittsburgh dissertation nearing completion by Richard Simon on the economic history of the West Virginia coalfields promises to contribute a great deal to our understanding of this portion of southern economic development.
44. Also see John Foster, *Class Struggle and the Industrial Revolution*, for an exemplary study of a textile community (Oldham) in England, where members of a cohesive craft community fought mechanization to prevent their loss of control over the work process. These workers achieved a heightened class consciousness during their struggles very

much unlike that of most southern workers in the American textile industry.

45. This is the central argument of Harry Braverman, *Labor and Monopoly Capital*.

46. Ben Lemert, *The Cotton Textile Industry of the Southern Appalachian Piedmont*, especially pp. 31–45.

47. McLaurin, *Paternalism and Protest*, pp. 157–61.

48. More research is needed on the specific conditions of conflict in the textile industry.

49. Harry M. Douty, "The North Carolina Industrial Worker, 1880–1930," p. 81.

50. Ibid., p. 61; McLaurin, *Paternalism and Protest*, p. 59.

51. Boyte, "Textile Industry," p. 32.

52. Mitchell and Mitchell, *Industrial Revolution*, p. 33.

53. The phrase is from the title of Thomas Tippett's account of the Gastonia strike.

54. Liston Pope, *Millhands and Preachers*, p. 231.

55. See Dell Bush Johannesin, "Development of Labor Law in North Carolina."

56. Luther Hodges, *Businessman in the Statehouse*, pp. 224–50.

57. McLaurin, *Paternalism and Protest*, pp. 65, 63, and 64.

58. The development of furniture manufacturing in western North Carolina during the 1890s appears also to have been an exception to the pattern of planter sponsorship. Early developers of the industry included local merchants, lumbermen, and northern furniture makers. Since the initial construction of small furniture factories required far less capital than was necessary for building textile mills, these represented opportunities for small, local businessmen. See David Thomas, "Early History of the North Carolina Furniture Industry, 1880–1921."

59. Nannie May Tilley, *The Bright-Tobacco Industry*, pp. 91 and 89–92.

60. See ibid., pp. 489–544, for a history of small-scale manufacturing from 1865 to 1885.

61. John Samuel Ezell, *The South since 1865*, pp. 144–48.

62. Alfred Chandler, "The Beginnings of 'Big Business' in American Industry," pp. 79–101.

63. See John David Rice, "The Negro Tobacco Worker and His Union in Durham, North Carolina," especially chap. 2.

64. Harriet Herring, *The Southern Industry and Regional Development*, p. 11.

65. Tilley, *Tobacco*, pp. 634–43, describes the extensive investments of tobacco manufacturers in other North Carolina industries. According to the United States census of manufacturing, the total value of manufactured products in North Carolina amounted to $94,919,633 in 1900.

Of this total, textile products contributed $28,372,798 and tobacco products contributed $13,620,816.

66. Rice, "Tobacco Worker," pp. 83, 128.

67. Reavis Cox, *Competition in the American Tobacco Industry, 1911–1932,* quoted in Rice, "Tobacco Worker," p. 14.

68. Rice, "Tobacco Worker," p. 21.

69. Ibid., p. 62.

70. Pope, *Millhands and Preachers,* p. 12; Hyland Lewis, *Blackways of Kent,* p. 114.

71. Rice, "Tobacco Worker," pp. 62, 22.

72. Robert F. Durden, *The Dukes of Durham, 1865–1929,* p. 127.

73. Walter B. Weare, *Black Business in the New South,* pp. 40–41.

74. Durden, *Dukes,* p. 147.

75. Weare, *Black Business,* p. 20.

76. Quoted in Rice, "Tobacco Worker," p. 34.

77. E. Franklin Frazier, "Durham," p. 333.

78. Robert Cannon, "The Organization and Growth of Black Political Participation in Durham, North Carolina, 1933–1958," p. ii.

79. Bill Phillips, "Piedmont Country Blues," p. 56. For a more extensive treatment of the Piedmont blues see Bruce Bastin, *Crying for the Carolines.*

80. Lewis, *Kent,* p. 114.

81. Carl N. Degler, *The Other South,* p. 336.

82. Hugh Lefler and Albert Newsome, *North Carolina* (1973), pp. 513 and 511.

83. Ezell, *The South,* p. 388.

84. Reinhard Bendix, *Work and Authority in Industry,* pp. 438, 445.

85. Moore, *Social Origins,* p. 447.

86. Cole, *Japanese Blue Collar,* p. 272.

87. Paul Gaston, "The 'New South,'" p. 326.

88. Bendix, *Work and Authority,* p. 20.

89. C. B. Macpherson, *The Political Theory of Possessive Individualism,* p. 3.

90. Bendix, *Work and Authority,* p. 11.

91. Gaston, "The 'New South,'" pp. 316–17.

92. McLaurin, *Paternalism and Protest,* p. 44.

93. Woodward, *Origins,* p. 148. Actually, Tompkins did not oppose all forms of regulation although he did oppose limits on the length of the work week and on child labor in the textile industry. In "The Real Grievances against the Railroads," he advocated federal rather than state regulations on interstate railroad traffic, a position favored by many railroad leaders who wished to eliminate cutthroat competition.

On the latter point see Gabriel Kolko, *Railroads and Regulation, 1877–1916.*

94. Paul Gaston, *The New South Creed*, pp. 6–7.

95. Quoted in Paul H. Buck, *The Road to Reunion, 1865–1900*, p. 173.

96. Gaston, *Creed*, p. 184.

97. A good study of William Gregg is Ernest McPherson Lander, Jr., *The Textile Industry in Antebellum South Carolina.*

98. Howard B. Clay, "Daniel Augustus Tompkins," p. 60.

99. Boyte, "Textile Industry," p. 5.

100. Quoted in Gilman, *Human Relations*, pp. 81–82.

101. Mitchell and Mitchell, *Industrial Revolution*, p. 34.

102. Gilman, *Human Relations*, p. 88.

103. Woodward, *Origins*, p. 133.

104. E. P. Thompson, *The Making of the English Working Class*, p. 445.

105. See Genovese, *Political Economy*, pp. 157–80.

106. Gaston, *Creed*, p. 20.

107. Fitzhugh's principal works include *Sociology for the South* and *Cannibals All!* Interesting secondary sources are Eugene Genovese, "The Logical Outcome of the Slaveholders' Philosophy: An Exposition, Interpretation, and Critique of the Social Thought of George Fitzhugh of Port Royal, Virginia," in *The World the Slaveholders Made*, pp. 118–244, and C. Vann Woodward, "A Southern War against Capitalism" in *American Counterpoint*, pp. 107–39.

108. Woodward, *Counterpoint*, p. 117.

109. Ibid., pp. 134–35.

110. Harvey Wish, *George Fitzhugh*, p. viii, quoted in Genovese, *World Slaveholders Made*, p. 232.

111. Woodward, *Counterpoint*, p. 118.

112. Ibid., p. 110.

113. Several of Fitzhugh's articles appeared in *DeBow's Review* as late as the 1880s. *DeBow's Review* reflected the philosophy of conservative modernization, advocating that industrial development be grafted onto a white supremacist agrarian order. Gaston cites a typical article in *DeBow's Review* by an author who called on southern legislatures to appropriate money for cotton manufacturing, arguing that "the state must [either] build a poor-house and a prison, or a cotton factory, in every county or parish" (Gaston, *Creed*, p. 26).

114. See McLaurin, *Paternalism and Protest*, p. 30, for evidence of high profits in cotton manufacturing, much of which were used to finance further industrial expansion.

Chapter 7

1. V. O. Key, *Southern Politics*, pp. 205, 211.

2. Glenn Gilman, *Human Relations in the Industrial Southeast*, pp. 48–49, 149.

3. Ibid., p. 49.

4. Hugh Lefler and Albert Newsome, *North Carolina* (1973), p. 570.

5. S. N. Eisenstadt, *The Political System of Empires.*

6. S. P. Huntington, *Political Order of Changing Societies.*

7. Randall Collins, *Conflict Sociology,* p. 350.

8. Lucien Pye, "The Concept of Political Development," p. 50.

9. Lester Seligman, "Elite Recruitment and Political Development," p. 240.

10. Lester Salamon, "Leadership and Modernization," pp. 615–16.

11. In using the term "modern," I do not intend to commit myself to the simplistic traditional-modern dichotomy that underlies so much of sociological theory or to subscribe to the values implicit in this distinction. It is merely convenient for purposes of organizing the discussion that follows.

12. Sheldon Hackney, *Populism to Progressivism in Alabama,* p. 329.

13. Hugh Lefler and Albert Newsome, *North Carolina: History, Geography, Government,* p. 356.

14. Ibid., p. 550.

15. Ibid., p. 562.

16. Key, *Southern Politics,* p. 208.

17. Public school textbooks are a fascinating data source. They reveal today's political socialization as well as indicating the "presentation of self" with which political leaders feel most comfortable. Hugh Lefler has been North Carolina's "official" historian in this sense. His interpretations have prevailed at both the public school and college levels. Some of North Carolina's historians, although I believe not Lefler, have been socially and familially connected with important political leaders. J. G. de R. Hamilton was from a prominent old North Carolina family. He became a principal in the Wilmington public schools shortly after the Wilmington race riot that brutally restored white supremacy to that city's politics. R. D. W. Connor, another important historian who also wrote of the period under investigation, was the son of the Speaker of the House of the North Carolina General Assembly, one of the principal architects of the disfranchisement laws of 1900. The history department at Chapel Hill was established by Kemp P. Battle.

18. Lefler and Newsome, *North Carolina: History, Geography, Government,* p. 358.

19. J. Morgan Kousser, *The Shaping of Southern Politics,* pp. 185–87.

20. Ibid., p. 195.

21. For a discussion of the concept of critical elections see Walter Dean Birnham, *Critical Elections and the Mainsprings of American Politics.*

22. Hackney, *Populism to Progressivism,* p. 72. Hackney's research has been influential in correcting the view that Progressivism was not simply Populism that had "shaved its whiskers, washed its shirt, put on a derby and moved up into the middle class." A good general intro-

duction to the relationship between the two movements is Roberta Ash, *Social Movements in America*, pp. 127–34 and 154–63.

23. Hackney, *Populism to Progressivism*, pp. 328–29.

24. Kousser, *Southern Politics*, p. 246.

25. Ibid., pp. 191–92.

Chapter 8

1. Peter Bachrach and Morton Baratz, *Power and Poverty*, p. 43.

2. V. O. Key, *Southern Politics*, p. 211. Italics added.

3. Phillip Muller, "New South Populism," p. 14.

4. Ibid.

5. Poor white farmers sometimes seem to have expressed their hostility to the plantation system that pushed them onto marginal lands as hatred of blacks. In *Reluctant Reformers*, p. 55, Robert Allen notes that during the antebellum period "the poor whites were prone to identify their distress not with the slave system but with the slaves themselves."

6. Muller, "New South Populism," p. 16.

7. William E. Laird and James R. Rinehart, "Deflation, Agriculture, and Southern Development," pp. 115–24.

8. Herbert Mitchell, "A Forgotten Institution—Private Banks in North Carolina," pp. 34–49.

9. Laird and Rinehart, "Agriculture," p. 117.

10. Roberta Ash, *Social Movements in America*, p. 131.

11. Bruce Johnson, "The Democratic Mirage," p. 368.

12. Allen, *Reluctant Reformers*, pp. 53–54.

13. Roger Ransom and Richard Sutch, "Debt Peonage in the Cotton South after the Civil War," p. 643.

14. Stephen DeCanio, "Cotton 'Overproduction' in Late Nineteenth-Century Southern Agriculture," pp. 608–33.

15. Ibid., p. 614. DeCanio writes: "After correcting for chemical and physical soil differences, farm capital, stocks, race of farmers and size of the respective labor forces, cotton acres tended to produce a greater dollar volume of outputs than acres devoted to alternative crops and livestock" (p. 612).

16. Ibid., pp. 631–32.

17. James C. Davies, "Toward a Theory of Revolution."

18. Simeon Alexander Delap, "The Populist Party in North Carolina," p. 49.

19. John D. Hicks, "The Farmers' Alliance in North Carolina," p. 163.

20. Robert C. McMath, Jr., *Populist Vanguard*, pp. xi and 45.

21. Lawrence Goodwyn, *Democratic Promise*, McMath, *Populist Vanguard*, and Michael Schwartz, *Radical Protest and Social Structure*.

22. Schwartz, *Radical Protest*, p. 15.
23. Goodwyn, *Democratic Promise*, p. 196.
24. McMath, *Populist Vanguard*, p. 29.
25. Schwartz, *Radical Protest*, p. 217.
26. Goodwyn, *Democratic Promise*, p. xii.
27. McMath, *Populist Vanguard*, p. 50.
28. Schwartz, *Radical Protest*, p. 218.
29. The best treatment of the history of Alliance Exchanges is Schwartz, *Populist Protest*, pp. 217–34. See especially p. 229.
30. McMath, *Populist Vanguard*, pp. 53–54.
31. Goodwyn, *Democratic Promise*, p. 31.
32. Robert Wayne Smith, "A Rhetorical Analysis of the Populist Movement in North Carolina, 1892–1896," p. 5.
33. McMath, *Populist Vanguard*, p. 64. See especially McMath's excellent chapter 5, "Brothers and Sisters: The Alliance as Community," for this aspect of Alliance influence. Also see Hicks, "Farmers' Alliance," p. 185.
34. McMath, *Populist Vanguard*, p. 133. The link between southern clergy and the textile industry is best documented by Liston Pope, *Millhands and Preachers*.
35. One of the best treatments of the role of religion in the Populist movement is Frederick Bode, "Religion and Class Hegemony," in which he examines the reaction in North Carolina to state Alliance President Cyrus Thompson's charge that in his day, the church stood where it had always stood, "on the side of human slavery."
36. McMath, *Populist Vanguard*, pp. 38, 66.
37. Schwartz, *Radical Protest*, pp. 116, 97.
38. Ibid., p. 266, 269–78.
39. Goodwyn, *Democratic Promise*, p. 217; McMath, *Populist Vanguard*, pp. 90–109.
40. McMath, *Populist Vanguard*, p. 72.
41. Ibid., p. 31.
42. Goodwyn, *Democratic Promise*, p. 139.
43. Schwartz, *Radical Protest*, p. 113.
44. Hugh Lefler and Albert Newsome, *North Carolina* (1973), p. 547.
45. Allen, *Reluctant Reformers*, pp. 59–60.
46. John Samuel Ezell, *The South since 1865*, p. 162.
47. McMath, *Populist Vanguard*, p. 90.
48. John D. Hicks, *The Populist Revolt*, p. 189. This is contested by Goodwyn, *Democratic Promise*, pp. 565–70, who attributes principal authorship of the concept to Charles Macune.
49. J. Morgan Kousser, *The Shaping of Southern Politics*, pp. 185–86.
50. Muller, "New South Populism," p. 8.
51. Sheldon Hackney, *Populism to Progressivism in Alabama*, p. 31.

52. Goodwyn, *Democratic Promise*, p. 539.
53. Hackney, *Populism to Progressivism*, p. 87.
54. Norman Pollack, *The Populist Response to Industrial America*, p. 12.
55. Christopher Lasch, *The Agony of the American Left*, pp. 3–31.
56. Allen, *Reluctant Reformers*.
57. Hackney, *Populism to Progressivism*, p. 72.
58. Muller, "New South Populism," p. 207.
59. The data source for the analysis of county-level voting was Donald R. Mathews, ed., *North Carolina Votes*.
60. Paul H. Buck, *The Road to Reunion, 1865–1900*, p. 72.
61. Hicks, "Farmers' Alliance," p. 181.
62. Helen G. Edmonds, *The Negro and Fusion Politics in North Carolina, 1894–1901*, p. 56.
63. G. F. Weaver, "The Politics of Local Democratic-Populist Fusion in the Election of 1896 in North Carolina."
64. Edmonds, *Fusion Politics*, p. 52.
65. Carl N. Degler, *The Other South*, pp. 335–36. For Gutherie's repudiation of fusion see Edmonds, *Fusion Politics*, p. 55.
66. Weaver, "Democratic-Populist Fusion," p. 22.
67. Smith, "Rhetorical Analysis," especially chap. 3.
68. On the impact of commercialization on farmers' movements, see Anne Mayhew, "A Reappraisal of the Causes of Farm Protest in the United States, 1870–1900."
69. Schwartz, *Radical Protest*, p. 113. According to Goodwyn, a history of Alliance organizing experience, rather than relative degrees of agricultural distress, prepared regions for Populist sympathy by contributing to mass political consciousness. See Goodwyn, *Democratic Promise*, p. 314.
70. Schwartz, *Radical Protest*, p. 262.
71. For a general discussion of the problems of elite analysis, see Lewis Edinger and Donald Searing, "Social Background in Elite Analysis." Also see Barrington Moore's reservations regarding quantitative research on class origins and behavior in the appendix to his *Social Origins of Dictatorship and Democracy*.
72. The classic recognition of this phenomenon is Robert Michels, *Political Parties*.
73. Muller, "New South Populism," pp. 150–51. This observation by Muller is very significant. Unfortunately, his usage of an elite-mass conceptualization blinds him to subtle but important distinctions among powerful political figures in North Carolina. Generally, class conceptions are more useful analytically than simple elite-mass distinctions.
74. Hackney, *Populism to Progressivism*, p. 31.
75. Biographical information for this chapter has been pieced to-

gether from numerous sources unless a particular source is cited. My extensive use of biographical information was made possible by the existence of a huge biographical index in the North Carolina Collection of the Louis Round Wilson Library, The University of North Carolina at Chapel Hill. The index will enable researchers to locate information on thousands of North Carolinians.

76. Throughout "New South Populism," Muller speculates that conservatives may have struggled for leadership in the North Carolina Farmers' Alliance in order to prevent the movement from becoming radical. This view is plausible and consistent with an observation in Arthur Stinchcombe, "Agricultural Enterprises and Rural Class Relations," that in general farmers' movements are often deficient in leadership and thus especially vulnerable to cooptation.

77. The following sketches of Butler, Thompson, and to a lesser extent Skinner are derived from Muller, "New South Populism," pp. 59–61.

78. H. Larry Ingle, "A Southern Democrat at Large."

79. Ibid., p. 188.

80. The best account of the session and indeed of the period is Edmonds, *Fusion Politics.*

81. Hackney, *Populism to Progressivism*, p. 28.

82. Ibid., p. 29.

83. Status differences are, of course, difficult to determine with such data. Often biographers simply used such terms as "farmer," "successful farmer," and "planter," but the inclusiveness or consistency of these usages is unreliable. It is safe to assume, however, that a "farmer" with a college degree dating from the 1860s or 1870s was, if not always a "planter," certainly not an ordinary farmer.

84. The state did not begin publishing legislative handbooks until 1913. See D. C. Mangum, *Biographical Sketches*, for several 1897 legislators.

85. For a discussion of the application of multidimensional scaling techniques to the analysis of roll call voting, see John F. Hoadley, "Spatial Analysis of Senate Voting Patterns." More generally, see George Rabinowitz, "Introduction to Nonmetric Multidimensional Scaling."

86. Hackney, *Populism to Progressivism*, p. 72.

87. The results of multidimensional scaling programs can be interpreted either as clusters or as dimensions of voting behavior. The latter requires more assumptions about the data. The nineteenth-century senate *Journals* do not always describe the content of enough roll call votes to permit an interpretation of the "dimensions" of voting in the spatial representation, other than to note that the horizontal dimension can be interpreted as a Democrat-Democrat opposition dimension. The vertical dimension moderately differentiates the opposition parties (Re-

publicans, upper, and Populists, lower). I examined how tightly the Populists were clustered because I was interested in the extent to which they were, like the Alabama Populists, "inconsistent and divided."

88. The specific content of many motions and amendments can be obtained only by studying the handwritten minutes of each day. These are stored, unindexed and unordered, in boxes at the North Carolina Department of Archives and History in Raleigh.

89. Edmonds, *Fusion Politics*, pp. 34–47.

90. The extent to which this was in violation of political norms is demonstrated by the fact that one of the most damning things the Democrats could think to say of the fusionists was that they "increased the tax on real and personal property and on the poll, levied new and hitherto unheard of special taxes and increased appropriations by the enormous sum of $100,000 over those of the Legislature of 1893." This charge was made in a propaganda pamphlet that somewhat exaggerated the facts entitled *History of the General Assembly: January 9– March 13, 1895, Inclusive* (anonymous), p. 5.

91. Rosalie Fitzhugh McNeill, "The First Fifteen Months of Governor Daniel Lindsay Russell's Administration," chap. 1.

92. Joseph F. Steelman, "The Progressive Era in North Carolina, 1884–1917," p. 122.

93. McNeill, "Russell's Administration," p. 35.

94. Edmonds, *Fusion Politics*, p. 62.

95. McNeill, "Russell's Administration," p. 40.

96. Ibid., chap. 2.

97. *Inaugural Address of Governor Daniel L. Russell*, Document No. A, North Carolina Senate, Session 1897, pp. 13, 8.

98. McNeill, "Russell's Administration," pp. 33–34.

99. Steelman, "Progressive Era," pp. 148–49.

100. McNeill, "Russell's Administration," p. 34.

101. The analysis technique, multidimensional scaling with KYST, is the same here as described in Figure 8.1.

102. Smith, "Rhetorical Analysis," p. 165.

103. McNeill, "Russell's Administration," p. 41.

104. See Ash, *Social Movements*, pp. 127–34. Also see Goodwyn's discussion of the Populists' "brokerage approach to the political process" in *Democratic Promise*, p. 312.

105. Smith, "Rhetorical Analysis," p. 172.

106. Goodwyn, *Democratic Promise*, p. 180.

107. McMath, *Populist Vanguard*, p. 94.

108. Goodwyn, *Democratic Promise*, p. xiii.

109. Degler, *Other South*, pp. 316–71.

110. Ibid., pp. 331, 319.

111. Ibid., p. 330.

112. Ibid., pp. 338, 351. As Degler notes, however (p. 335), few blacks in North Carolina are likely to have supported Gutherie in the 1896 election after he urged fusion with the Democrats.

113. See Norbert Wiley, "America's Unique Class Politics," for a fine discussion of this aspect of Weber's approach to social stratification.

114. Jeffery M. Paige, *Agrarian Revolution*, especially pp. 1–71.

115. Allen, *Reluctant Reformers*, p. 61.

Chapter 9

1. Helen G. Edmonds, *The Negro and Fusion Politics in North Carolina, 1894–1901*, p. 178.

2. Ibid., p. 55.

3. On the concept of symbolic politics, see Murray Edelman, *Politics as Symbolic Action*. Earlier I noted the tendency for poor whites to direct their hostility to the plantation system that pushed them onto inferior lands toward black slaves who were also victimized by plantation agriculture. It is interesting to view southern racism as a vocabulary of acceptable public sentiments that functioned to maintain order and divert attention from stratification differences in the white caste. This is a distinctively sociological interpretation of racism that contrasts with the popular social psychological view that sees racial hostility as a personality defect to which lower-class whites are especially prone.

4. For a good discussion of how language may repress communication see Claus Mueller, "Notes on the Repression of Communicative Behavior." My notion of a public vocabulary is an extension to the cultural level of C. Wright Mills's social psychological concept of a "vocabulary of motives" discussed in Hans Gerth and C. Wright Mills, *Character and Social Structure*. A vocabulary of motives is a collection of idealized explanations of behavior—"I was angry" or "I was jealous"—from which a social actor selects in order to interpret his actions to others. These motives are not internal drive states but understandable ways of talking. At the societal level, racism may be thought of as the same kind of artifact, rather than as a psychological trait.

5. Carl N. Degler, *The Other South*, pp. 342, 341.

6. Edmonds, *Fusion Politics*, p. 178.

7. Christopher Lasch, *The Agony of the American Left*, pp. 3–31.

8. See J. Morgan Kousser, *The Shaping of Southern Politics*, p. 191–92.

9. Quoted in John D. Hicks, "The Farmers' Alliance in North Carolina," p. 187.

10. Edmonds, *Fusion Politics*, p. 179.

11. Kousser, *Southern Politics*, p. 191.

12. Originally I planned to compare the earlier structure of roll call voting in this session with that of the earlier sessions. The senate *Journal* reports hundreds of unanimous votes during this session and

almost no votes in which there were conflicts among Democrats. I was thus unable to perform a scaling analysis parallel to the ones for 1895 and 1897. The Democrats were unanimous on the crucial disfranchisement vote; the Republicans and one Populist voted against it.

13. V. O. Key, *Southern Politics*, p. 211.

14. Ibid., p. 206.

15. Hugh Lefler and Albert Newsome, *North Carolina* (1973), p. 562.

16. Joseph Steelman, "The Progressive Era in North Carolina, 1884–1917," pp. 197–98.

17. Donald R. Matthews, ed., *North Carolina Votes*.

18. John Samuel Ezell, *The South since 1865*, p. 253; Hugh Lefler and Albert Newsome, *North Carolina: History, Geography, Government*, p. 356.

19. Rupert Vance, "Aycock of North Carolina," p. 288.

20. R. D. W. Connor and Clarence Poe, eds., *Life and Speeches of Charles Brantley Aycock*, p. 3.

21. Key, *Southern Politics*, pp. 211–13, 217, 218.

22. Lefler and Newsome, *North Carolina* (1973), p. 564.

23. Steelman, "Progressive Era," p. 312.

24. Quoted in Lefler and Newsome, *North Carolina* (1973), p. 558.

25. Ibid., p. 558.

26. Steelman, "Progressive Era," p. 200.

27. Connor and Poe, eds., *Aycock*, p. 82.

28. Ibid., pp. 82–83.

29. Steelman, "Progressive Era," p. ii.

30. Vance, "Aycock," p. 306.

31. Steelman, "Progressive Era," p. 211.

32. For biographical accounts of these important reformers see B. J. Hendrick, *The Training of an American*, and Joseph L. Morrison, *Josephus Daniels*. A new work by John Milton Cooper, Jr., *Walter Hines Page*, is especially helpful.

33. Cooper, *Page*, p. 5.

34. Morrison, *Josephus Daniels*, p. 12.

35. Quoted in Cooper, *Page*, p. 79.

36. Morrison, *Josephus Daniels*, p. 22.

37. Phillip Muller, "New South Populism," p. 26.

38. The Wataugans have yet to receive the analysis they merit. A partial list of members can be found in ibid., p. 26. I located biographical information through the North Carolina Collection index at the Louis Round Wilson Library, The University of North Carolina at Chapel Hill.

39. Muller, "New South Populism," pp. 20–32.

40. Lefler and Newsome, *North Carolina* (1973), p. 533.

41. Muller, "New South Populism," p. 44.

42. Ibid., p. 29.

43. Quoted in Steelman, "Progressive Era," p. 297.

44. Politically, this has its analogue today in the "culture of poverty" literature used by many middle-class social scientists to interpret the persistence of poverty in American life.

45. Steelman, "Progressive Era," p. 208.

46. These lines are from a letter to Alice Wilson Page, 2 March 1899, the year of North Carolina's conservative restoration, quoted in Steelman, "Progressive Era," p. 207.

47. Walter Hines Page, "The Forgotten Man," p. 83.

48. For a general view of the relationship between Progressivism and American political economy see Gabriel Kolko, *The Triumph of Conservatism*, Christopher Lasch, *The New Radicalism in America, 1889–1963*, and James Weinstein, *The Corporate Ideal in the Liberal State, 1900–1918*.

49. Lasch, *Agony*, p. 10.

50. See Harry Gracey, "Learning the Student Role," a participant observation study that demonstrates that the principal function of early schooling is to train conformity to what, from the child's perspective, are arbitrary demands by adults. An excellent historical study that makes the same social psychological point but better relates educational philosophy to class ideology is Richard Johnson's "Educational Policy and Social Control in Early Victorian England." The best general treatment of the contribution of education to the reproduction of capitalist labor relations is Samuel Bowles and Herbert Gintis, *Schooling in Capitalist America*.

51. See Ivan Illich's *Deschooling Society* for a discussion of how educational establishments in developing societies legitimate the stratification system. It was a common experience when I worked for an Appalachian state welfare department to hear poor people explain their poverty to themselves and others as a consequence of their personal failure to get an education.

52. Connor and Poe, eds., *Aycock*, p. 318.

53. Ibid., p. 126.

54. Ibid., p. 281.

55. Ibid., p. 132.

56. Barrington Moore, *Social Origins of Dictatorship and Democracy*, p. 437.

57. I have found some intriguing hints that educators may have felt more comfortable with the Democrats than with the Populists. The latter, perhaps, challenged their professional authority. I sensed this, for example, in several newspaper accounts of legislative conflicts over statewide textbook adoption. Although most arguments involved the expense of the books—the Populists typically suspected a conspiracy between the state Board of Education and textbook publishers—in at

least one instance, arguments were made in defense of local control. For instance, the *News and Observer* (6 March 1895) reported that Populist Senator J. M. Moody in the 1895 General Assembly argued that local boards should have the right to select their own books. "He said the county boards of education had enough sense to know what books were best." Recently publicized conflict in West Virginia's Kanawha County over textbook selection, as well as the issue of neighborhood control of schools throughout the nation (which has been discounted as racist), both seem to reflect a status conflict between rural or working-class people and the urban, professionally employed persons whose decisions usually determine school policy. I suspect that research into the relations between Populists and professionals in North Carolina at the turn of the century would reveal such a status conflict, even though these groups are usually thought to have been allied.

58. Steelman, "Progressive Era," p. 251.

59. Quoted in Lester Salamon, "Leadership and Modernization," p. 615.

60. Inequity in the distribution of benefits from Progressive measures is well documented. In *Origins of the New South, 1877–1913*, pp. 369–95, Woodward emphasized how progressive reforms ("For Whites Only") were grafted onto a caste society. More recently, in "Consequences of Disfranchisement," J. Morgan Kousser examined class and racial biases in North Carolina educational expenditures from 1880 to 1910. In an admission that contradicts his position in *The Shaping of Southern Politics*, where he argues that southern Democrats cut expenditures after 1900, Kousser concludes: "The burgeoning expenditures of the Progressive Era, then, were inequitably distributed—biased against poor whites, and even more biased against the blacks. Unable to protect themselves at the polls, robbed of the shelter provided by sympathetic political parties, and incapable, therefore, of prevailing upon the legislature to repeal laws which favored the wealthy whites in the black belt counties at the expense of both Negroes and poor hill country whites, the lower-class could only watch helplessly as they fell educationally further and further behind the middle and upper class whites who supported, and benefited most from, the so-called Progressive movement" (pp. 17–18).

Chapter 10

1. Kirkpatrick Sale, "Six Pillars of the Southern Rim," p. 165.

2. An example is George B. Tindall's "Beyond the Mainstream," which treats the persistence of "southernism" as a matter of ethnicity. He supports this interpretation with evidence of attitudinal persistence from John Shelton Reed's *The Enduring South*.

3. Eugene Genovese, *The World the Slaveholders Made*, p. 230.

4. Quoted in Paul Gaston, *The New South Creed*, pp. 158–59.

5. V. O. Key, *Southern Politics*, pp. 207–8, 210.

6. Genovese, *World Slaveholders Made*, p. 141.

7. C. Vann Woodward, *American Counterpoint*, pp. 264–66.

8. W. J. Cash, *The Mind of the South*, pp. x, 177, 183.

9. Ibid., p. 177.

10. Ibid., p. 188.

11. Woodward, *Counterpoint*, pp. 282, 276, and 281.

12. Sheldon Hackney, "Origins of the New South in Retrospect," p. 197.

13. Michael O'Brien, "C. Vann Woodward and the Burden of Southern Liberalism," p. 596.

14. Hackney, "*Origins*," p. 193.

15. Woodward, *Counterpoint*, p. 273.

16. In part, this may be because of Woodward's equal, though contradictory, stress on the South as an absentee-owned "colony."

17. C. Vann Woodward, *Origins of the New South, 1877–1913*, p. 20.

18. Ibid., p. 133. The reader should compare Broadus Mitchell, *The Rise of Cotton Mills in the South*, with Broadus Mitchell and George Mitchell, *The Industrial Revolution in the South*, a publication that appeared in 1930.

19. See especially William B. Hesseltine, *Confederate Leaders in the New South*.

20. Lester Salamon, *The Social Origins of Mississippi Backwardness*. Jonathan M. Wiener, "Planter-Merchant Conflict in Reconstruction Alabama," pp. 73–94, and also "Planter Persistence and Social Change," pp. 235–60.

21. Hackney, "*Origins*," p. 200.

22. William J. Cooper, Jr., *The Conservative Regime*, pp. 120, 40.

23. Raymond Pulley, *Old Virginia Restored, 1870–1930*, p. 151.

24. Floyd Hunter, *Community Power Succession*, in press.

25. See Jonathan Wiener, "Review of Reviews," pp. 146–75, for a response to critics and an assessment of this contribution.

26. Although Moore does not develop a theory of backwardness, this statement is not altogether accurate because his discussion of India's lack of development is critical to his central contention that before industrialization can occur, an elite must emerge with enough power to force change, as has not been the case in India.

27. See Theda Skocpol's "Old Regime Legacies and Communist Revolutions in Russia and China" for an excellent analysis of how such historical legacies influence and limit the course of modernization.

28. Stephen J. DeCanio, *Agriculture in the Postbellum South*, p. 260.

29. Eugene Genovese, *Roll, Jordan, Roll*, p. 665.

30. Anthony M. Tang, *Economic Development in the Southern Pied-*

mont, 1860–1950, pp. 66–95 and 219. Although Tang analyzed only South Carolina and Georgia counties, there is no reason to believe that his conclusions would not also hold for counties in the North Carolina Piedmont.

31. George B. Tindall, *The Emergence of the New South, 1913–1945*, pp. 127, 392.

32. See Francis Fox Piven and Richard A. Cloward, *Regulating the Poor*, pp. 200–221, on agricultural modernization and mass unemployment. Also see Tony Dunbar, *Our Land Too*, pp. 6–104.

33. A good overview is Tindall, *Emergence*, chap. 12.

34. Lowell Ashby, *The North Carolina Economy*, p. 239.

35. North Carolina *Census of Agriculture*, 1974.

36. *Abstract of the 15th Census of the United States, 1930*, p. 512.

37. Raleigh *News and Observer*, 7 September 1975.

38. Luther Hodges, *Businessman in the Statehouse*, chaps. 9 and 10.

39. See for example, Robert Agger, Daniel Goldrich, and Burt S. Swanson, *The Rulers and the Ruled*, who report business opposition to new industries in Winston-Salem and Durham.

40. Hodges, *Businessman*, p. 203.

41. None of the "Six Pillars" that according to Sale are the basis for "sunbelt" growth—agribusiness, defense, technology including research and development, oil, real estate, and leisure—depend upon large numbers of high-wage industrial workers.

42. This is consistent with Glaucio Soares, "Economic Development and Class Structure," who has shown statistically that controlling for the level of industrialization, North Carolina and the other southern states except Louisiana have too small a middle class for their levels of economic development as predicted from the relationship between the variables for the United States as a whole.

43. Steve Berg, "Prison Observers Confront State's Burdened System."

44. Emil Malizia, "The Earnings of North Carolina Workers," pp. 1 and 3.

45. Barbara Koeppel, "Something Could Be Finer Than to Be in Carolina," pp. 21–22.

46. George Adcock, "Is International Status Taking the South by Surprise?"

Bibliography

Manuscripts
Chapel Hill, North Carolina. Southern Historical Collection, The University of North Carolina at Chapel Hill. The Cameron Family Papers, no. 133.

Government Documents
State of North Carolina. *The Public Documents, 1907*, Vol. 1. Raleigh: E. M. Uzzell and Co., State Printer, 1907.

United States Census Office. *Abstract of the Fifteenth Census of the United States, 1930*. Washington: Government Printing Office, 1933.

———. *Census of Agriculture, 1974*, Vol. 1, part 33 (North Carolina State and County Data). Washington: Government Printing Office, 1977.

———. *Compendium of the Tenth Census of the United States, 1880*. Washington: Government Printing Office, 1885.

———. *Eighth Census of the United States, 1860*, Vol. 1 (Population). Washington: Government Printing Office, 1864.

———. *Eighth Census of the United States, 1860*, Vol. 2 (Agriculture). Washington: Government Printing Office, 1864.

———. *Eighth Census of the United States, 1860*, Vol. 3 (Manufactures). Washington: Government Printing Office, 1865.

———. *Eighth Census of the United States, 1860*, Vol. 4 (Vital Statistics). Washington: Government Printing Office, 1866.

———. *Tenth Census of the United States, 1880*, Vol. 1 (Population). Washington: Government Printing Office, 1883.

———. *Tenth Census of the United States, 1880*, Vol. 2 (Manufactures). Washington: Government Printing Office, 1883.

———. *Tenth Census of the United States, 1880*, Vol. 3 (Agriculture). Washington: Government Printing Office, 1883.

———. *Tenth Census of the United States, 1880*, Vol. 6 (Cotton Production). Washington: Government Printing Office, 1884.

———. *Twelfth Census of the United States, 1900*, Vol. 1 (Population). Washington: Government Printing Office, 1901.

———. *Twelfth Census of the United States, 1900*, Vol. 2 (Population). Washington: Government Printing Office, 1902.

———. *Twelfth Census of the United States, 1900*, Vols. 5 and 6 (Agriculture). Washington: Government Printing Office, 1902.

———. *Twelfth Census of the United States, 1900*, Vols. 8 and 9 (Manufactures). Washington: Government Printing Office, 1902.

Books and Articles

Adcock, George. "Is International Status Taking the South by Surprise?" *The South Magazine: Journal of Southern Business* (1975).

Agger, Robert; Goldrich, Daniel; and Swanson, Burt S. *The Rulers and the Ruled: Political Power and Impotence in American Communities.* New York: John Wiley and Sons, 1964.

Allen, Robert L. *Reluctant Reformers: Racism and Social Reform Movements in the United States.* Washington, D.C.: Howard University Press, 1974.

Ash, Roberta. *Social Movements in America.* Chicago: Markham, 1962.

Ashby, Lowell. *The North Carolina Economy.* Research Paper 7. Chapel Hill: School of Business Administration, University of North Carolina, 1961.

Ashe, Samuel A. "Duncan Cameron." In Samuel A. Ashe, ed., *Biographical History of North Carolina*, Vol. 3, pp. 43–47. Greensboro, N.C.: C. L. Van Noppen, 1905.

_____. "Paul Carrington Cameron." In Samuel A. Ashe, ed., *Biographical History of North Carolina*, Vol. 3, pp. 48–55. Greensboro, N.C.: C. L. Van Noppen, 1905.

_____. *Biographical History of North Carolina*, 6 vols. Greensboro, N.C.: C. L. Van Noppen, 1905.

Bachrach, Peter, and Baratz, Morton. *Power and Poverty: Theory and Practice.* New York: Oxford University Press, 1970.

Baran, Paul. "On the Political Economy of Backwardness." In Robert Rhodes, ed., *Imperialism and Underdevelopment*, pp. 285–301. New York: Monthly Review Press, 1970.

Bastin, Bruce. *Crying for the Carolines.* London: Studio Vista Limited, 1971.

Battle, Kemp P. "James Smith Battle." In Samuel Ashe, ed., *Biographical History of North Carolina*, Vol. 6, pp. 12–19. Greensboro, N.C.: C. L. Van Noppen, 1905.

Beckford, George. *Persistent Poverty: Underdevelopment in Plantation Economies of the Third World.* New York: Oxford University Press, 1972.

Bendix, Reinhard. *Nation Building and Citizenship.* Garden City: Anchor Books, 1969.

_____. "Tradition and Modernity Reconsidered." *Comparative Studies in Society and History* 9 (1967): 292–346.

_____. *Work and Authority in Industry.* Berkeley: University of California Press, 1974.

Berg, Steve. "Prison Observers Confront State's Burdened System." *Raleigh News and Observer*, 13 April 1975.

Berghe, Pierre van den. "Education, Class and Ethnicity in Southern Peru: Revolutionary Colonialism." In Philip Altback and Gail Kelly, eds., *Education and Colonialism: Comparative Perspectives*. New York: McKay, forthcoming.

Birnham, Walter Dean. *Critical Elections and the Mainsprings of American Politics*. New York: W. W. Norton and Co., 1970.

Blauner, Robert. *Alienation and Freedom*. Chicago: University of Chicago Press, 1964.

Blum, Jerome. "The Rise of Serfdom in Eastern Europe." *American Historical Review* 62 (1957): 807–36.

Bode, Frederick. "Religion and Class Hegemony: A Populist Critique in North Carolina." *Journal of Southern History* 38 (1971): 417–38.

Bodenheimer, Susanne. "Dependency and Imperialism: The Roots of Latin American Underdevelopment." *Politics and Society* 1 (1971): 327–58.

Bowles, Samuel, and Gintis, Herbert. *Schooling in Capitalist America: Educational Reform and the Contradictions of Economic Life*. New York: Basic Books, 1976.

Boyte, Harry. "The Textile Industry: Keel of Southern Industrialization." *Radical America* 6 (1972): 4–49.

Branson, Levi. *Branson's North Carolina Business Directory*. Raleigh, N.C.: Levi Branson Office Publishing Co., 1869, 1872, 1877–78, and 1884.

Braverman, Harry. *Labor and Monopoly Capital*. New York: Monthly Review Press, 1974.

Brown, C. K. "The Southern Railway Security Company, an Early Instance of a Holding Company." *North Carolina Historical Review* 3 (1926): 158–70.

Buck, Paul H. *The Road to Reunion, 1865–1900*. Boston: Little, Brown and Co., 1937.

Busch, Lawrence, "Patterns of Dependence: The Case of Three African Nations." Unpublished paper, University of Kentucky, 1974.

Cannon, Robert. "The Organization and Growth of Black Political Participation in Durham, North Carolina, 1933–1958." Ph.D. dissertation, University of North Carolina, 1975.

Casanova, Pablo Gonzalez. "Internal Colonialism and National Development." *Studies in Comparative International Development* 1 (1965): 27–37.

Cash, W. J. *The Mind of the South*. New York: Vintage Books, 1941.

Chandler, Alfred. "The Beginnings of 'Big Business' in American Industry." In Thomas Cochran and Thomas Brewer, eds., *Views of American Economic Growth: The Industrial Era*, pp. 79–101. New York: McGraw-Hill, 1966.

Chilcote, Ronald, and Edelstein, Joel. *Latin America: The Struggle with Dependency and Beyond*. New York: Halsted Press, 1974.

Chirot, Daniel. "The Growth of the Market and Servile Labor Systems in Agriculture." *Journal of Social History* 8 (1975): 67–80.

_____. *Social Change in a Peripheral Society*. New York: Academic Press, 1976.

Clay, Howard B. "Daniel Augustus Tompkins: An American Bourbon." Ph.D. dissertation, University of North Carolina, 1950.

Cochran, Thomas, and Miller, William. *The Age of Enterprise: A Social History of Industrial America* (Revised Edition). New York: Harper and Row, 1961.

Cole, Robert. *Japanese Blue Collar*. Berkeley: University of California Press, 1971.

Collins, Herbert. "The Idea of a Cotton Textile Industry in the South, 1870–1890." *North Carolina Historical Review* 34 (1957): 358–92.

Collins, Randall. *Conflict Sociology: Toward an Explanatory Science*. New York: Academic Press, 1975.

Conner, R. D. W., and Poe, Clarence, eds. *Life and Speeches of Charles Brantley Aycock*. New York: Doubleday, Page & Co., 1912.

Cooper, John Milton, Jr. *Walter Hines Page: The Southerner as American, 1855–1918*. Chapel Hill: The University of North Carolina Press, 1977.

Cooper, William J. *The Conservative Regime: South Carolina, 1877–1890*. Baltimore: The Johns Hopkins Press, 1968.

Cox, Reavis. *Competition in the American Tobacco Industry, 1911–1932*. New York: Columbia University Press, 1933.

Danhof, Clarence. "Thoughts on the South's Economic Problems." In Melvin Greenhut and W. T. Whitman, eds., *Essays in Southern Economic Development*, pp. 7–68. Chapel Hill: The University of North Carolina Press, 1964.

David, Paul, and Temin, Peter. "Slavery: The Progressive Institution?" In Paul David, Herbert Gutman, Richard Sutch, Peter Temin, and Gavin Wright, eds., *Reckoning with Slavery*, pp. 165–230. New York: Oxford University Press, 1976.

Davies, James C. "Toward a Theory of Revolution." *American Sociological Review* 27 (1962): 5–19.

Davis, Kingsley, and Moore, Wilbert E. "Some Principles of Stratification." In Reinhard Bendix and Seymour M. Lipset, eds., *Class, Status, and Power*, pp. 47–53. New York: Free Press, 1966.

Davis, Lance; Easterlin, Richard; et al., eds. *American Economic Growth*. New York: Harper and Row, 1972.

DeCanio, Stephen J. *Agriculture in the Postbellum South: The Economics of Production and Supply*. Cambridge, Mass.: MIT Press, 1974.

_____. "Cotton 'Overproduction' in Late Nineteenth-Century Southern Agriculture." *Journal of Economic History* 33 (1973): 608–33.

Degler, Carl N. *The Other South*. New York: Harper and Row, 1974.

Delap, Simeon Alexander. "The Populist Party in North Carolina." *His-*

torical Papers, Series XIV. Durham, N.C.: Trinity College Historical Society, 1922.

Douty, Harry M. "The North Carolina Industrial Worker, 1880–1930." Ph.D. dissertation, University of North Carolina, 1936.

Dowd, Jerome. *Sketches of Prominent Living North Carolinians*. Raleigh, N.C.: Edwards and Broughton, 1888.

Dreiser, Theodore, ed. *Harlan Miners Speak: Report on Terrorism in the Kentucky Coal Fields*. New York: Harcourt, Brace, and Co., 1932.

Dunbar, Tony. *Our Land Too*. New York: Vintage Books, 1969.

Durden, Robert F. *The Dukes of Durham, 1865–1929*. Durham, N.C.: Duke University Press, 1975.

Easterlin, Richard A. "Regional Income Trends, 1840–1950." In Seymour E. Harris, ed., *American Economic History*, pp. 525–47. New York: McGraw-Hill Book Company, 1961.

Eaton, Clement. *The Growth of Southern Civilization, 1790–1860*. New York: Harper and Row, 1961.

Edelman, Murray. *Politics as Symbolic Action*. Chicago: Markham, 1971.

Edinger, Lewis, and Searing, Donald. "Social Background in Elite Analysis: A Methodological Inquiry." *American Political Science Review* 61 (1967): 428–45.

Edmonds, Helen G. *The Negro and Fusion Politics in North Carolina, 1894–1901*. Chapel Hill: The University of North Carolina Press, 1951.

Edwards, George. "Development of American Security Capitalism." In Thomas Cochran and Thomas Brewer, eds., *Views of American Economic Growth: The Industrial Era*, pp. 115–33. New York: McGraw-Hill, 1966.

Eisenstadt, S. N. *The Political System of Empires*. New York: Free Press, 1963.

Eller, Ron. "Coal, Culture, and Community." Unpublished paper, Mars Hill College, 1976.

Eutsler, Roland. "The Cape Fear and Yadkin Valley Railroad." *North Carolina Historical Review* 2 (1925): 427–41.

Eyck, Erich. *Bismarck and the German Empire*. London: George Allen and Unwin, 1950.

Ezell, John Samuel. *The South since 1865*. New York: MacMillan Co., 1963.

Faux, Geoffrey. "Colonial New England." *New Republic* 167 (1972): 16–19.

Fitzhugh, George. *Cannibals All!, or Slaves Without Masters*. Edited by C. Vann Woodward. Cambridge, Mass.: Harvard University Press, 1960.

———. *Sociology for the South, or The Failure of Free Society*. Richmond, Va.: A. Morris, 1854.

Fogel, Robert, and Engerman, Stanley. *Time on the Cross*. New York: Little, Brown, and Co., 1974.

Foster, John. *Class Struggle and the Industrial Revolution*. New York: St. Martin's Press, 1974.

Frank, Andre Gunder. "The Development of Underdevelopment." In Robert Rhodes, ed., *Imperialism and Underdevelopment*, pp. 4–17. New York: Monthly Review Press, 1970.

————. "Economic Dependence, Class Structure, and Underdevelopment Policy," In James D. Cockcroft, Andre Gunder Frank, and Dale Johnson, *Dependence and Underdevelopment*, pp. 19–45. New York: Doubleday and Co., 1972.

Frazier, E. Franklin. "Durham: Capital of the Black Middle Class." In Alain Locke, ed., *The New Negro*, pp. 333–40. New York: Albert and Charles Boni Co., 1925.

Gaston, Paul. "The 'New South.'" In Arthur Link and Rembert Patrick, eds., *Writing Southern History*, pp. 316–36. Baton Rouge: Louisiana State University Press, 1965.

————. *The New South Creed: A Study in Southern Mythmaking*. New York: Vintage Books, 1973.

Genovese, Eugene. "The Fate of Paternalism in Modern Bourgeois Society: The Case of Japan." In Eugene Genovese, *Roll, Jordan, Roll: The World the Slaves Made*, pp. 661–65. New York: Vintage Books, 1976.

————. *The Political Economy of Slavery*. New York: Vintage Books, 1967.

————. *Roll, Jordan, Roll: The World the Slaves Made*. New York: Vintage Books, 1976.

————. *The World the Slaveholders Made*. New York: Vintage Books, 1971.

Gerth, Hans, and Mills, C. Wright. *Character and Social Structure*. New York: Harcourt, Brace, and World, 1953.

Giddens, Anthony. *The Class Structure of the Advanced Societies*. New York: Harper Torchbooks, 1973.

Gilman, Glenn. *Human Relations in the Industrial Southeast*. Chapel Hill: The University of North Carolina Press, 1956.

Goodwyn, Lawrence. *Democratic Promise*. New York: Oxford University Press, 1976.

Gordon, Milton. *Social Class in American Sociology*. New York: McGraw-Hill, 1958.

Gracey, Harry. "Learning the Student Role: Kindergarten as Academic Boot Camp." In Dennis Wrong and Harry Gracey, eds., *Readings in Introductory Sociology*, pp. 243–254. New York: Macmillan Co., 1972.

Grady, Henry, "Cotton and Its Kingdom." *Harper's Magazine* 68 (1881): 719–34.

Griffin, Richard. "Reconstruction of the North Carolina Textile Industry, 1865–1885." *North Carolina Historical Review* 41 (1964): 34–53.

————, and Standard, Diffee. "The Cotton Textile Industry in Antebellum North Carolina, Part II: The Era of Boom and Consolidation, 1830–1860." *North Carolina Historical Review* 34 (1957): 131–64.

Gutman, Herbert. *The Black Family in Slavery and Freedom, 1750–1925.* New York: Pantheon, 1976.

Hackney, Sheldon. "*Origins of the New South* in Retrospect." *Journal of Southern History* 38 (1972): 191–216.

————. *Populism to Progressivism in Alabama.* Princeton, N.J.: Princeton University Press, 1969.

Hamerow, Theodore S. *Restoration, Revolution, Reaction: Economics and Politics in Germany, 1815–1871.* Princeton, N.J.: Princeton University Press, 1958.

Hechter, Michael. *Internal Colonialism: The Celtic Fringe in British National Development, 1536–1966.* Berkeley: University of California Press, 1975.

————. "Regional Inequality and National Integration: The Case of the British Isles." *Journal of Social History* 5 (1971): 96–117.

Hendrick, B. J. *The Training of an American: The Earlier Life and Letters of Walter Hines Page, 1855–1913.* New York: Doubleday, Page, & Co., 1928.

Herring, Harriet. "Early Industrial Development in the South." *Annals of the American Academy* 153 (1931): 1–10.

————. *Passing of the Mill Village.* Chapel Hill: The University of North Carolina Press, 1949.

————. *Southern Industry and Regional Development.* Chapel Hill: The University of North Carolina Press, 1940.

————. *Welfare Work in Mill Villages.* Chapel Hill: The University of North Carolina Press, 1929.

Hesseltine, William. *Confederate Leaders in the New South.* Baton Rouge: Louisiana State University Press, 1950.

Hicks, John D. "The Farmers' Alliance in North Carolina." *North Carolina Historical Review* 2 (1925): 162–87.

————. *The Populist Revolt: A History of the Farmers' Alliance and the People's Party.* Minneapolis: University of Minnesota Press, 1931.

Hoadley, John F. "Spatial Analysis of Senate Voting Patterns." Thesis, University of North Carolina, 1974.

Hobbs, Samuel Huntington, Jr. *North Carolina: Economic and Social.* Chapel Hill: The University of North Carolina Press, 1930.

Hodges, Luther. *Businessman in the Statehouse: Six Years as Governor of North Carolina.* Chapel Hill: The University of North Carolina Press, 1962.

Hofstadter, Richard. *The Age of Reform.* New York: Random House, 1955.

Hunter, Floyd. *Community Power Succession.* Chapel Hill: The University of North Carolina Press, forthcoming.

Huntington, S. P. *Political Order of Changing Societies.* New Haven: Yale University Press, 1968.

Illich, Ivan. *Deschooling Society.* New York: Harper and Row, 1971.

Ingle, H. Larry. "A Southern Democrat at Large: William Hodge Kitchin and the Populist Party." *North Carolina Historical Review* 45 (1968): 161–83.

Johannesin, Dell Bush. "Development of Labor Law in North Carolina." Ph.D. dissertation, University of North Carolina, 1955.

John, Maxcy L. "Mark Morgan." In Samuel Ashe, ed., *Biographical History of North Carolina,* Vol. 2, pp. 282–92. Greensboro, N.C.: C. L. Van Noppen, 1905.

Johnson, Bruce. "The Democratic Mirage: Notes Toward a Theory of American Politics." In Milton Mankoff, ed., *The Poverty of Progress,* pp. 362–90. New York: Holt, Rinehart, and Winston, 1972.

Johnson, Dale L. "Dependence and the International System." In James D. Cockcroft, Andre Gunder Frank, and Dale L. Johnson, eds., *Dependence and Underdevelopment,* pp. 71–111. New York: Doubleday and Co., 1972.

Johnson, Guion. *Ante-Bellum North Carolina.* Chapel Hill: The University of North Carolina Press, 1937.

———. "Social Characteristics of Ante-Bellum North Carolina." *North Carolina Historical Review* 6 (1929): 140–57.

Johnson, Richard. "Educational Policy and Social Control in Early Victorian England." *Past and Present* 49 (1970): 98–119.

Key, V. O. *Southern Politics.* New York: Random House, 1949.

Koeppel, Barbara. "Something Could Be Finer Than to Be in Carolina." *The Progressive* 40 (1976): 20–23.

Kolko, Gabriel. *Railroads and Regulation, 1877–1916.* Princeton, N.J.: Princeton University Press, 1965.

———. *The Triumph of Conservatism.* Chicago: Quadrangle, 1967.

Konkle, Burton Alva. *John Motley Morehead and the Development of North Carolina, 1796–1866.* Philadelphia: William J. Campbell, 1922.

Kousser, J. Morgan. "Consequences of Disfranchisement: Race and Class Discrimination in North Carolina, 1880–1910." Paper presented at the American Historical Association, December 1974.

———. *The Shaping of Southern Politics.* New Haven: Yale University Press, 1964.

Lacy, Dan. "The Beginnings of Industrialism in North Carolina, 1865–1900." Ph.D. dissertation, University of North Carolina, 1935.

Laird, William E., and Rinehart, James R. "Deflation, Agriculture, and Southern Development." *Agricultural History* 42 (1968): 115–24.

Lander, Ernest McPherson, Jr. *The Textile Industry in Antebellum South Carolina.* Baton Rouge: Lousiana State University Press, 1969.

Lasch, Christopher. *The Agony of the American Left.* New York: Alfred A. Knopf, 1969.

────. *The New Radicalism in America, 1889–1963*. New York: Alfred A. Knopf, 1965.

Lefler, Hugh, ed. *North Carolina History Told by Contemporaries*. Chapel Hill: The University of North Carolina Press, 1955.

────, and Newsome, Albert. *North Carolina: History, Geography, Government*. New York: Scribner, 1959.

────. *North Carolina: The History of a Southern State*. Chapel Hill: The University of North Carolina Press, 1973.

Lemert, Ben F. *The Cotton Textile Industry of the Southern Appalachian Piedmont*. Chapel Hill: The University of North Carolina Press, 1953.

────. *Tobacco Manufacturing Industry in North Carolina*. Raleigh, N.C.: National Youth Administration of North Carolina, 1939.

Lenski, Gerhard E. *Power and Privilege*. New York: McGraw-Hill, 1966.

Lewis, Hylan. *Blackways of Kent*. Chapel Hill: The University of North Carolina Press, 1955.

Lynd, Robert S., and Lynd, Helen Merrell. *Middletown: A Study in Modern American Culture*. New York: Harvest Books, 1956.

McGuire, Peter S. "The Seaboard Air Line." *North Carolina Historical Review* 11 (1934): 94–115.

McLaurin, Melton. *Paternalism and Protest*. Westport: Greenwood, 1971.

McMath, Robert C., Jr. *Populist Vanguard*. Chapel Hill: The University of North Carolina Press, 1975.

MacPherson, C. B. *The Political Theory of Possessive Individualism*. New York: Oxford University Press, 1962.

Malizia, Emil. "The Earnings of North Carolina Workers." *University of North Carolina News Letter* 60 (1975): 1–3.

Mangum, D. C. *Biographical Sketches of the Members of the Legislature of North Carolina, Session 1897*. Raleigh, N.C.: Edwards and Broughton, Printers, 1897.

Matthews, Donald R., ed. *North Carolina Votes*. Chapel Hill: The University of North Carolina Press, 1962.

Mayhew, Anne. "A Reappraisal of the Causes of Farm Protest in the United States, 1870–1900." *Journal of Economic History* 32 (1972): 464–75.

Michels, Robert. *Political Parties*. New York: Free Press, 1962.

Mills, C. Wright. *The Sociological Imagination*. New York: Oxford University Press, 1959.

Mitchell, Broadus. "Growth of Manufactures in the South." *Annals of the American Academy* 153 (1931): 21–29.

────. *The Rise of Cotton Mills in the South*. Baltimore: The Johns Hopkins Press, 1921.

────, and Mitchell, George. *The Industrial Revolution in the South*. Baltimore: The Johns Hopkins Press, 1930.

Mitchell, Herbert. "A Forgotten Institution—Private Banks in North Carolina." *North Carolina Historical Review* 35 (1958): 34–49.

Moore, Barrington. *Social Origins of Dictatorship and Democracy.* Boston: Beacon Press, 1966.

Morrison, Joseph L. *Josephus Daniels: The Small-d Democrat.* Chapel Hill: The University of North Carolina Press, 1966.

Mueller, Claus. "Notes on the Repression of Communicative Behavior." In Hans Peter Dreitzel, ed., *Recent Sociology*, No. 2, pp. 101–13. New York: Macmillan, 1972.

Muller, Phillip. "New South Populism." Ph.D. dissertation, University of North Carolina, 1971.

Myrdal, Gunnar. "The Drift Towards Regional Economic Inequalities in a Country." In George Dalton, ed., *Economic Development and Social Change*, pp. 386–400. Garden City, N.Y.: Natural History Press, 1971.

Nicholls, William. *Southern Tradition and Regional Progress.* Chapel Hill: The University of North Carolina Press, 1960.

North, Douglass C. "Agriculture in Regional Economic Growth." *Journal of Farm Economics* 41 (1959): 943–51.

O'Brien, Gail. "A Study of Power and Influence in Mecklenburg County, 1844–1854." Unpublished paper, University of North Carolina, 1970.

————. "War and Social Change: An Analysis of Community Power Structure, Guilford County, North Carolina, 1848–1882." Ph.D. dissertation, University of North Carolina, 1975.

O'Brien, Michael. "C. Vann Woodward and the Burden of Southern Liberalism." *American Historical Review* 78 (1973): 589–604.

Odum, Howard W. *Southern Regions of the United States.* Chapel Hill: The University of North Carolina Press, 1936.

————. *The Way of the South.* New York: Macmillan Co., 1947.

Page, Walter Hines. "The Forgotten Man." *State Normal Magazine* 1 (1897): 74–88.

Paige, Jeffery M. *Agrarian Revolution.* New York: Free Press, 1975.

Palmer, Alan. *Bismarck.* New York: Charles Scribners' Sons, 1976.

Parkin, Frank. *Class Inequality and Political Order.* New York: Praeger, 1971.

Peirce, Neal. *The Border South States.* New York: Norton, 1975.

Phillips, Bill. "Piedmont Country Blues." *Southern Exposure* 2 (1974): 56–62.

Piven, Frances Fox, and Cloward, Richard A. *Regulating the Poor: The Functions of Public Welfare.* New York: Vintage Books, 1971.

Pollack, Norman. *The Populist Response to Industrial America.* Cambridge: Harvard University Press, 1962.

Pope, Liston. *Millhands and Preachers.* New Haven: Yale University Press, 1942.

Pulley, Raymond. *Old Virginia Restored, 1870–1930*. Charlottesville: University of Virginia Press, 1968.

Pye, Lucien. "The Concept of Political Development." In Jason Finkle and Richard Gable, eds., *Political Development and Social Change*, pp. 43–51. New York: John Wiley and Sons, 1971.

Rabinowitz, George. "Introduction to Nonmetric Multidimensional Scaling." *American Journal of Political Science* 19 (1975): 343–90.

Ransom, Roger, and Sutch, Richard. "Debt Peonage in the Cotton South after the Civil War." *Journal of Economic History* 32 (1972): 641–69.

Reed, John Shelton. *The Enduring South: Subcultural Persistence in Mass Society*. Lexington, Mass.: Lexington Books, 1972.

Reissman, Leonard. "Social Development and the American South." *Journal of Social Issues* 22 (1966): 101–16.

Rice, John David. "The Negro Tobacco Worker and His Union in Durham, North Carolina." Master's thesis, University of North Carolina, 1941.

Rubinson, Richard. "The World-Economy and the Distribution of Income within States: A Cross-National Study." *American Sociological Review* 41 (1976): 638–59.

Russell, Daniel Lindsay. *Inaugural Address of Governor Daniel L. Russell*. Document No. A, North Carolina Senate, Session 1897.

Salamon, Lester. "Leadership and Modernization: The Emerging Black Political Elite in the American South." *Journal of Politics* 35 (1973): 615–46.

———. *The Social Origins of Mississippi Backwardness*. Bloomington: Indiana University Press, forthcoming.

Sale, Kirkpatrick. "Six Pillars of the Southern Rim." In Roger Alcaly and David Mermelstein, eds., *The Fiscal Crisis of American Cities*, pp. 165–80. New York: Vintage Books, 1977.

Sanders, Charles Richard. *The Cameron Plantation of Central North Carolina*. Durham: Seeman Printing Co., 1974.

Santos, Theotonio dos. "The Structure of Dependence." *American Economic Review* 60 (1970): 231–36.

Schwartz, Michael. *Radical Protest and Social Structure*. New York: Academic Press, 1976.

Seers, Dudley. "The Stages of Growth of a Primary Producer in the Middle of the Twentieth Century." In Robert Rhodes, ed., *Imperialism and Underdevelopment*, pp. 163–80. New York: Monthly Review Press, 1970.

Seligman, Lester. "Elite Recruitment and Political Development." In Jason Finkle and Richard Gable, eds., *Political Development and Social Change*, pp. 240–49. New York: John Wiley and Sons, 1971.

Silver, James. *Mississippi: The Closed Society*. New York: Harcourt, Brace, and World, 1963.

Sitterson, J. Carlyle. "Business Leaders in Post–Civil War North Carolina, 1865–1900." In J. Carlyle Sitterson, ed., *Studies in Southern History,* pp. 111–21. The James Sprunt Studies in History and Political Science, Vol. 39. Chapel Hill: The University of North Carolina Press, 1957.

Skocpol, Theda. "Old Regime Legacies and Communist Revolution in Russia and China." *Social Forces* 55 (1976): 284–315.

Smith, R. T. "Social Stratification, Cultural Pluralism, and Integration in West Indian Societies." In S. Lewis and T. G. Mathews, eds., *Caribbean Integration.* Rio Piedras: Puerto Rico Press, 1967.

Smith, Robert Wayne. "A Rhetorical Analysis of the Populist Movement in North Carolina, 1892–1896." Ph.D. dissertation, University of Wisconsin, 1957.

Smith, Thomas C. *The Agrarian Origins of Modern Japan.* Stanford, Calif.: Stanford University Press, 1959.

Soares, Glaucio. "Economic Development and Class Structure." In Reinhard Bendix and Seymour M. Lipset, eds., *Class, Status, and Power,* pp. 190–99. New York: Free Press, 1966.

Spengler, J. L. "Southern Economic Trends and Prospects." In John C. McKinney and Edgar Thompson, eds., *The South in Continuity and Change,* pp. 101–31. Durham, N.C.: Duke University Press, 1965.

Standard, Diffee, and Griffin, Richard. "The Cotton Textile Industry in Antebellum North Carolina, Part I: Origin and Growth to 1830." *North Carolina Historical Review* 34 (1957): 15–35.

Steelman, Joseph F. "The Progressive Era in North Carolina, 1884–1917." Ph.D. dissertation, University of North Carolina, 1955.

Stinchcombe, Arthur. "Agricultural Enterprises and Rural Class Relations." *American Journal of Sociology* 67 (1961): 165–76.

Stover, John F. *The Railroads of the South, 1865–1900.* Chapel Hill: The University of North Carolina Press, 1955.

Sunkel, Osvald. "Big Business and 'Dependencia.'" *Foreign Affairs* 50 (1972): 517–31.

Tang, Anthony M. *Economic Development in the Southern Piedmont, 1860–1950.* Chapel Hill: The University of North Carolina Press, 1958.

Thomas, David. "Early History of the North Carolina Furniture Industry, 1880–1921." Ph.D. dissertation, University of North Carolina, 1964.

Thompson, E. P. *The Making of the English Working Class.* New York: Vintage Books, 1963.

Thompson, Edgar. *Plantation Societies, Race Relations and the South: The Regimentation of Populations.* Durham, N.C.: Duke University Press, 1975.

Thompson, Holland. "The Civil War and Social and Economic Changes." *Annals of the American Academy* 153 (1931): 11–20.

————. *The New South*. New Haven: Yale University Press, 1919.

Tilley, Nannie May. *The Bright-Tobacco Industry, 1860–1929*. Chapel Hill: The University of North Carolina Press, 1948.

Tindall, George B. "Beyond the Mainstream: The Ethnic Southerners." *Journal of Southern History* 40 (1974): 3–18.

————. *The Emergence of the New South, 1913–1945*. Baton Rouge: Louisiana State University Press, 1967.

————. "The South Pits Itself against History as It Rises Once Again." Raleigh *News and Observer*, 19 January 1975, IV-6.

Tippett, Tom. *When Southern Labor Stirs*. New York: Jonathan Cape and Harrison Smith, 1931.

Tompkins, Daniel. "The Real Grievances against the Railroads." *South Atlantic Quarterly* 6 (1907): 317–22.

U.S. Department of Labor. *State Economic and Social Indicators*. Washington, D.C.: U.S. Government Printing Office, 1970.

Vance, Rupert. "Aycock of North Carolina." *Southwest Review* 18 (1933): 288–306.

————. *Human Geography of the South*. Chapel Hill: The University of North Carolina Press, 1935.

————, and Sutker, Sara. "Metropolitan Dominance and Integration." In Rupert Vance and N. J. Demerath, eds., *The Urban South*, pp. 114–34. Chapel Hill: The University of North Carolina Press, 1954.

Wagley, Charles. "Plantation America: A Culture Sphere." In Vera Rubin, ed., *Caribbean Studies: A Symposium*. Seattle: University of Washington Press, 1960.

Wallerstein, Immanuel. "Class-Formation in the Capitalist World-Economy." *Politics and Society* 5 (1975): 367–75.

————. "Dependence in an Interdependent World: The Limited Possibilities of Transformation within the Capitalist World Economy." *African Studies Review* 17 (1974): 1–26.

————. *The Modern World-System: Capitalist Agriculture and the Origins of the European World Economy in the Sixteenth Century*. New York: Academic Press, 1974.

————. "The Rise and Future Demise of the World Capitalist System: Concepts for Comparative Analysis." *Comparative Studies in History and Society* 16 (1974): 387–415.

————. "Three Paths of National Development in the Sixteenth Century." *Studies in Comparative International Development* 8 (1972): 95–101.

Walls, David. "Central Appalachia: A Peripheral Region within an Advanced Capitalist Society." *Journal of Sociology and Social Welfare* 4 (1976): 232–42.

Weare, Walter B. *Black Business in the New South: A Social History of the North Carolina Mutual Life Insurance Company*. Champaign: University of Illinois Press, 1976.

Weaver, G. F. "The Politics of Local Democratic-Populist Fusion in the Election of 1896 in North Carolina." M.A. thesis, University of North Carolina, 1968.

Webb, Lee. "Colonialism and Underdevelopment in Vermont." *Liberation* 16 (1971): 29–33.

Weinstein, James. *The Corporate Ideal in the Liberal State, 1900–1918.* Boston: Beacon Press, 1968.

Whitehill, Arthur M., Jr., and Takezawa, Shin'ichi. *Cultural Values in Management-Worker Relations.* Chapel Hill: School of Business Administration, University of North Carolina, 1961.

———. *The Other Worker.* Honolulu: East-West Center Press, 1968.

Wiener, Jonathan M. "Planter-Merchant Conflict in Reconstruction Alabama." *Past and Present* 68 (1975): 73–94.

———. "Planter Persistence and Social Change: Alabama, 1850–1870." *Journal of Interdisciplinary History* 7 (1976): 235–60.

———. "Review of Reviews." *History and Theory* 15 (1976): 146–75.

Wiley, Norbert. "America's Unique Class Politics: The Interplay of Labor, Credit, and Commodity Markets." In Hans Peter Dreitzel, ed., *Recent Sociology No. 1,* pp. 188–213. London: Macmillan Co., 1969.

Williams, William Appleman. "The Vicious Circle of American Imperialism." *New Politics* 4 (1965): 49–55.

Wilson, Robert. *Southern Exposure.* Chapel Hill: The University of North Carolina Press, 1927.

Winsborough, H. H. "The Changing Regional Character of the South." In John C. McKinney and Edgar Thompson, eds., *The South in Continuity and Change,* pp. 34–52. Durham, N.C.: Duke University Press, 1965.

Winston, Robert. "North Carolina: A Militant Mediocracy." *The Nation* 112 (1921): 731.

Wish, Harvey. *George Fitzhugh.* Baton Rouge: Louisiana State University Press, 1943.

Woodward, C. Vann. *American Counterpoint.* New York: Little, Brown, and Co., 1971.

———. *Origins of the New South, 1877–1913.* Baton Rouge: Louisiana State University Press, 1951.

———. *Tom Watson, Agrarian Rebel.* New York: Macmillan, 1938.

Wright, Gavin. "Prosperity, Progress, and American Slavery." In Paul David, Herbert Gutman, Richard Sutch, Peter Temin, and Gavin Wright, eds., *Reckoning with Slavery,* pp. 302–36. New York: Oxford University Press, 1976.

Zimmerman, L. J. *Poor Lands, Rich Lands: The Widening Gap.* New York: Random House, 1965.

Index

A

Absentee ownership, 60, 94–95, 227. *See also* Colonialism
Addams, Jane, 208
Alderman, Edwin A., 93, 199
Alexander, Sydenham B., 163, 165
Allen, Robert, 147, 156, 187
Andrews, Alexander Boyd, 77, 163
American South: impact of slavery, 3; impact of Civil War, 3; as colony, 25, 32–35, 94–95; political economy, 25–41; economic dependency, 25–27, 30, 94–95, 130; personal incomes, 28–30; compared with North, 28–29; postbellum economic development, 30–32; conservative modernization of, 99–100; patterns of domination, 231
American Tobacco Company, 81, 82, 115, 116, 120
Apter, David, 135
Ash, Roberta, 183
Ashe, Samuel, 86
Aycock, Benjamin, 198
Aycock, Charles B., 81, 137, 138, 139, 140, 194, 197, 198, 199, 201, 202, 205, 207, 209, 210, 220

B

Banks, 36, 46, 78, 79–80, 84, 146–47, 159–61, 189–90; planter dominance, 19, 78–91
Baran, Paul, 16–17, 38
Battle, Elisha, 82
Battle, George Gordon, 85, 93
Battle, Herbert B., 84
Battle, James Smith, 82, 85
Battle, Joel, 58, 82, 83
Battle, Kemp Plummer, 83, 84
Battle, Richard H., 83–84
Battle, Samuel Westray, 85
Battle, Thomas H., 84
Battle, Turner, 85
Battle, William Horn, 83
Battle, William Smith, 82, 83, 85
Battle family, 82–85
Beckford, George, 13–14
Bendix, Reinhard, 99, 100, 121, 122
Bennehan, Rebecca, 86
Bennehan, Richard, 86
Berghe, Pierre van den, 34
Bismarck, Otto von, 98
Black, Cyril, 135, 213
Black, Julius C., 193, 196
Blacks: in textile industry, 112–13, 117; in tobacco industry, 117–18; creation of middle class, 118–19; political participation, 119, 144, 159, 175–76; labor, 130; and Democratic party, 138, 189–91, 197–98; and Populism, 184, 187–90; disfranchisement, 190–92; and education, 208–11. *See also* Racial stratification; Slavery
Blackwell, W. T., 113, 120
"Bolters," 178, 180, 182, 183. *See also* Populist party
Boone, Daniel, 86
Bourbons, 136–37, 185, 196, 200
Boyte, Harry, 40, 60, 100

Brooks, Aubrey, 211, 212
Bridges, Robert Rufus, 75, 77
Brown, Joseph A., 193, 196
Brown, Joseph Hill, 206
Bryan, James A., 193
Bryan, William Jennings, 158
Buck, Paul H., 71, 93, 94, 157
Butler, Marion, 8, 120, 154, 159, 165, 178, 183, 184

C
Caldwell, J. P., 212
Calhoun, John C., 124
Cameron, Bennehan, 89–90, 92, 93, 94, 114, 202
Cameron, Duncan, 86, 87, 91
Cameron, John, 86
Cameron, Paul Carrington, 8, 87–89, 93, 95, 124, 218
Cameron family, 85–91
Cannon, G. H., 182
Cannon, Robert, 119
Capitalism. *See* World system; Plantation society
Carlyle, Thomas, 127
Carnegie, Andrew, 123
Carr, Elias, 90, 152, 163, 165
Carr, Julian S., 114, 118, 120, 158, 204, 205
Carter, David, 166
Carter, Jimmy, 155
Casanova, Pablo Gonzales, 33
Cash, W. J., 102, 108, 133, 216, 217, 218, 219
Chandler, Alfred, 115
Cheek, Thomas, 194, 196
Chiba, Kaguo, 230, 231
Chirot, Daniel, 12
Clark, E. T., 182
Clark, Walter, 163, 212
Clark, W. W., 212
Clay, Cassius, 20
Cochran, Thomas C., 25, 105
Coffin, John, 113

Cole, Robert, 97, 105, 106
Coleman, W. C., 118
Colonialism, 9–12, 19; American South, 25, 32–35, 94–95; celtic periphery, 33–34
Colored Farmers' Alliance, 150, 187
Communications Workers of America, 230
Compromise of 1877, 93
Cone, Caesar, 212
Connor, R. D. W., 198
Conservative modernization, 217, 223–26; restrictive nature of, 96, 99; of South, 99–100; role of state in, 99, 227–30
Cooley, R. A., 194
Cooper, William J., Jr., 220
Corporate farming, 226
Cotterill, Robert, 216
Cotton, 25, 68, 101; alliance with commerce, 36–38; prices, 146; "overproduction" thesis, 148; comparative advantage in North Carolina, 148–49. *See also* Plantation agriculture
Cotton Growers' Protective Society, 89
Cowper, George, 194
Cowper, Richard Green, 194
Craig, Locke, 191, 199
Credit problems, 52, 146–48, 153, 159–61. *See also* Subtreasury plan
Critical elections, 138, 140
Crop lien system, 147, 151
Cunningham, John S., 114

D
Dabney, Charles, 206
Danhof, Clarence, 32–33
Daniels, Frank, 205
Daniels, Frank A., 194
Daniels, Jonathan, 32

Daniels, Josephus, 8, 69, 203, 204, 205, 206
David, Paul, 23
Davis, Angela, 228
DeCanio, Stephen, 148, 223
Degler, Carl N., 158, 184
Delap, Simeon A., 149
Democratic party: political modernization, 132–34, 136–44, 197–203, 213; manufacturing and business interests, 133, 137, 192–96, 201; education, 137, 202–12; popular image, 137–38; political modernization, 138; and blacks, 138–39, 189–91, 197–98; expenditures, 140; legislation, 140, 197–98; class composition of leadership, 169–72, 191–96, 198–201
Dewey, John, 208
Disfranchisement, 142–44, 197–98
Dixon, Thomas, 85–86
Donaldson, Henry, 58
Doughton, Rufus, 177, 199
Douty, Harry, 111
Duke, Benjamin Newton, 114, 117, 118, 120, 158
Duke, James B., 8, 114, 120
Duke, Washington, 113, 114, 118
Durden, Robert, 118

E
Eastern Europe: political economy, 11, 12
Edmonds, Helen G., 134, 175, 176, 188, 190, 191
Education: and populism, 175, 206–7; and economic development, 203–12 passim; as middle class reform, 203–8; as social control, 208–12; and race, 210
Eisenstadt, S. N., 134, 135
Elite recruitment, 135
Engels, Friedrich, 11, 210

Engerman, Stanley, 21–22, 23–24, 28, 32, 59
Ervin, W. C., 66
Exum, W. J., 120
Ezell, John S., 198, 215

F
Farm ownership, 72–76, 225–26
Farmers' Alliance: origins, 149; exchanges, 150–53, 162; community basis, 151; and religion, 151; internal stratification, 151–52; leadership, 152, 165–72; relation to Populist party, 153; legislation, 153; relation to Democratic party, 153. *See also* Populism; Populist party
"Farmers' Legislature," 153
Ferree, John H., 66
Fields, William C., 194, 196
Filmer, Robert, 127
Finley, John, 80
Fitzhugh, George, 127, 128, 129, 217
Fogel, Robert, 21–22, 23–24, 28, 32, 59
Forbes, A. A., 174, 175
Fowle, Daniel, 90
Fowler, J. E., 174, 175
Frank, Andre Gunder, 9, 12
Frazier, E. Franklin, 118
Freud, Sigmund, 189
Fries, Francis, 81
Fries, John, 211, 212
Fries, Mary, 81
Fuller, Blind Boy, 119
Fusion: and political reform, 138–39; legislation, 138, 172–78; politics, 157–58, 180–83; breakdown of party cooperation, 176–87; reasons for failure, 190. *See also* Populism; Populist party

G

Gardner, O. Max, 133
Gaston, Paul, 122, 123, 124, 125, 127
Genovese, Eugene, 12–13, 18–21, 23–24, 40, 55, 102, 215, 217, 225
Geography: economic impact of, 44
Germany, 97–99, 127
Gilman, Glenn, 39, 100, 108, 126, 133
Glenn, Robert B., 194, 196
Goffman, Erving, 18
Goodwyn, Lawrence, 150, 152, 153, 155, 184
Grady, Henry, 70, 71, 88, 124, 125, 129
Graham, William A., 45, 163
Gramsci, Antonio, 219
Greenbackers, 157
Gregg, William, 124
Griffin, Richard, 23, 58, 61, 62
Gutherie, W. A., 120, 157, 158

H

Hackney, Sheldon, 40, 136, 140, 155, 156, 164, 168, 174, 183, 219, 220
Hairston, Frank C., 194
Hamerow, Theodore S., 98
Hamilton, Alexander, 57
Hampton, Wade, 88
Harris, Fred, 155
Hawkins, John D., 77
Hawkins, William J., 77
Hechter, Michael, 33–34
Hegemony. *See* Planters
Helper, Hinton, 20
Herring, Harriet, 53, 56–57, 59, 60, 115
Hicks, Archibald, 194
Hicks, John D., 155, 156, 157
Hill, Isham, 194
Hobby, Wilbur, 230

Hobsbawm, Eric, 156
Hodges, Luther, 226, 227, 228
Hofstadter, Richard, 155, 156
Holt, Edwin M., 65, 66
Holt, Thomas M., 65–66, 67, 90, 107
Hunter, Floyd, 221
Huntington, S. P., 134

I

Ideology: persistence of Southern tradition, 35–37, 99–100, 123–26; New South myths, 70–71, 123–26, 215–16; planters and white supremacy, 92–93; functions of, 121; industrial, 121–22; contradictions of Southern philosophy, 123–27; agrarian roots of, 124–25
Industrialization, 30, 42, 50–51, 130–32, 217, 224; and agriculture, 70–95, 99, 101, 107, 223. *See also* Manufacturing; Revolution from above; Textile industry; Tobacco industry
Ingle, H. Larry, 166
Internal colonialism: applied to South, 33–35

J

Jackson, Andrew, 133
Jackson, John Q., 194
James, Fernando, 194, 196
Japan, 16, 96–99, 105–7, 127, 225, 231
Jarvis, Thomas, 90, 166, 201
Jefferson, Thomas, 57, 184, 217
Jerome, Thomas J., 194
Johnson, Guion, 44, 47, 49
Johnson, Lyndon, 155
Johnston, William, 86
Jones, Edmund W., 80
Jones, F. P., 194
Jones, J. A. T., 194

Joyner, James, 199
Junkers, 77, 97. *See also* Germany
Justice, Edwin, 211
Justice, Michael Hoke, 194, 196

K
Kerr, William, 81
Key, V. O., 5, 132, 137, 139, 140, 145, 192, 196, 197, 198, 199, 200, 216
Kitchin, William Hodge, 166, 167, 200, 211
Kitchin, W. W., 200
Knights of Labor, 111
Koeppel, Barbara, 229, 230
Kousser, J. Morgan, 6, 138, 139, 140, 142, 144, 191

L
Lacy, Dan, 60
Laird, William E., 146, 147
Lambert, Wiley L., 194
Lanier, Sidney, 70
Lasch, Christopher, 156, 190, 208
Leake, John, 64
Ledbetter, J. S., 65
Ledbetter, T. B., 65
Lee, Fitzhugh, 93
Lee, Robert E., 88, 93, 200
Lefler, Hugh, 44, 45, 49, 72, 120, 134, 137, 196, 197, 199, 206
Legislature: turnover, 140–41; expenditures, 140, 142; social class composition, 167–72, 191–97
Lenoir, William, 80
Lenski, Gerhard, 7
Lewis, Hylan, 117
Lewis, Richard H., 206
Lincoln, Nancy, 133
Lincoln, Tom, 133
Locke, John, 128
Long, Huey, 216
Lost Cause: myth of, 123–26
Lowe, David, 194, 196

Lynd, Helen M., 110
Lynd, Robert S., 110

M
McCarthy, Joe, 155
McGee, Brownie, 119
McIntyre, Stephen, 195
McIver, Charles D., 93, 199, 206
McLaurin, Melton, 40, 100, 104, 112, 113, 123
McLean, Malcolm, 226
McMath, Robert C., 150, 151, 152, 172, 184
MacPherson, C., 122
Macune, Charles, 150, 153
Maddox, Lester, 155
Malizia, Emil, 229
Malloy, Charles, 64, 107
Manufacturing: lag in South, 27–30; indigenous source, 35, 60; in Piedmont, 47; geared to planters' needs, 38
Marx, Karl, 7, 10, 11, 210
Mason, Oscar, 195
Mayo, Peter, 89
Mechanization, 226
Meiji Restoration, 16, 97
Mercantilism, 15
Middle class: dependency on planters, 20–21, 36–37, 14, 203–7; role in New South, 38–41, 42, 52; blacks, 118–19; and educational reform, 203–11
Mill builders: typology of, 65–67. *See also* Textile industry
Mill village: racial exclusivity of, 102; paternalism in, 102–4; as industrial plantation, 104
Miller, William, 25, 105
Mills, C. Wright, 8
Mississippi: persistent backwardness, 36–38
Mitchell, Broadus, 39, 54, 55, 56, 100, 103, 104, 107, 111, 126, 219

Mitchell, George, 100, 103, 104, 107, 111, 126
Mitchell, Herbert, 146
Mobilization of bias, 145
Modernization, 96–99, 221–25. *See also* Conservative modernization; Political modernization; Revolution from above
Monetary system, 52, 159, 189. *See also* Banks; Credit problems; Populism
Moore, Barrington, 7, 36, 37, 38, 77, 96, 97, 99, 130, 203, 210, 221, 222
Mordecai, George, 87
Morehead, Eugene Lindsay, 79, 89
Morehead, James, 79
Morehead, James T., Jr., 80
Morehead, James Turner, 79, 92, 93
Morehead, John Motley, 45, 59, 78, 81, 82, 129, 212
Morehead, Joseph Motley, 80
Morehead family, 78–80
Morgan empire, 77
Morgan, J. P., 32, 94, 139
Morgan, Mark, 107, 108
Morrison, Joseph L., 204
Moses, Edward, 206
Moving, Frank, 206
Muller, Phillip, 146, 163, 165, 166, 207
Murchison, David Reid, 78
Murchison, Duncan, 78
Murchison, John R., 78
Murchison, Kenneth McKenzie, 78
Murphy, Archibald, 45
Murray, Thomas J., 195
Mussolini, Benito, 128
Myrdal, Gunnar, 9, 14

N
Nash, Abner, 86
Nash, Francis, 86

Newsome, Albert, 44, 45, 49, 72, 120, 134
Nicholls, William, 35–36, 38
North, Douglass, 14, 28
North Carolina: position in old South, 4; industrial leader of New South, 4–6; economic development of, 6, 52–53; ambiguous political development, 6; as test of middle class hypothesis, 42, 62–69; antebellum characteristics, 43–47

O
O'Brien, Gail, 50
O'Brien, Michael, 219
O'Dell, John M., 66, 67, 211
Odum, Howard, 33, 39
Osborne, Francis, 195
Overman, Lee, 191

P
Page, Anderson, 203
Page, Frank, 204
Page, Henry, 212
Page, Walter Hines, 8, 93, 203, 204, 205, 206, 207, 212
Paige, Jeffery, 185
Panic of 1873, 55
Parker, Alton B., 139
Parker, David Reid, 182
Paternalism: relationship of planter to yeomen, 102; plantation model, 102, 123; in mill villages, 103–4; and personalistic orientation, 103, 107–8; as means of cultural control, 109; decline of, 111; and industrialization, 127–28, 131, 225; and education, 203–11
Patterson, Lindsay, 212
Patterson, Rufus, Jr., 81–82
Patterson, Rufus Lenoir, 80–81, 92, 212
Patterson, Samuel F., 80, 91, 212

Patterson, Samuel Legerwood, 81, 92
Patterson family, 80–82
Peabody, George, 93
Peele, William, 206
Plantation agriculture: world periphery, 11, 215; labor, 12, 17, 36, 185–87; preconditions, 13; under development, 14; expansion and diversification, 15; profitability, 19–24; cotton exports, 25; postbellum myths, 70–71; dynamics of, 231–32. *See also* Cotton; Planters
Plantation society: political economy, 9, 10, 13–17, 22; trade dependency, 12, 16; class structure, 12–13, 17–24, 101–2, 185–87, 231; authority relations, 17–19; relation to capitalism, 18–23; development limits, 18–20; ideology, 102, 127–28; community development, 146. *See also* Plantation agriculture; Planters
Planters: profit seeking, 18–24; hegemony of, 18, 36, 49–50, 77, 91, 130, 211–12, 217, 232; conspicuous consumption, 19; resistance to manufacturing, 22, 23, 35; gentry class, 49; perceived threat of 'poor whites,' 59; as industrialists, 70–95, 99, 101, 226–28; myth of postbellum fall, 71; land ownership in N.C., 73–76; merger of agricultural and industrial interests, 70–95; limits on political power, 74, 100, 129; landed families as unit of stratification system, 77–91; social basis for class unity, 91–92; cooperation with northern capitalists, 93–94; and Democratic party, 134, 152, 169–72, 191–96, 198–201; tenant

conflict, 185–87. *See also* Plantation agriculture; Cotton
Poe, Clarence, 198
Political economy: methodology of, 7–8; of plantation society, 9–10, 13–17; of Eastern Europe, 11–12
Political crises: methodological significance, 145
Political culture, 132–34, 137, 145
Political modernization: defined, 134–35, 142; in North Carolina, 136–44; and participation, 142–44
Political sociology, 134
Polk, Leonidas, 8, 153, 154, 159, 165, 182, 190, 206
Pollack, Norman, 156
Pope, Liston, 39–40, 54, 100, 112, 117, 126
Populism: political philosophy, 150; and cooperative movement, 150; interpretations of, 155, 183–84; social support, 178–81; goals, 183; internal stratification, 183–90; and race relations, 184, 187–90; relation to rural class structure, 185–87; reasons for failure, 187–90. *See also* Farmers' Alliance; Fusion; Populist party
Populist party: and political modernization, 140–41, 186; political philosophy, 150; platform, 153; North Carolina's role in national party, 154; subtreasury plan, 154; election of 1896, 156–58; speeches, 158–59; monetary policy, 159, 161, 189–90; leadership, 163–72; and planters, 167, 172, 183; state legislature, 167–87 passim; conservatism, 174–76, 183–84, 190; education, 175; government spending, 176; disunity,

178–82. *See also* Bolters; Farmers' Alliance; Fusion; Populism
Possessive individualism, 122. *See also* Ideology
Prisons: prisoner/citizen ratio, 228. *See also* State
Pritchard, Jeter C., 163, 177, 178, 182
"Progressive Plutocracy," 133
Progressives: in North Carolina, 137–44, 188–212 passim; in Alabama, 140–41; in Virginia, 220–21
Prohibitionists, 157
Public health, 211
Pulley, Raymond, 220
Pye, Lucien, 134

R

Racial stratification: in plantation societies, 18; master-slave relations, 19–21; in textile industry, 102. *See also* Blacks
Railroads, 46, 75, 77, 79, 80, 81, 82, 84, 94; in antebellum North Carolina, 46; and landed upper class, 78, 79, 80, 81, 82, 87, 90, 94
Ransom, Matt Whitaker, 163, 197, 200, 205
Ransom, Roger, 147
Ray, Frank, 191
Reconstruction, 101, 132, 136
Reissman, Leonard, 40–41
Republican party: basis for support, 137, 162; southern antipathy toward, 157; leadership, 169–72; platform, 177; legislative program, 177
Research Triangle, 227–28
Revolution from above: defined, 38; as interpretation of North Carolina, 70–95, 113; continuity with the past, 219–21

Reynolds, R. J., 114, 226
Ricks, Robert Henry, 74, 77, 92
Rinehart, James R., 146, 147
Robinson, J. W. S., 195, 196
Rockefeller, John D., 93
Rountree, George, 142, 144, 191
Ruffin, Anne, 87
Ruffin, Thomas, 87
Russell, Daniel, 133, 158, 177, 182, 188

S

Salamon, Lester, 36–37, 38, 135, 136, 220
Sale, Kirkpatrick, 215
Sanders, O. M., 174
Sanders, Richard, 87, 90
Santos, Theotonio, 14
Scales, Alfred, 80
Schenck mills, 57
Schwartz, Michael, 73, 150, 152, 161, 172, 187
Second serfdom, 11
Settle, Thomas, 163
Sherman, William T., 60
Simmons, Furnifold M., 120, 199, 200, 201
Sinclair, P. J., 212
Sitterson, J. Carlyle, 60, 61
Skinner, Harry, 154, 164, 165, 178, 180, 195
Skinner, Thomas Gregory, 164, 195, 196
Slavery: investments, 21; in North Carolina, 46; ideological defense of, 127–28. *See also* Racial stratification; Blacks; Plantation society
Smelser, Neil, 156
Smith, Adam, 127
Smith, Robert, 158, 159
Smith, Robert Lee, 195, 196
Social Darwinism: and white supremacy, 123
Social stratification: in study of

social change, 6–7; in antebellum North Carolina, 47–52; perceived threat of poor whites, 59; social unity of landed class, 91–92; patterns of, 185–87, 216, 222, 231. *See also* Planters; Racial stratification; Middle class; Tenant farmers; Yeomen farmers; Blacks
Speight, R. H., 195, 196
Spencer, Herbert, 123
Stanback, Charles, 195, 196
Standard, Diffee, 23, 58
State: role in conservative modernization, 99, 228–30; instrument of repression, 99, 131, 228; preventing unionization, 112; sponsor of economic development, 227–28
Steele, R. J., 65
Steele, Walter Leake, 65, 66, 67
Steelman, Joseph, 6, 134, 176, 197, 202
Stoneman, George, 60
Stuart, Jeb, 218
Stubbs, H. W., 191
Subtreasury plan, 154
Sutch, Richard, 147

T
Tang, Anthony, 225
Tariff, 149
Temin, Peter, 23
Tenant farmers, 72, 73, 147–49, 185–87, 225–26
Terry, Sonny, 119
Textile industry: in postbellum North Carolina, 42; cotton outlet, 43; as test of middle class thesis, 53–54, 57–69; significance for South's industrial revolution, 53; romantic interpretation, 54–56; social history, 55–62; antebellum foundations, 56, 59–60, 64–66; mill

builders, 58–62; incentives for, 59; growth factors, 68–69; rural social structure, 100–101; mill villages, 102–4; preventing high wage industries, 227–28
Thompson, Cyrus, 165, 177
Thompson, Edgar, 17, 18, 127
Thompson, E. P., 127
Thompson, Holland, 39, 54–55
Thompson, John W., 206
Tindall, George, 30, 225
Tobacco industry: leaders of, 113–14; impact of technology, 114; monopolistic nature of, 115; and Southern traditions, 116–20; Populist connections, 120
Tompkins, Daniel, 8, 64, 84, 123, 124, 125, 129, 201, 207, 212
Travis, Edwin L., 195
Turner, Frederick Jackson, 133

U
Unionization, 109–13, 227–31
Urbanism: and middle class, 37; lack of in North Carolina, 53

V
Vance, Rupert, 33, 198
Vance, Zebulon, 90, 154

W
Wages: in antebellum North Carolina, 46; of mill workers, 110; in tobacco industry, 116–17
Wallace, George, 155
Wallerstein, Immanuel, 9–11, 12, 15, 23, 221
Ward, Hallett S., 195
Washington, Booker T., 118
Waterson, Henry, 124
Watson, Tom, 155, 189
Watts, George W., 114, 118
Weber, Max, 185
Weiner, Jonathan M., 220

Whitaker, F. A., 195
White supremacy, 75, 79, 92, 101,
    112–13, 137, 188–91, 208–11
Williams, John D., 78
Williams, William Appleman, 33
Williams, William L., 195, 196
Williamson, Thomas, 66
Williamson, William Holt, 66
Wilson, James W., 84
Wilson, John N., 196
Wilson, Robert, 43
Winslow, Arthur, 206
Winston, Francis Donnell, 163,
    191, 199
Winston, George Taylor, 163
Winston, Patrick Henry, Jr., 163
Winston, Robert, 42
Winston, Robert Watson, 163

Wish, Harvey, 128
Woodruff, R. W., 221
Woodward, C. Vann, 3, 32, 38–39,
    40, 42, 54, 56, 90, 94–95, 103,
    123, 126, 129, 155, 156, 217, 218,
    219, 220
World system: division of labor,
    10, 11; development, 10–11;
    position of South, 12, 99–100;
    and historical contexts, 221–22
Wright, Gavin, 23–24, 30
Wright, Richard H., 114

Y
Yeomen farmers, 74, 76, 114,
    146–50, 186, 223. *See also*
    Farmers' Alliance; Populism;
    Populist party